Retained EU Law

Other titles available from Law Society Publishing:

SRA Standards and Regulations: November 2019 edition
Solicitors Regulation Authority

The Solicitor's Handbook 2019
Gregory Treverton-Jones QC, Nigel West, Susanna Heley and Robert Forman

Data Protection Toolkit, 2nd edition
Alison Matthews

Regulation and In-house Lawyers, 2nd edition
Tracey Calvert and Bronwen Still

Compliance and Ethics in Law Firms, 2nd edition
Tracey Calvert

Titles from Law Society Publishing can be ordered from all good bookshops or direct (telephone 0370 850 1422, or visit our online shop at **www.lawsociety.org.uk/bookshop**).

RETAINED EU LAW

A Practical Guide

Eleonor Duhs and Indira Rao

The Law Society

ISBN-13: 978-1-78446-164-5

Published in 2021 by the Law Society
113 Chancery Lane, London WC2A 1PL

Typeset by Columns Design XML Ltd, Reading
Printed by Hobbs the Printers Ltd, Totton, Hants

FSC
www.fsc.org
MIX
Paper from responsible sources
FSC® C020438

The paper used for the text pages of this book is FSC® certified. FSC (the Forest Stewardship Council®) is an international network to promote responsible management of the world's forests.

Contents

APPENDICES

Acknowledgements

We would like to thank Daniel Greenberg CB, Vina Shukla, Gustaf Duhs and Mohan Rao for reviewing the manuscript and for providing insightful comments and encouragement. We are grateful to Lim Yee for assistance with the references and footnotes and to Vanessa MacNair for guidance on the parliamentary scrutiny process. Any errors are the responsibility of the authors.

We both became EU lawyers through practice of the law, seeing it in action through negotiations in the EU institutions, hearings in the Court of Justice and in domestic courts, deliberations in Whitehall and through countless discussions over the course of our careers with expert, dedicated and brilliant colleagues. Their thoughts about EU law are woven through the fabric of this book. We would like to thank them for their contribution to it and for their generosity, time and support. It has been a privilege to work alongside them. Special thanks go to Sir Iain Macleod KCMG and Cathy Adams CMG.

We would like to express our appreciation to our publishers. We are grateful to Laura Armentano for commissioning the book and to David Crosby and Suzanne Giles for taking it forward.

The beginning and the end of the UK's membership of the EU are marked, respectively, by the European Communities Act 1972 and the European Union (Withdrawal) Act 2018. The drafting of both these Acts is remarkable: they deal with an unparalleled breadth and complexity of subject matter with great skill. We would like to pay tribute to the drafters of this legislation. Their public service rightly deserves acknowledgement.

Eleonor would like to thank Martyn, Molly and Oscar for their enormous contribution – their encouragement throughout was invaluable. The same thanks and acknowledgement are due to her parents, Rosalind and Staffan, and siblings Gustaf and Alex.

Indira would like to thank her parents, Srinivasa and Usha, for their inspiration, support and encouragement. Warm thanks also go to Mohan and Debbie, Anna, Frankie, Meredith and OSC colleagues.

We wrote this book against the turbulent backdrop of 2020. The process of researching and writing was an escape and gave us a sort of normality. Modern technology has played a central role in enabling us to share texts, thoughts and to collaborate in a way which would have been unthinkable for authors in the past. For that too we are grateful.

Finally, 2020 marks 100 years since women were allowed to take degrees at the university where we were both educated. We would like to pay tribute to those who have given us the privilege of knowing what it is to have 'money and a room of one's own'.

The law is stated as at 10 November 2020.

Eleonor Duhs and Indira Rao
London, November 2020

About the authors

Eleonor Duhs was a senior lawyer at the Department for Exiting the European Union. She was the lead lawyer on the core provisions of the European Union (Withdrawal) Act 2018 and led on aspects of the EU–UK Withdrawal Agreement and the Framework for the Future EU–UK relationship. She negotiated the General Data Protection Regulation in Brussels and was a senior lawyer in the EU law team at the Foreign, Commonwealth & Development Office.

Eleonor is currently a Director (Barrister) at Fieldfisher LLP where she advises governments, public sector bodies and businesses on the implications of Brexit. She regularly speaks about Brexit in the media and at national and international conferences.

Indira Rao MBE is Counsel for EU and International Law in the House of Commons. She has over 20 years' experience advising on EU law, public international law and constitutional and administrative law in Parliament and government, following five years at a Magic Circle law firm. She was the lead lawyer at the Foreign, Commonwealth & Development Office advising on legal issues arising from the UK's withdrawal from the EU.

Her previous roles include senior legal adviser on EU and international law at the Attorney General's Office, First Secretary (Legal) at the UK Permanent Representation to the EU and UK Agent to the Court of Justice of the European Union.

Table of cases

Table of statutes

Table of statutory instruments

Table of EU legislation

Other jurisdictions

Table of treaties

Abbreviations and definitions

CFSP	Common Foreign and Security Policy
Charter	Charter of Fundamental Rights of the European Union
CJEU or European Court	Court of Justice of the European Union
Community Charter	Community Charter of the Fundamental Social Rights of Workers
ECA 1972	European Communities Act 1972
ECHR	European Convention on Human Rights
ECtHR	European Court of Human Rights
EEA Agreement	Agreement on the European Economic Area, signed at Oporto on 2 May 1992
EEA EFTA Separation Agreement	The Agreement on arrangements between Iceland, the Principality of Liechtenstein, the Kingdom of Norway and the United Kingdom of Great Britain and Northern Ireland following the withdrawal of the United Kingdom from the European Union, the EEA Agreement and other agreements applicable between the United Kingdom and the EEA EFTA States by virtue of the United Kingdom's membership of the European Union
ESC	European Social Charter
ESMA	European Securities and Markets Authority
EU or Union[1]	European Union
EUWA 2018	European Union (Withdrawal) Act 2018
EU(WA)A 2020	European Union (Withdrawal Agreement) Act 2020

[1] The terms 'EU' or 'Union' are used where the original reference was in fact to the European Communities. This has been done to simplify the terminology. Similarly, treaty article numbering is based on the TEU and TFEU even in respect of cases decided under previous treaties.

GDPR	General Data Protection Regulation
GOWA 2006	Government of Wales Act 2006
HRA 1998	Human Rights Act 1998
ICCPR	International Covenant on Civil and Political Rights
ILO	International Labour Organization
IPCD	Implementation Period completion day (11.00 p.m. GMT on 31 December 2020)
JCHR	Joint Committee on Human Rights
JHA	justice and home affairs (also known as freedom, security and justice)
Lisbon Treaty	Treaty of Lisbon amending the Treaty on European Union and the Treaty establishing the European Community, signed at Lisbon on 13 December 2007
NIA 1998	Northern Ireland Act 1998
OJ	Official Journal of the European Union
Swiss Citizens' Rights Agreement	The Agreement between the United Kingdom of Great Britain and Northern Ireland and the Swiss Confederation on citizens' rights following the withdrawal of the United Kingdom from the European Union, and the free movement of persons agreement
TEU	Treaty on European Union
TFEU	Treaty on the Functioning of the European Union
White Paper	Department for Exiting the European Union, *Legislating for the United Kingdom's withdrawal from the European Union* (White Paper, Cm 9446, 2017)
Withdrawal Agreement	Agreement on the withdrawal of the United Kingdom of Great Britain and Northern Ireland from the European Union and the European Atomic Energy Community of 19 October 2019

CHAPTER 1

Introduction

1.1 AIM OF THE BOOK

The main aim of this book is to provide the reader with a practical understanding of retained EU law. Retained EU law is a new concept in domestic law, introduced by the European Union (Withdrawal) Act 2018 (EUWA 2018), as amended by the European Union (Withdrawal Agreement) Act 2020 (EU(WA)A 2020).

1.2 BACKGROUND

The government set out its legislative plans to deliver the result of the EU referendum of 23 June 2016 in its White Paper, *Legislating for the United Kingdom's withdrawal from the European Union*,[1] published in March 2017 (the 'White Paper'). The government indicated that it would bring forward legislation to repeal the European Communities Act 1972 (ECA 1972), the statute which gave effect to EU law in the UK.

The White Paper said that 'simply repealing the ECA would lead to a confused and incomplete legal system'. It explained that this was because EU law which had effect in the UK without the need to pass specific UK implementing legislation (such as EU regulations) would 'cease to have effect in the UK once we have left the EU and repealed the ECA'. This would leave 'large holes in the statute book'. In addition, the secondary legislation made under ECA 1972 to implement obligations arising from EU membership would fall away when ECA 1972 was repealed. This would also 'leave a significant gap in the statute book'.

The White Paper also pointed to the fact that there were over 12,000 EU regulations in force, around 7,900 statutory instruments which implemented EU legislation and 186 Acts of Parliament incorporating a degree of EU influence.

[1] Department for Exiting the European Union, *Legislating for the United Kingdom's withdrawal from the European Union* (White Paper, Cm 9446, 2017).

Although the White Paper did not say so in such terms, it would not be feasible to replace this volume of law with new domestic legislation ready to come into force on exit.[2]

The government's chosen method of addressing these issues was to convert EU law into UK law and to preserve the laws that were made in the UK to implement EU obligations, as they stood just before the point at which EU law ceased to apply to the UK, in order to ensure continuity and legal certainty.

The policy behind the creation of retained EU law was to 'ensure that wherever possible, the same rules and laws apply on the day after we leave the EU as before' (White Paper, p.14) in order to 'give businesses, workers, investors and consumers the maximum possible certainty as we leave the EU'. As the White Paper explained:

> **1.12** In order to achieve a stable and smooth transition, the Government's overall approach is to convert the body of existing EU law into domestic law, after which Parliament (and, where appropriate, the devolved legislatures) will be able to decide which elements of that law to keep, amend or repeal once we have left the EU. This ensures that, as a general rule, the same rules and laws will apply after we leave the EU as they did before.
>
> **1.13** If the Great Repeal Bill[3] did not convert existing EU law into domestic law at the same time as repealing the ECA, the UK's statute book would contain significant gaps once we left the EU. There are a large number of EU regulations and many other EU-derived laws which form part of our law which, if we were to repeal the ECA without making further provision, would no longer apply, creating large holes in our statute book.

The Secretary of State for Exiting the European Union described the approach as:

> [taking] a snapshot of the body of EU law that currently forms part of the United Kingdom legal system and [ensuring] that it will continue to apply in the United Kingdom after we leave.
>
> (HC Deb 7 September 2017, vol.628, col.342)

This new body of law came to be known as 'retained EU law'.

The White Paper noted that converting EU law into UK law would not be sufficient to provide 'a smooth and orderly exit' because a large proportion of the converted law would not function properly when transplanted from the EU context to the new domestic context. The proposed Bill would therefore contain powers to enable corrections to be made to the new body of law to overcome this issue. These laws would apply until Parliament and/or the devolved legislatures decided whether to retain, amend or replace them.

In terms of how this new body of law would be interpreted, the White Paper said (at para.2.14):

---

[2] The White Paper was published before a transition or implementation period was contemplated (see **10.3**). At the time, it was contemplated that EU law would cease to apply to the UK on exit day. References in the White Paper to exit or exit day should be read with this in mind.

[3] The Great Repeal Bill was the working title of the Bill. It was introduced to Parliament as the European Union (Withdrawal) Bill.

> ... for as long as [retained EU law] remains on the UK statute book, it is essential that there is a common understanding of what that law means. The Government believes that this is best achieved by providing for continuity in how that law is interpreted before and after exit day. To maximise certainty, therefore, the Bill will provide that any question as to the meaning of [retained EU law] will be determined in the UK courts by reference to the CJEU's case law as it exists on the day we leave the EU.

1.3 STRUCTURE OF THE BOOK

EUWA 2018 is an Act of constitutional significance. The long title of the Act is deceptively simple:

> An Act to repeal the European Communities Act 1972 and make other provision in connection with the withdrawal of the United Kingdom from the EU.

The scope of application of EUWA 2018 is extremely wide. It operates across a huge swathe of the UK statute book.

This work is intended as a practical guide to what retained EU law is and how it functions, illustrated with examples. It is intended to equip the practitioner with the tools to delve into the detail of how retained EU law affects their own area of expertise. At the time of writing, retained EU law has not yet come into force. It is a novel area which will develop as theory is put into practice and cases reach the courts.

Retained EU law is a new concept in our domestic law, but its roots are in EU law and in the operation of ECA 1972. It is impossible to understand how retained EU law operates without an understanding of its EU law origins and of how EU law was given effect in the UK during EU membership.

EUWA 2018 presupposes an understanding of EU concepts such as the 'principle of the supremacy of EU law' and 'the rule in *Francovich*'. For this reason, this book explains the key concepts of EU law that are a prerequisite for an understanding of retained EU law, before turning to the provisions of EUWA 2018. Getting to grips with these EU concepts is essential to understanding the intricacies of retained EU law.

Many of the concepts in EU law which EUWA 2018 builds on are complex and contested. For example, the operation of the supremacy of EU law in the courts of the EU Member States is controversial. The way in which the duty of consistent interpretation operates in the courts of the Member States is unpredictable. These issues will still matter when interpreting retained EU law.

EUWA 2018 is not the easiest Act to navigate. That is not a criticism of the drafting. The subject matter is dense and complex. Different concepts are interlinked in nuanced ways; significant issues are signposted in a subtle manner which can be easy to miss. For example, phrases such as 'so far as relevant' and 'as it has effect' carry significant meaning. There are general rules with exceptions and then an exception to the exceptions. There is a lot of detail in the Schedules. There is a huge volume of secondary legislation made under the Act.

To assist the reader, we have illustrated the operation and effect of EUWA 2018 by using examples. We have used actual cases as far as possible. Where the combined complexity of the existing case law and the effect of EUWA 2018 would have complicated rather than clarified matters – or where no case law yet exists – we have used fictional examples.

Given the interconnected nature of the concepts involved, some points are relevant at several places along the way. We have in some cases repeated a point to avoid an excess of cross-references and to reflect the fact that practitioners may be dipping in rather than reading the book from cover to cover.

We refer to the Explanatory Notes to EUWA 2018 which received Royal Assent on 26 June 2018. It is useful to bear in mind how the courts regard Explanatory Notes. The position was explained as follows in *Westminster City Council* v. *National Asylum Support Service* [2002] 1 WLR 2956 (HL):

> Insofar as the Explanatory Notes cast light on the objective setting or contextual scene of the statute, and the mischief at which it is aimed, such materials are therefore always admissible aids to construction ... What is impermissible is to treat the wishes and desires of the Government about the scope of the statutory language as reflecting the will of Parliament. The aims of the Government in respect of the meaning of clauses as revealed in Explanatory Notes cannot be attributed to Parliament. The object is to see what is the intention expressed by the words enacted.

This book is up to date as at 10 November 2020. At the time of writing, negotiations between the UK and EU on their future relationship are ongoing. It is not clear how any ensuing agreement will be implemented or whether it might have an effect on retained EU law. A large volume of secondary legislation under EUWA 2018 is expected before the end of the year.[4]

1.4 CHANGE AND CONTINUITY

As detailed in the White Paper, the driving policy behind EUWA 2018 is continuity. By converting EU law into domestic law and preserving UK laws made to implement EU obligations, the Act ensures that there is continuity and certainty for businesses, individuals and government. However, EUWA 2018 does bring about radical change to the UK's legal system:

- it transforms the statute book by repealing ECA 1972;
- it creates a new and unique category of domestic law;
- it gives wide-ranging powers to ministers;

[4] In July 2020, the government estimated that it would lay 250–300 EU exit statutory instruments between September and the end of December 2020. See letter of 27 July 2020 from the Leader of the House to the Chair of the European Statutory Instruments Committee: **https://committees.parliament.uk/publications/2223/documents/20324/default/** (accessed 10 November 2020).

- it has given rise to a huge volume of secondary legislation; and
- it amends the devolution statutes.

EUWA 2018 aims to navigate this tension between change and continuity. But there are obvious contradictions. The Act painstakingly and meticulously incorporates EU secondary legislation into domestic law but the Charter of Fundamental Rights is no longer part of domestic law.

A potent example of this tension is found in the saving of the principle of the supremacy of EU law. EUWA 2018 retains it as a way of ensuring that there is clarity in the statute book in terms of how different legislation interacts. But it is difficult to see how it can mean the same thing when its essential qualities – a means of harmonising law but also the expression of a legal system in which 'Member States have limited their sovereign rights' – no longer pertain. The resolution of these complex issues will lie in the decisions of the UK courts when applying and interpreting EUWA 2018.

CHAPTER 2

Types of EU law and EU institutions

2.1 OVERVIEW

This chapter explains the main types of EU law and their relative position in the EU legal hierarchy. An understanding of the different types of EU law and their particular features is a prerequisite for understanding how EU law is incorporated into domestic law as retained EU law.

2.2 EU TREATIES

The Union is founded on two treaties – the Treaty on European Union (TEU) and the Treaty on the Functioning of the European Union (TFEU) (the 'EU Treaties'[1]): see the TFEU, Art.1(2).

The EU Treaties perform a number of functions. For example, they set out the EU's:

- core constitutional principles
- objectives
- values
- powers
- institutional framework
- law-making processes
- rules on accession and withdrawal.

The EU Treaties are primary law[2] in the EU legal system.

The extent to which rights in treaty articles form part of retained EU law is discussed in **Chapter 13**.

---

1 The term 'EU Treaties' is used in this book to mean the TEU and TFEU, unless otherwise specified. It should not be confused with the definition of 'EU Treaties' in the Interpretation Act 1978 which has a broader meaning.

2 Primary law is not a term used by the EU treaties. However, it is useful to categorise EU law into primary, secondary and tertiary law to understand its hierarchy.

2.3 EU SECONDARY LEGISLATION

The EU Treaties confer powers on EU institutions to adopt legal acts.

The institutions may adopt the types of legal act shown in Figure 2.1 (see the TFEU, Art.288).

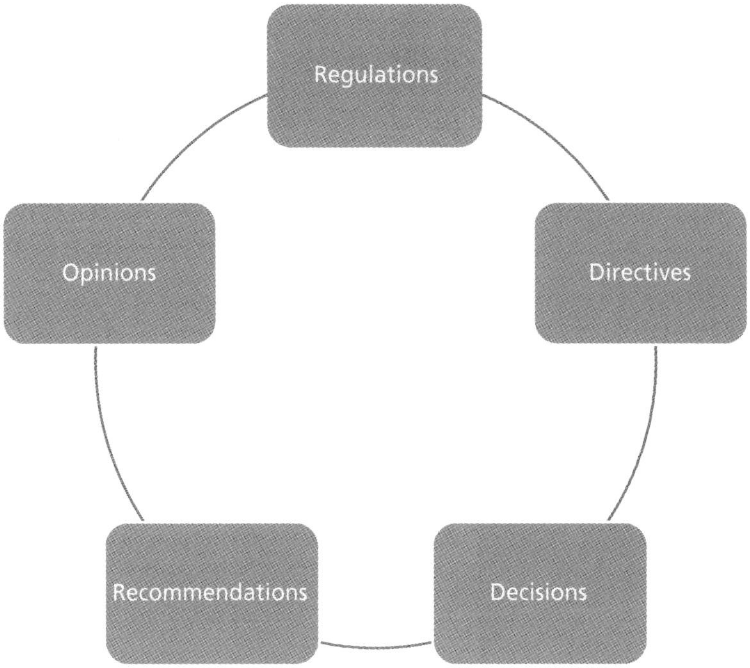

Figure 2.1 Types of legal act

2.3.1 Regulations

The key features of a regulation, in general terms, are as follows:

- First, it is directly applicable. This means that it takes effect in Member State law without the need for the Member State to take any implementing action. This ensures uniform application of a regulation throughout the EU.
- Second, a regulation has general application, meaning that it applies in all Member States. It is binding in its entirety.

The extent to which regulations form part of retained EU law is discussed in **Chapter 12**.

Example

Regulation (EC) No 763/2008 on population and housing censuses establishes common rules for the provision of comprehensive data on population and housing to ensure that comparable data is available from all the Member States.

2.3.2 Directives

A directive is binding on a Member State as to the result to be achieved but the Member State has a choice as to *how* it achieves that result.

Example

Council Directive on the education of the children of migrant workers (77/486/EEC) applies to the dependants of any worker who is a national of another Member State. It provides, among other things, that Member States should, in accordance with their national circumstances and legal systems, take appropriate measures to ensure that free tuition to facilitate initial reception is offered in their territory to these children.

In the normal course of events, a Member State makes domestic legislation which gives effect to the directive. An individual then relies on the domestic legislation to enforce their rights.

Example

The Working Time Regulations 1998 were made in domestic law to implement Directive 93/104/EC concerning certain aspects of the organisation of working time.

Not every provision of a directive will necessarily require domestic implementing legislation. For example, the transposition table published to show how the EU Emissions Trading System Directive was implemented by the UK says that Art.9 on an EU-wide quantity of allowances did not require domestic implementation because it was only applicable to the Commission.[3]

If a Member State fails to implement a directive within the stated deadline or implements it incorrectly, an individual can rely directly on the rights in the

[3] See Transposition Table: Directive 2003/87/EC as amended by Directive 2009/29/EC, establishing a scheme for greenhouse gas emission allowance trading within the Community (EU Emissions Trading System Directive): **https://assets.publishing.service.gov.uk/government/uploads/system/uploads/attachment_data/file/42948/5221-transposition-table-transposition-cons.pdf** (accessed 10 November 2020).

directive if they can show that the relevant provision in the directive has direct effect; that is to say it is clear, precise and unconditional.

Example

In Case 41/74, Ms Van Duyn, a national of the Netherlands, was refused leave to enter the UK to take up a job as a secretary with the Church of Scientology. The reason given was that the activities of the organisation were considered to be socially harmful.

The Court of Justice of the European Union (CJEU) considered Directive 64/221, Art.3(1) which said that measures taken on grounds of public policy or public security must be based on the personal conduct of the individual. The Court held that this provision conferred rights on individuals which were enforceable by them in national courts and which the national courts must protect.

Directives can have 'vertical direct effect' but not 'horizontal direct effect'. This means that an individual may rely on a provision of a directive against the state but not against another individual. There are, however, cases where the CJEU has recognised 'incidental direct effect'. These are cases where an individual relies on a directly effective provision in a directive against the state but this has an incidental effect on another individual.[4]

The saving of domestic legislation which implements directives is discussed in **Chapter 11**.

The extent to which directly effective rights in directives form part of retained EU law is discussed in **Chapters 11** and **13**. Directives themselves are not incorporated into domestic law as retained EU law (see **11.4**).

2.3.3 Decisions

A decision is binding on those to whom it is addressed. It may be addressed to a Member State, an individual or a company. Some decisions are directly applicable and some require implementation in domestic law.

Example

Council Decision No 940/2014/EU concerning the dock dues in the French outermost regions is addressed to France.

---

[4] For example, in Case C–201/02 *Wells* v. *Secretary of State for Transport*, EU:C:2004:12, the competent planning authority granted consent for mining operations at a privately owned quarry. Mrs Wells challenged the authority's decision on the basis that the authority had failed to carry out an environmental impact assessment as required by Directive 85/337. The Court held that Mrs Wells could rely on the directive even if this could ultimately result in another individual suffering a detriment in the form of loss of planning consent.

The extent to which decisions form part of retained EU law is discussed at **12.4.2**.

2.3.4 Recommendations and opinions

Recommendations and opinions are not legally binding. The Court of Justice has, however, held that they can have legal effects:

> The national courts are bound to take recommendations into consideration in order to decide disputes submitted to them, in particular where they cast light on the interpretation of national measures adopted in order to implement them or where they are designed to supplement binding [EU] provisions.
>
> (Case 322/88 *Grimaldi* v. *Fonds de Maladies Profesionnelles*, EU:C:1989:646, para.18)

Recommendations and opinions do not form part of retained EU law but they may be relevant to the interpretation of retained EU law.

Examples

Council Recommendation (2009/1019/EU) recommends that Member States adopt and implement national, regional or local action plans, aimed at improving seasonal influenza vaccination coverage.

Council Opinion (2010/C 146/02) sets out the Council's opinion on the updated convergence programme of Sweden for the period 2009–12.

2.4 EU TERTIARY LEGISLATION

The next level of EU law is commonly referred to as 'tertiary legislation' and is made up of delegated acts and implementing acts. These acts can take the form of a regulation, directive or decision. The extent to which tertiary legislation forms part of retained EU law is discussed in **Chapter 12**.

2.4.1 Delegated acts

A legislative act at the level of EU secondary legislation (the parent act) may confer a power on the Commission to make a non-legislative act which supplements or amends the parent act (see the TFEU, Art.290). This is known as a delegated act. A delegated act can only supplement or amend non-essential elements of the parent act.

The EU Treaties draw a distinction between legislative acts and non-legislative acts. The difference is one of procedure. Legislative acts are those made under the ordinary legislative procedure or under a special legislative procedure (see the TFEU, Art.297). Non-legislative acts are not made under a legislative procedure. However, non-legislative acts may still be legally binding.

Delegated acts are useful where a parent act requires frequent amendment to keep it up to date, for example to take account of the latest scientific evidence. The procedure for making a delegated act is much quicker than that for making EU secondary legislation.

Example

Regulation (EU) 2016/2031 on protective measures against pests of plants establishes criteria for the identification of pests for which the adoption of measures is necessary to prevent their introduction into and spread within Union territory. Pests which meet the criteria are listed in the Annex to the regulations and must not be introduced into the EU. The regulation gives the Commission the power to update the list in the Annex by delegated act as pests are identified which meet the criteria.

Commission Delegated Regulation (EU) 2019/1702 supplements the list in the Annex by adding pests based on the latest research from the Commission's Joint Research Centre and the European Food Safety Authority.

2.4.2 Implementing acts

A power to adopt an implementing act may be conferred on the Commission or, in duly justified cases, the Council where uniform conditions are needed to implement a legally binding EU act (see the TFEU, Art.291).

Example

Directive 2003/87/EC establishes a Modernisation Fund to support investments in modernising energy systems and improving energy efficiency in Member States. The directive confers a power on the Commission to adopt implementing acts setting out detailed rules on the operation of the Modernisation Fund. The Commission adopted an implementing act, Commission Implementing Regulation (EU) 2020/1001, which lays down detailed rules on the operation of the Modernisation Fund such as the specific information that must be provided in an application for funding.

2.5 INTERNATIONAL AGREEMENTS

The EU may conclude international agreements with third countries or international organisations. The agreements are binding on the EU institutions and the Member States. The EU Treaties do not specify where international agreements sit in the EU legal hierarchy. The case law of the CJEU has established that international agreements prevail over provisions of EU secondary legislation (see, for example, Case C–344/04 *IATA and ELFAA*, EU:C:2006:10 at para.35).

Example

The EU is a party to an Agreement with the Republic of Chile on trade in organic products.

The extent to which rights in international agreements form part of retained EU law is discussed in **Chapter 13**.

2.6 GENERAL PRINCIPLES AND THE CHARTER OF FUNDAMENTAL RIGHTS

General principles of EU law and the Charter of Fundamental Rights (the 'Charter') are considered separately in **Chapters 6** and **7**, respectively.

2.7 EU INSTITUTIONS AND OTHER EU BODIES

The interpretation of retained EU law will involve consideration of retained EU case law (as explained in **Chapter 15**). Retained EU case law makes frequent reference to the EU institutions and other EU bodies and it is useful to be familiar with what they do.

Table 2.1 summarises the role of the bodies which are defined as EU institutions in the TEU, Art.13. In addition to the institutions, there are a number of EU bodies and agencies with specialised roles.[5]

Domestic regulations made using the deficiencies-correcting power in EUWA 2018, s.8 (explained in **Chapter 17**) can replace references in retained EU law to EU institutions and other EU bodies with references to UK bodies where this is necessary to make the retained EU law operate properly. For example, a requirement to send a report to the Commission may be changed to a requirement to send a report to the Secretary of State.

It is useful in this context to have an understanding of the role of the original EU entity. There is no requirement in EUWA 2018 that a function or rule-making power which was previously exercised by an EU entity in relation to the UK is transferred to the closest UK equivalent. For example, a power to make rules which was exercised by an EU regulatory body could be transferred to ministers. The choice of UK body may have an impact on how a function is carried out or how the rules are made going forward.

[5] A full list of EU bodies and agencies can be found at: **https://europa.eu/european-union/contact/institutions-bodies_en#agencies** (accessed 10 November 2020).

Table 2.1 EU institutions

	Role	Composition	Default voting rule
European Parliament	Co-legislator with the Council Exercises budgetary functions Exercises political control and consultation Elects the President of the Commission	705 directly elected representatives of the EU's citizens	Majority of votes cast
European Council	Sets the EU's political direction and priorities	Heads of state or government of the Member States	Consensus
Council	Co-legislator with the European Parliament Exercises budgetary functions Carries out policy-making and coordinating functions	One ministerial representative from each Member State	Qualified majority
European Commission	'Guardian of the EU Treaties' Proposes legislative acts Executes the budget Manages the EU's funding programmes Represents the EU internationally (with exceptions)	27 Commissioners	Majority of Commissioners

	Role	Composition	Default voting rule
Court of Justice of the European Union (CJEU)	Ensures that in the interpretation and application of the EU Treaties the law is observed Reviews the legality of the acts of EU institutions Ensures that the Member States comply with obligations under the EU Treaties Interprets EU law at the request of the national courts and tribunals	The CJEU consists of two courts: • Court of Justice: 27 judges and 11 Advocates General • General Court: 2 judges from each Member State	Decisions are taken by majority
European Central Bank	Conducts the EU's monetary policy	Governing Council made up of 6 members of the Executive Board and governors of the national central banks of the euro area countries	Majority of members of the Governing Council having a voting right (there is a system of rotation of voting rights)
Court of Auditors	Carries out the EU's audit	One national of each Member State	Majority of members of the Court

CHAPTER 3

Case law of the Court of Justice of the European Union

3.1 OVERVIEW

The Court of Justice of the European Union is the EU's judicial body. It is made up of two courts – the Court of Justice (often referred to as the ECJ) and the General Court. Its primary task is to ensure that the law is observed in the interpretation and application of the EU Treaties. EUWA 2018 uses the term 'European Court' to refer to the CJEU.

As explained in **Chapter 15**, the CJEU's case law will remain relevant to the interpretation of retained EU law. Under EUWA 2018, s.6, in general terms, domestic courts must interpret unmodified retained EU law in accordance with CJEU decisions which were made before the end of the transition period, and they may have regard to CJEU decisions made after implementation period completion day (IPCD) so far as it is relevant.

Given that pre-IPCD CJEU case law may be determinative of a domestic case and post-IPCD CJEU case law has the potential to be influential, it is important to be familiar with the methods of interpretation that the CJEU employs in reaching its decisions. Interpreting retained EU law in accordance with relevant CJEU case law will also involve the UK courts applying the CJEU's methods of interpretation.

This chapter explains how the CJEU interprets EU law in order to inform an understanding of EUWA 2018, s.6. It also sets out the different types of action that can come before the Court of Justice and the General Court under the EU Treaties to assist the practitioner in navigating CJEU case law.

3.2 METHODS OF INTERPRETATION

The CJEU's primary methods of interpretation focus on text, context and purpose.[1] The methods are not mutually exclusive. For example, in *easyCar*, the Court said:

[1] See Lenaerts, K. and Gutiérrez-Fons, J.A. (6 July 2013) 'To say what the law of the EU is: Methods of interpretation and the European Court of Justice', Distinguished Lecture delivered on the occasion of the XXIV Law of the European Union course of the Academy of European Law.

> It is settled case-law that the meaning and scope of terms for which [EU] law provides no definition must be determined by considering their usual meaning in everyday language, while also taking into account the context in which they occur and the purposes of the rules of which they are part[.]
>
> (Case C–336/03 *easyCar (UK) Ltd* v. *Office of Fair Trading*, EU:C:2005:150, para.21)

3.2.1 Textual interpretation

A textual approach concentrates on the literal or plain meaning of the provision to be interpreted. Where the meaning of a provision is clear and unambiguous or leaves little room for doubt, the CJEU has said that a purposive or contextual interpretation may not call into question the literal meaning of the provision. For example, in Case C–48/07 *Les Vergers du Vieux Tauves*, EU:C:2008:458, para.44, the CJEU rejected the interpretation put forward by the Commission of a directive on corporation taxes because it would go against the 'clear and unambiguous' wording of the directive.

However, a textual approach may give way to a contextual or purposive approach where different language versions of an EU provision diverge. The CJEU has said:

> The different language versions of [an EU] text must be given a uniform interpretation and hence in the case of divergence between the versions the provision in question must be interpreted by reference to the purpose and general scheme of the rules of which it forms part.[2]

3.2.2 Contextual and purposive interpretation

Where the CJEU does not consider a provision to be clear and unambiguous, it applies a contextual and/or purposive method of interpretation:

- Contextual interpretation involves taking account of the scheme of the legislation and its place in the framework constituted by the EU Treaties and EU law in general.
- Purposive interpretation involves identifying the purpose of a legal act, interpreting it in light of the objectives it pursues and seeking to give effect to the legislative purpose behind it. It has been described as the 'characteristic element' of the CJEU's interpretative method.[3]

These two methods of interpretation are often used side by side and it is not always easy to separate them out. The following are examples of some of the matters to which the Court has regard in applying these methods of interpretation.

---

2 See, for example, Case 30/77 *R* v. *Bouchereau*, EU:C:1977:172, para.14.

3 Fennelly, N. (1996) 'Legal interpretation at the European Court of Justice', 20 *Fordham International Law Journal* 656.

Legal basis

The CJEU may look at the legal basis of the EU act in question to ascertain the purpose of the act (see, for example, Case C–173/99 *The Queen* v. *Secretary of State for Trade and Industry, ex parte Broadcasting, Entertainment, Cinematographic and Theatre Union (BECTU)*, EU:C:2001:356, para.37).

Recitals

The CJEU may look to the recitals of EU legislation to ascertain the purpose and intent behind the legal instrument. However, recitals cannot displace the operative provisions of a legal instrument. The CJEU has said:

> Whilst a recital in the preamble to a regulation may cast light on the interpretation to be given to a legal rule, it cannot in itself constitute such a rule.
>
> (Case 215/88 *Casa Fleischhandels* v. *BALM*, EU:C:1989:331, para.31)

Travaux préparatoires

Travaux préparatoires (or *travaux*) are the documentary evidence of the negotiation and drafting of a treaty. Traditionally, the CJEU has not tended to have recourse to the *travaux* relating to the EU Treaties when interpreting treaty articles but that has started to change in recent years. For example, in Case C–370/12 *Thomas Pringle* v. *Government of Ireland*, EU:C:2012:756, the Court did look to the *travaux* relating to the Treaty of Maastricht in determining the aim of the TFEU, Art.125, the so-called ‘no bail-out’ provision.

Legislative background

The Court has had regard to documents produced as part of the process of adopting EU secondary legislation as an aid to interpretation, for example the Commission’s legislative proposal or explanatory memorandum (see, for example, Case C–924/19 PPU *Országos Idegenrendészeti Föigazgatóság Dél-alföldi Regionális Igazgatóság*, EU:C:2020:367).

Soft law

In the EU context, the term ‘soft law’ has been used to include non-legally binding documents such as action plans, guidelines, notices and communications. While not legally binding, they can have legal effects as an aid to interpretation.

3.2.3 Consistent interpretation with international law

According to CJEU case law, provisions of EU secondary legislation 'must, as far as possible, be interpreted in a manner that is consistent with [international] agreements' (see, for example, Joined Cases C–335/11 and C–337/11 *HK Danmark*, EU:C:2013:222, para.29).

3.2.4 Legal principles and constitutional traditions common to the Member States

In interpreting an undefined EU law term, the Court may have regard to the position in the domestic law of Member States. For example, in Case 59/85 *Netherlands* v. *Ann Florence Reed*, EU:C:1986:157, the Court looked at the position in the Member States when considering whether the term 'spouse' included an unmarried partner.

3.3 TYPES OF ACTION BEFORE THE COURT OF JUSTICE

Table 3.1 sets out the different types of action that can be brought before the Court of Justice to assist the practitioner in navigating CJEU case law.

Table 3.1 Types of action before the Court of Justice

Type of action	**Features**	**Treaty article**	**Example**
Infringement/infraction proceedings	The Commission may bring an action against a Member State for a breach of EU law	TFEU, Art.258	Case C–512/08 *Commission* v. *Republic of France*
Member State v. Member State	A Member State may bring an action against another Member State for a breach of EU law. This type of action is not common	TFEU, Art.259	Case C–145/04 *Kingdom of Spain* v. *United Kingdom*
Reference for a preliminary ruling	A national court or tribunal may refer a question about the interpretation, application or validity of EU law to the Court of Justice for an authoritative view which it then applies. The highest national court in a Member State is obliged to make a reference unless the answer is clear The procedure is often characterised as a dialogue between the national court and the Court of Justice. It plays a fundamental role in ensuring that EU law is applied correctly and consistently in all Member States	TFEU, Art.267	Case C–428/07 *Horvath*
Action for annulment	A review of the legality of legislative acts and acts of the Council, Commission, European Parliament, European Council or European Central Bank intended to produce legal effects vis-à-vis third parties.	TFEU, Art.263	Case C–428/08 *United Kingdom* v. *Council*

Type of action	Features	Treaty article	Example
	Also covered are acts of bodies, offices or agencies of the EU intended to produce legal effects vis-à-vis third parties. The potential grounds of challenge are: • lack of competence • infringement of an essential procedural requirement • infringement of the EU Treaties or any rule of law relating to their application • misuse of powers		
Action for failure to act	An action to review the legality of a failure to act by the European Parliament, European Council, Council, Commission or European Central Bank or by bodies, offices or agencies of the EU	TFEU, Art.265	Case C–196/12 *Commission* v. *Council*
Opinion	A Member State, the European Parliament, the Council or the Commission may request an opinion from the Court as to whether an international agreement which the EU proposes to enter is compatible with the EU Treaties	TFEU, Art.218(11)	*Opinion 1/09*
Appeal from the General Court	Decisions of the General Court may, within two months, be subject to an appeal before the Court of Justice, on a point of law	TFEU, Art.256	Case C–106/09P *Commission* v. *Government of Gibraltar and United Kingdom*

3.4 TYPES OF ACTION BEFORE THE GENERAL COURT

Table 3.2 sets out the different types of action that can be brought before the General Court.

Table 3.2 Types of action before the General Court

Type of action	Features	Treaty article	Example
Natural or legal person v. EU institution	Action brought by natural or legal persons against acts of the institutions, bodies, offices or agencies of the EU	TFEU, Art.256	Case T–111/08 *MasterCard* v. *Commission*
Member State v. Commission	Action brought by a Member State against the Commission	TFEU, Art.256	Case T–57/07 *French Republic* v. *Commission*
Action against specific acts of the Council	Action brought against the Council relating to acts adopted in the field of State aid, trade protection measures (dumping) and acts by which it exercises implementing powers	TFEU, Art.256/ Statute of the Court of Justice, Art.51	Case T–276/13 *Growth Energy* v. *Council*
Non-contractual liability	Action seeking compensation for damage caused by the institutions or the bodies, offices or agencies of the EU or their staff	TFEU, Arts.256, 268	Case T–309/10 *Klein* v. *Commission*
Contractual disputes	A contract made by the EU may give the General Court the jurisdiction to resolve a dispute arising under that contract	TFEU, Arts.256, 272	Case T–242/17 *SC* v. *EULEX Kosovo*
Intellectual property action	Action relating to intellectual property brought against the EU Intellectual Property Office and against the Community Plant Variety Office	TFEU, Art.256	Case T–336/08 *Lindt* v. *OHIM*
Staff disputes	Action between the EU and its staff concerning employment relations	TFEU, Arts.256, 270	Case T–283/17 *SH* v. *Commission*

CHAPTER 4

Key concepts: supremacy of EU law

4.1 OVERVIEW

Chapters 4 to **8** explain the key concepts of EU law that are essential to an understanding of the operation of retained EU law. EUWA 2018 presupposes a detailed knowledge of these concepts.

It may seem odd that the principle of the supremacy of EU law needs to feature in this book at all. The House of Lords Select Committee on the Constitution said in its report on the European Union (Withdrawal) Bill that it considered that it was:

> impossible to see in what sense 'the principle of the supremacy of EU law', set out in clause 5, could meaningfully apply in the UK once it has left the EU.
>
> (Select Committee on the Constitution, *European Union (Withdrawal) Bill* (HL 2017-09, 69), para.88)

The reason why the principle of the supremacy of EU law appears in EUWA 2018, s.5 stems from one of the stated aims of the Act which is to incorporate EU law into domestic law. The principle of the supremacy of EU law is fundamental to the way EU law functions. To incorporate EU law into the domestic statute book on IPCD without retaining the principle of the supremacy of EU law would remove one of its key features. It would also unbalance the statute book.

In broad terms, EU law had supremacy over domestic law while the UK was a Member State. Removing that hierarchy while simultaneously aiming to retain a 'snapshot' of EU law as it applied in the UK immediately before IPCD would create uncertainty about how the different parts of the statute book would interact.

But the relevance of the principle of the supremacy of EU law is broader: direct effect, the duty of consistent interpretation and the disapplication of conflicting domestic law are all aspects of supremacy. Retaining the effect of the supremacy of EU law was therefore crucial to the continuity which is a central theme of EUWA 2018.

EUWA 2018 does not define the principle of the supremacy of EU law. This chapter aims to elucidate this complex principle in order to assist with an understanding of the relationship between retained EU law and supremacy.

4.2 SUPREMACY OF EU LAW

As a matter of EU law, where there is a conflict between national law and EU law, EU law will prevail. The conflicting national law will be set aside in favour of the EU rule. The supremacy of EU law over national law is of fundamental importance in the EU legal order. Without it there is no harmonisation of standards across the Member States, and the EU legal order would lack coherence and effectiveness.

The three key ways in which the EU's legal system confers rights on individuals in national law – direct effect, indirect effect and liability of the state in damages under the rule in *Francovich*[1] – are all expressions of the supremacy of EU law. These are discussed in detail in **Chapter 5**.

4.3 DEVELOPMENT OF THE SUPREMACY OF EU LAW

The principle of the supremacy of EU law is not found in the EU Treaties. Instead, it was developed by the CJEU.

The CJEU's development of the principle of supremacy reflects two main propositions:[2]

- that supremacy reflects the nature of the EU legal order;
- that supremacy facilitates the purposes of the EU.

The first proposition is illustrated in Case 26/62 *Van Gend en Loos*, EU:C:1963:1, in which the CJEU stated that:

> the [EU] constitutes a new legal order of international law, for the benefit of which the states have limited their sovereign rights, albeit within limited fields ...

The second proposition is a practical one: EU law cannot be coherent unless it operates in a consistent fashion. The EU Treaties and EU secondary legislation must apply in such a way as to achieve the same outcome in the different Member States. This approach is illustrated in Case 106/77 *Simmenthal*, EU:C:1978:49. The CJEU stated (at para. 18) that:

> any recognition that national legislative measures which encroach upon the field within which the [EU] exercises its legislative power or which are otherwise incompatible with the provisions of [EU] law had any legal effect would amount to a corresponding denial of the effectiveness of obligations undertaken unconditionally and irrevocably by Member States pursuant to the Treaty and would thus imperil the very foundations of the [EU].

The principle of supremacy applies irrespective of the status of the domestic rule. In Case 11/70 *Internationale Handelsgesellschaft mbH* v. *Einfuhr- und Vorratsstelle für Getreide und Futtermittel*, EU:C:1970:114 there was a conflict between an EU regulation and a provision of the German constitution. The German Court's

[1] Joined Cases C–6/90 and C–9/90 *Francovich and Bonifaci* v. *Italy*, EU:C:1991:428.

[2] See Steiner, J. and Woods, L. (2010) *EU Law* (10th edn: OUP) at 4.3.1.

position (as explained at para.2 of the judgment) was that provisions of the EU regulation were contrary to:

> certain structural principles of national constitutional law … which must be protected within the framework of [EU] law, with the result that the primacy of [EU] law must yield before the principles of the [German constitution].

The CJEU disagreed. National law had to give way to EU law. The principle of the supremacy of EU law was the foundation which held the EU together. The Court said (at para.3):

> the law stemming from the Treaty … cannot because of its very nature be overridden by rules of national law, however framed, without being deprived of its character as [EU] law and without the legal basis of the [EU] itself being called in question.

4.4 EFFECT OF THE SUPREMACY OF EU LAW

The effect of the principle of supremacy is that, in the event of a conflict between EU law and national law, the domestic courts must apply EU law in its entirety. The domestic courts must therefore set aside any provision of national law which may conflict with EU law. The requirement to give precedence to EU law applies whether the relevant domestic law was implemented 'prior or subsequent to the [EU] rule' (see *Simmenthal*, para.21).

The early judgments of the CJEU in relation to supremacy suggest that supremacy only applies where the rule in question has direct effect.[3] However, the development of the principle of indirect effect, also described as the duty of consistent interpretation, and *Francovich* damages suggest that supremacy is not confined to circumstances where a provision of EU law has direct effect. In the cases of *Brasserie du Pêcheur* and *Factortame*, the CJEU acknowledged that the limits of direct effect make it a 'minimum guarantee' which is 'not sufficient in itself to ensure the full and complete implementation of the Treaty' (see Joined Cases C–46/93 and C–48/93 *Brasserie du Pêcheur* v. *Bundesrepublik Deutschland* and *The Queen and Secretary of State for Transport, ex parte Factortame*, EU:C:1996:79, para.20).

4.4.1 Supremacy of EU law in the national courts of the Member States

The ways in which the supremacy of EU law manifests itself in the legal systems of the Member States are complex. National courts have accepted the supremacy of EU law where the provisions in question have direct effect (for a discussion on direct effect see **5.4**). However, their acceptance of the principle of supremacy is

[3] See how the issue is framed at paras.7 and 13 of the judgment in *Simmenthal* in terms of 'directly applicable … provisions'.

conditional. The German Federal Constitutional Court, for example, has taken the view that EU law could not operate to override core principles of the German constitution.[4]

4.5 SUPREMACY OF EU LAW IN THE UK LEGAL SYSTEM

The supremacy of EU law, at its most basic, operated as an exception to the doctrine of implied repeal. In essence, the doctrine of implied repeal means that where there is a conflict between an earlier statute and a later one, the later statute takes precedence. Inconsistent provisions in the earlier statute are treated as if they had been repealed even though the later statute does not expressly repeal them. That is because the assumption is that the will of Parliament in passing the later statute was to change the law. The latest expression of Parliament's will should therefore prevail. This is linked to the principle of the sovereignty of Parliament, and in particular that no Parliament can bind its successor.

Example: Doctrine of implied repeal

An earlier Parliament passed legislation to say that ladders for use in the home could be no higher than four metres. A later Parliament enacts legislation which states that the maximum height of ladders for domestic use is six metres. Under the doctrine of implied repeal, the earlier Act of Parliament no longer has legal effect. The law is as set out in the later Act of Parliament, and the maximum height of ladders for domestic use is six metres.

---

[4] See cases such as *Brunner* v. *European Union Treaty* [1994] 1 CMLR 57. In May 2020, the German Federal Constitutional Court held that the European Central Bank's decisions on the Public Sector Purchase Programme and the CJEU's judgment on the legality of those decisions were legally invalid (see BVerfG, Judgment of the Second Senate of 5 May 2020, 2 BvR 859/15, paras.1–237). The German Federal Constitutional Court held that the CJEU's proportionality review was so inadequate that it exceeded the judicial mandate conferred on the CJEU under the TEU, Art.19(1). This had the effect of making the judgment of the CJEU *ultra vires*. This approach has the potential to undermine both the principle of the supremacy of EU law and direct effect. See the analysis of Dimitros Kyriazis in the blog 'The PSPP judgment of the German Constitutional Court: An abrupt pause to an intricate judicial tango': **https://europeanlawblog.eu/2020/05/06/the-pspp-judgment-of-the-german-constitutional-court-an-abrupt-pause-to-an-intricate-judicial-tango/** (accessed 13 May 2020). It remains to be seen whether this is a case which turns on its own facts or whether it has wider implications for the supremacy of EU law.

Example: How supremacy of EU law created an exception to the doctrine of implied repeal

This is a fictional example which simply describes the effect of ECA 1972 on the doctrine of implied repeal.

Legislation

The EU's Domestic Appliances Directive applies to any equipment used inside the home. It states that ladders must be no more than four metres tall. The directive was implemented in UK law by the Domestic Appliances (EU Directive) Act (the 'Domestic Appliances Act'). A later UK Act, the DIY Miscellaneous Provisions Act (the 'DIY Act') is a piece of entirely domestic law. It stipulates that ladders used on private premises must be no more than eight metres tall.

Analysis

The DIY Act is not fully in conflict with the Domestic Appliances Act because the Domestic Appliances Act only applies to ladders used inside the home. So the provisions of the DIY Act which apply in private premises but outside the home do not conflict with the Domestic Appliances Act. To the extent that there is a conflict between the Domestic Appliances Act and the DIY Act (i.e. in relation to ladders within, as opposed to outside, the home) there is no implied repeal of the Domestic Appliances Act by the DIY Act because the Domestic Appliances Act gave effect to EU law.

4.5.1 Supremacy in the UK courts

As discussed in **Chapter 9**, the supremacy of EU law in the UK legal system was given effect through ECA 1972. In the case of *Factortame* (*R* v. *Secretary of State for Transport, ex p. Factortame (No.2)* [1991] 1 All ER 70), Lord Bridge stated that:

> Under the terms of the 1972 Act [i.e. ECA 1972] it has always been clear that it was the duty of a United Kingdom court, when delivering final judgment, to override any rule of national law found to be in conflict with any directly enforceable rule of [EU] law. Similarly, when decisions of the European Court of Justice have exposed areas of United Kingdom statute law which failed to implement Council directives, Parliament has always loyally accepted the obligation to make appropriate and prompt amendments. Thus there is nothing in any way novel in according supremacy to rules of [EU] law in those areas to which they apply and to insist that, in the protection of rights under [EU] law, national courts must not be inhibited by rules of national law from granting interim relief in appropriate cases is no more than a logical recognition of that supremacy.

The reference to 'directly enforceable' (or in other words directly effective: see **Chapter 5**) provisions of EU law overriding national law raises the question of the extent to which EU provisions which are not directly effective had effect in the UK's legal system. This issue was the subject of litigation in the case of *Duke* v. *GEC Reliance Ltd* [1988] AC 618. The House of Lords held that ECA 1972, s.2(1) and (4) only applied to directly effective [EU] law (see **Chapter 9** for further discussion of these sections of ECA 1972). Lord Templeman stated that:

> Section 2(4) of the European Communities Act 1972 does not … enable or constrain a British court to distort the meaning of a British statute in order to enforce against an individual [an EU] directive which has no direct effect between individuals.

The view that only directly effective provisions of EU law took effect through ECA 1972 is arguably an overly narrow reading and gives insufficient weight to other ways in which supremacy manifests itself, such as under the duty of consistent interpretation or indirect effect and the principle of state liability as expressed in *Francovich*. In the case of *Litster* v. *Forth Dry Dock & Engineering Co Ltd* [1990] 1 AC 546, the House of Lords held that domestic legislation introduced to implement a directive should be interpreted so as to comply with the directive. The court was enabled 'where necessary, to supply by implication words appropriate to comply with those obligations'. The court made no reference to *Duke* v. *GEC Reliance Ltd*, or to the fact that provisions of the directive were not directly effective.[5]

In the case of *Benkharbouche* v. *Secretary of State for Foreign and Commonwealth Affairs* [2017] UKSC 62, the Supreme Court disapplied provisions of the State Immunity Act 1978 because they conflicted with the Charter of Fundamental Rights, Art.47 (right to an effective remedy and to a fair trial). The Supreme Court took a broad approach to the application of the principle of supremacy, stating simply that 'a conflict between EU law and English domestic law must be resolved in favour of the former, and the latter must be disapplied'.[6]

---

[5] See Steiner, J. and Woods, L. (2010) *EU Law* (10th edn: OUP) at 4.4.2.2.

[6] See para.78 of the judgment. The arguments relating to the supremacy of EU law, the Charter of Fundamental Rights, Art.47 and horizontal direct effect were considered in detail by the Court of Appeal. See *Benkharbouche* v. *Embassy of the Republic of Sudan* (Rev 1) [2015] EWCA Civ 33, paras.76–81. The Court of Appeal stated that the claimants were entitled to rely on the Charter, Art.47 as having horizontal direct effect.

CHAPTER 5

Key concepts: direct effect, indirect effect and *Francovich* damages

5.1 OVERVIEW

An understanding of how direct effect, indirect effect and the rule in *Francovich* operated in domestic law when the UK was an EU Member State is fundamental to an appreciation of how EUWA 2018 deals with these concepts.

Direct effect is relevant to the issue of how rights in EU law are converted into retained EU law. Indirect effect – also known as the duty of consistent interpretation or *Marleasing*,[1] after the leading case in this area – will continue to be an important aspect of the interpretation of retained EU law by the UK courts. Claims for *Francovich* damages will no longer be capable of being brought after IPCD (although this is subject to transitional provisions: see **18.3** and **Appendix C**). EUWA 2018 does not elucidate these concepts. A clear grasp of how they operate in EU law is therefore key to comprehending their significance under the Act.

Direct effect, indirect effect and *Francovich* damages are interrelated. The principle which underpins them is that EU law is capable of conferring rights on individuals, not just on the Member States.

The principle of direct effect was developed in order to allow individuals to access the rights conferred on them where the state in question had failed to implement EU law correctly or alternatively had failed to implement the relevant measures at all.

However, direct effect of directives can only be relied upon in vertical situations (i.e. against state bodies). This left a gap in enforceability in horizontal situations (i.e. in litigation between private parties). In response to this potential unfairness, the CJEU developed the principle of indirect effect. Indirect effect, also known as consistent interpretation, requires the courts to read national law which is intended to implement EU law in a way that gives proper effect to EU law, and was considered in detail in *Marleasing*.

The principle of indirect effect, however, has its limits. The requirement is to read national law so that it is consistent with EU law, as far as this is possible. In some

[1] Case C–106/89 *Marleasing SA* v. *La Comercial Internacional de Alimentación SA*, EU:C:1990:395.

cases this may not be possible. In those circumstances there is a third remedy which can allow individuals to enforce the rights conferred under EU law, namely through bringing a claim against the state for *Francovich* damages. In terms of the relationship between the three concepts, Case C–150/99 *Stockholm Lindöpark*, EU:C:2001:34, para.35 suggests that bringing a *Francovich* claim is unnecessary if an alternative cause of action is available. This points to the following approach:[2]

- The national court should consider whether the provision in question can be interpreted so as to give effect to the relevant EU rights.
- Where this is not possible, the court should consider whether the provisions can be said to have direct effect.
- Where the tests for direct effect are not met, the final step is to consider whether the conditions for state liability have been met.

5.2 DIRECT EFFECT AND DIRECT APPLICABILITY

The concepts of direct effect and direct applicability are often viewed as interchangeable. However, it is useful to draw a distinction between them (at least at a high level). EU law is directly applicable where it does not require implementation in Member State law.[3] EU regulations, such as the General Data Protection Regulation (GDPR) are said to be directly applicable (see the TFEU, Art.288) and therefore do not require implementing legislation at domestic level. This is in contrast with directives, which require Member State implementation. Directives can be thought of as instructions to Member States to legislate to achieve a certain outcome. They do not achieve that outcome of themselves. The difference is clear from the way in which they are drafted.

Example: Provision in a regulation

General Data Protection Regulation (EU) 2016/679

Article 6

Lawfulness of processing

1. Processing shall be lawful only if and to the extent that at least one of the following applies:

   (a) the data subject has given consent to the processing of his or her personal data for one or more specific purposes

[2] See Costa, M. and Peers, S. (2020) *Steiner & Woods EU Law* (14th edn: OUP) at 9.2.5. It appears that there is no formal requirement to follow a particular order.

[3] As far as the UK was concerned, ECA 1972 enabled the interaction between the EU and UK legal spheres. For example, EU regulations were available automatically in UK law by virtue of ECA 1972, s.2(1). For further discussion see **Chapter 9**.

Explanation: Note that this provision can apply directly in Member State law. It sets out a rule to be followed and requires no further implementation.

Example: Provision in a directive

Working Time Directive 2003/88/EC

Article 3

Daily rest

> Member States shall take the measures necessary to ensure that every worker is entitled to a minimum daily rest period of 11 consecutive hours per 24-hour period.

Explanation: This provision needs to be implemented in Member State law. It is drafted as an instruction to Member States to legislate so as to achieve the specified outcome.

An EU measure is directly effective where it is sufficiently clear, precise and unconditional to be relied on by individuals in domestic courts without implementing measures. So while a directive requires domestic implementation, where that implementation is incorrect or where there are no implementing measures, an individual may be able to rely on the direct effect of certain provisions of the directive in order to enforce their rights.

However, a closer look shows that the concepts of direct effect and direct applicability are not clear-cut. Although regulations are said to be directly applicable (i.e. they do not require specific implementing measures in order for them to be enforceable), in reality regulations do contain measures which need to be implemented. For example, Member States may need to set out proportionate penalties in domestic law for breaching the requirements in the regulation. The provision requiring Member States to set out penalties may not be sufficiently clear, precise and unconditional to confer rights on individuals. In other words, it may not meet the test for direct effect.

5.3 RELATIONSHIP BETWEEN DIRECT EFFECT AND THE SUPREMACY OF EU LAW

The basis for the principle of direct effect is the supremacy of EU law. As discussed at **4.2**, the supremacy of EU law is needed in order for consistent outcomes to be achieved across the Member States. If Member State law was able to interfere with those outcomes by creating differences this would undermine the harmonisation required for areas of EU law, such as the single market, to function properly. In broad terms, direct effect assists with achieving consistent and effective outcomes across the Member States by allowing individuals to bring a challenge in circumstances where the Member State has failed to give proper effect to particular measures in EU law (for example where it has failed to implement a directive properly).

5.4 DEVELOPMENT OF DIRECT EFFECT

The principle of direct effect was first developed in the landmark case of *Van Gend en Loos*. The issue in that case was whether a treaty article (now the TFEU, Art.30 on the prohibition of customs duties between Member States) was capable of having direct effect. The CJEU stated that the EU:

> constitutes a new legal order of international law for the benefit of which the states have limited their sovereign rights, albeit within limited fields, and the subjects of which comprise not only Member States but also their nationals. Independently of the legislation of Member States, [EU] law therefore not only imposes obligations on individuals but is also intended to confer upon them rights which become part of their legal heritage.

5.5 EXTENT OF THE PRINCIPLE OF DIRECT EFFECT

Direct effect is not confined to particular types of EU instrument. It is most important in the context of directives. Direct effect enables individuals to access their rights despite incomplete or inadequate implementation of a directive by a Member State. But direct effect can apply across the spectrum of EU law, as set out in Table 5.1.

5.6 TEST FOR THE APPLICATION OF DIRECT EFFECT

The test for direct effect is different according to the type of legal instrument under consideration. However, the core requirement is that the relevant measure is sufficiently clear, precise and unconditional and does not need further implementation in EU or Member State law.

The criteria for direct effect have been applied generously.[4] This means that provisions which do not necessarily appear to meet the core requirement of direct effect have nevertheless been deemed to be enforceable.

5.7 HORIZONTAL AND VERTICAL DIRECT EFFECT

Vertical direct effect means that direct effect can be invoked by an individual against a Member State. Horizontal direct effect applies as between two private parties. Notably, directives have been deemed not to have horizontal direct effect (see Case

[4] See Steiner, J. and Woods, L. (2010) *EU Law* (10th edn: OUP) at 5.2.3.3.

152/84 *Marshall* v. *Southampton & South West Hampshire Area Heath Authority (Teaching)*, EU:C:1986:84). This gave rise to seemingly unfair outcomes in certain cases which the CJEU resolved through development of the principle of indirect effect (see **5.11**).

5.8 DIRECT EFFECT IN THE IMPOSITION OF CRIMINAL LIABILITY

Criminal liability cannot be imposed through the principle of direct effect. This is because it would offend against the principle of legal certainty (see Joined Cases C–387/02, C–391/02 and C–403/02 *Berlusconi and Others*, EU:C:2004:624).

5.9 SUMMARY OF THE OPERATION OF DIRECT EFFECT

Table 5.1 summarises how direct effect operates in the context of different EU legal instruments.

5.10 INCIDENTAL DIRECT EFFECT

In some cases individuals have relied on a directly effective provision in a directive in a case which is brought against the state. However, the case also has an incidental effect on another individual. This is known as 'incidental direct effect'. In *Wells*, a planning authority granted consent for mining operations at a privately owned quarry. Mrs Wells challenged the authority's decision on the basis that the authority had failed to carry out an environmental impact assessment as required by Directive 85/337. The CJEU held that Mrs Wells could rely on the directive even if this could ultimately result in another individual suffering a detriment in the form of loss of planning consent.

5.11 INDIRECT EFFECT OR THE DUTY OF CONSISTENT INTERPRETATION

Indirect effect is also known as the duty of consistent interpretation or *Marleasing*, after the leading case in this area. It requires Member State authorities (including the courts) to interpret all national law in so far as possible in conformity with EU law.[5] This deals with the potential unfairness caused by the fact that directives do not have horizontal direct effect and therefore cannot be relied upon in a dispute between private parties.

---

5 See *Marleasing* as discussed in Costa, M. and Peers, S. (2020) *Steiner & Woods EU Law* (14th edn: OUP) at 5.3.

Table 5.1 Operation of direct effect

Type of instrument	Test	Vertical direct effect?	Horizontal direct effect?
TEU/TFEU	Provisions must be precise, clear and unconditional and should not require additional measures, at either EU or domestic level. An example of a treaty article which has been held to have direct effect is the TFEU, Art.157 (equal pay for male and female workers). See the case of *Defrenne*[6]	Yes	Yes[7]
Charter of Fundamental Rights	The Charter rights may have direct effect, but this depends on whether the source of the right as codified in the Charter is enforceable. Examples of fundamental rights in the Charter which have been held to have direct effect include Art.47 (right to an effective remedy and a fair hearing). See, for example, the Supreme Court case of *Benkharbouche*[8]	Will depend on the precise right in question	Will depend on the precise right in question

[6] Case 43/75 *Defrenne* v. *Société anonyme belge de navigation aérienne Sabena*, EU:C:1976:56. In this case an air stewardess brought a claim for equal pay against Sabena, an airline company, on the basis that paying male air stewards more than their female counterparts for the same tasks was a breach of the TFEU, Art.157. The CJEU held that Art.157 had direct effect, thus protecting Ms Defrenne's right to equal pay.

[7] In the case of *Defrenne*, the CJEU confirmed that the TFEU, Art.157 had horizontal direct effect. The Court held that the prohibition on discrimination between men and women not only applies to the action of public authorities, but also extends to all agreements which are intended to regulate paid labour collectively, as well as to contracts between individuals. There are some limited exceptions to the horizontal direct effect of treaty articles. For example, the TFEU, Arts.34 and 35 are considered not to have horizontal direct effect. See Costa, M. and Peers, S. (2020) *Steiner & Woods EU Law* (14th edn: OUP) at 5.2.3.

[8] See para.78 of the Supreme Court judgment.

Type of instrument	Test	Vertical direct effect?	Horizontal direct effect?
General principles of EU law	The general principles can be used so as to disapply incompatible domestic law. See, for example, *Walker (Appellant)* v. *Innospec Ltd and others (Respondents)* [2017] UKSC 47[9] where national law was disapplied on the basis of the general principle of non-discrimination. EU legislation which breaches the general principles must also be disapplied: see *Kadi*[10] where the CJEU annulled a regulation freezing assets on the basis that it constituted a disproportionate interference with the right to property which is a general principle of EU law[11]	Yes[12]	Will depend on the precise general principle in question[13]
EU international agreements	Provisions must be clear, unconditional and sufficiently precise. It is also necessary to consider whether or not the 'nature and broad logic' of the international agreement precludes direct effect[14]	Yes	Yes[15]

[9] Whether this is a question of direct effect (given that there is no application in the context of the general principles of the test for direct effect, i.e. that the measure is clear, precise and unconditional) or simply a question of how the general principles can be used is perhaps a moot point. Nevertheless, it is clear that the general principles can be used to disapply conflicting domestic legislation (such as in the case of *Walker*: see **6.2**) and to quash EU legislation which does not comply with the general principles.

[10] See Joined Cases C–402/05 P and C–415/05 P *Kadi and Al Barakaat International Foundation* v. *Council and Commission*, EU:C:2008:461.

[11] For further discussion, see Rossi, L.S. (2019) 'The relationship between the EU Charter of Fundamental Rights and Directives in horizontal situations', EU Law Analysis, 25 February.

[12] See the Opinion of Advocate General Sharpston in Case C–427/06 *Birgit Bartsch* v. *Bosch und Siemens Hausgeräte (BSH) Altersfürsorge GmbH*, EU:C:2008:297, para.79.

[13] Examples of the CJEU finding that the general principles have direct effect in horizontal situations include Case C–441/14 *Dansk Industri*, EU:C:2016:278, paras.22 and 27, Case C–555/07 *Kücükdeveci*, EU:C:2010:21, paras.50–51 and Case C–144/04 *Mangold*, EU:C:2005:709.

[14] See *C&J Clark International*, para.84.

[15] For example in Case C–265/03 *Simutenkov*, EU:C:2005:213, the CJEU held that Art.23(1) of the Agreement on Partnership and Cooperation, establishing a partnership between the EU, the member states and Russia which precluded discrimination on the grounds of nationality as regards working conditions, remuneration

Type of instrument	Test	Vertical direct effect?	Horizontal direct effect?
Regulations	Provisions must be clear, precise and unconditional. This is likely to be the case because regulations are intended to take effect without the need for specific implementing legislation at domestic level (although it does not follow that every provision necessarily has direct effect) (see **12.4.1**)	Yes	Yes
Directives	For provisions to have direct effect the following conditions must be met: ● the provision is unconditional ● the provision is sufficiently clear and precise ● the provision's operation is not dependent on further action being taken by EU or national authorities ● the time limit for implementation has expired ● rights are conferred on individuals or legal persons	Yes	No
Decisions	Provisions must be sufficiently clear, precise and unconditional	Yes, where the addressee is a Member State[16]	No[17]

or dismissal, had direct effect. Although the CJEU did not specifically address the issue of horizontal direct effect, it would appear that Art.23(1) had horizontal direct effect. The case was about a challenge to the rules of a sports federation which precluded Mr Simutenkov (a Russian national) from playing football in competitions on the grounds of his nationality. Further, Art.23(1) would have limited effect if it only applied where individuals were employed by the state. This suggests that the direct effect of Art.23(1) applied horizontally as well as vertically.

[16] See Case C–156/91 *Hansa Fleisch* v. *Landrat des Kreises Schleswig-Flensburg*, EU:C:1992:423.

[17] See EUR-Lex summary on EU decisions: **https://eur-lex.europa.eu/legal-content/EN/TXT/?uri=LEGISSUM:ai0036#:~:text=Decisions%20addressed%20to%20one%20or%20several%20specific%20individuals,the%20addressee%20%28s%29%20may%20have%20a%20direct%20effect** (accessed 10 November 2020).

Although the duty only applies 'in so far as possible', the duty of consistent interpretation has been used to read provisions into domestic law and to read other provisions down, such that the distinction between direct and indirect effect has become subtle and intricate.[18]

In the UK, a number of cases have clarified the extent of the duty of consistent interpretation. In the case of *Cutter* v. *Eagle Star Insurance Co Ltd* [1998] 1 WLR 1647 Lord Clyde stated that the duty of consistent interpretation meant that:

> it is proper to strain to give effect to the design and purpose behind the legislation, and to give weight to the spirit rather than the letter ... But even in this context the exercise must still be one of construction and it should not exceed the limits of what is reasonable.

In the case of *Assange* v. *The Swedish Prosecution Authority* [2012] UKSC 22 Lord Mance summarised the main principles. He stated that:

> domestic courts may depart from the precise words used, eg by reading words in or out. The main constraint is that the result must 'go with the grain' or 'be consistent with the underlying thrust' of the legislation being construed, that is, not 'be inconsistent with some fundamental or cardinal feature of the legislation': *Vodafone 2*, para 38, per The Chancellor and Test Claimants in the FII Group Litigation, para 97, per Arden LJ, in each case citing *Ghaidan v Godin-Mendoza* [2004] 2 AC 557.

5.12 *FRANCOVICH* DAMAGES

In the case of *Francovich*, the CJEU held that in some circumstances a Member State has to pay damages to an individual where loss has been suffered due to a failure to implement a directive, where transposition is inadequate or incomplete or where the State has failed to apply EU law correctly. In *Francovich*, the Italian government had failed to implement a directive on insolvency. The workers who had incurred losses as a result were unable to rely on the direct effect of the directive because the relevant provisions were insufficiently clear, precise and unconditional. However, the CJEU found that the Italian government was liable for the workers' losses and was therefore liable to pay compensation. The CJEU recalled that the EU Treaties were intended to confer rights on individuals. The CJEU stated that the effectiveness of EU law:

> would be impaired and the protection of the rights which they grant would be weakened if individuals were unable to obtain redress when their rights are infringed by a breach of [EU] law for which a Member State can be held responsible.
>
> (*Francovich*, para.33)

[18] See the discussion in Steiner, J. and Woods, L. (2010) *EU Law* (10th edn: OUP) at 5.3.2.

Francovich has therefore been an important means, along with the principles of direct and indirect effect, of enforcing rights, particularly where those rights are contained in directives.[19]

The test to be met in order to establish state liability under *Francovich* was reformulated by the CJEU in Joined Cases *Brasserie du Pêcheur* and *The Queen and Secretary of State for Transport, ex parte Factortame*,. The test is now as follows:

- The rule of law infringed must be intended to confer rights on individuals.
- The breach must be sufficiently serious.
- There must be a direct causal link between the breach of the obligation resting on the state and the damage sustained by the injured parties.

The use of *Francovich* claims during the UK's EU membership appears to have been relatively limited. During the progress of the European Union (Withdrawal) Bill, the government stated that there had been between 22 and 25 *Francovich* cases brought in the UK (HC Deb 21 November 2017, vol.631, col.978).

[19] See Costa, M. and Peers, S. (2020) *Steiner & Woods EU Law* (14th edn: OUP) at 9.2.5.

CHAPTER 6

Key concepts: the general principles

6.1 OVERVIEW

EUWA 2018 retains the general principles of EU law. They continue to apply to the interpretation of retained EU law after IPCD. However, one of the most significant exceptions in EUWA 2018 is that the retained general principles of EU law are not capable of being used after IPCD as the basis for a claim. The domestic courts cannot use the retained general principles of EU law to disapply domestic legislation (including retained EU law) or quash conduct or otherwise decide that it is unlawful on the basis of a breach of the general principles. An understanding of the general principles of EU law and how they functioned during the UK's EU membership is fundamental to an understanding of how the retained general principles of EU law function after IPCD and what the changes brought about by EUWA 2018 might mean in practice.

There is no definitive list of the general principles of EU law. They were developed by the CJEU, like the principle of supremacy discussed in **Chapter 4**, to give coherence to the EU legal order. They draw on the common legal traditions of the Member States as well as international treaties to which the Member States are parties, most notably the European Convention on Human Rights (ECHR).[1] Like the principle of supremacy, their development was crucial in order to ensure the compatibility of the EU legal order with the constitutions and international treaty obligations of the Member States.[2] The general principles have the status of primary law. In other words, they have the same legal status as the EU Treaties and the Charter of Fundamental Rights.

The general principles of EU law are referred to in the EU Treaties, but those references are few:

---

1 Other examples include the European Social Charter (1961), Convention 111 of the International Labour Organization (1958) and the UN Convention on the Rights of the Child. See Costa, M. and Peers, S. (2020) *Steiner & Woods EU Law* (14th edn: OUP) at 6.2.3.

2 See *Internationale Handelsgesellschaft mbH*: 'respect for fundamental rights forms an integral part of the general principles of law protected by the Court of Justice, the protection of such rights, whilst inspired by the constitutional traditions common to the Member States, must be ensured within the framework of the structure and objectives of the [EU].'

- The TEU, Art.6(3) states that fundamental rights 'shall constitute general principles of the Union's law'.
- The TFEU, Art.340 says that the principle of non-contractual liability of the Union should be developed 'in accordance with the general principles common to the laws of the Member States'.
- The TEU, Art.19(1) states that the CJEU 'shall ensure that in the interpretation and application of the Treaties the law is observed'. The reference to law is understood to encompass the general principles.[3]

6.2 FUNCTION OF THE GENERAL PRINCIPLES

In EU law, the general principles work in two main ways:

- as aids to interpretation of EU law;
- as the basis for claims.

The general principles apply to the EU institutions, as well as the Member States when acting within the scope of EU law.

Where the EU institutions are acting, they must do so in accordance with the general principles. EU secondary legislation which does not comply with the general principles will be invalid.

Where Member States are acting within the scope of EU law, those actions must also comply with the general principles. Member States will be acting within the scope of EU law where they are implementing EU law (for example by legislating or exercising powers conferred under EU law) or derogating from EU law (for example by acting within the scope of an exemption from EU obligations). Action by the Member States which does not comply with the general principles can be quashed. National legislation which falls within the scope of EU law and is incompatible with the general principles can be disapplied.

Example: General principles as aids to interpretation

Joined Cases C–402/07 and C–432/07 Sturgeon, EU:C:2009:716

Regulation 261/2004 established common rules on compensation and assistance to air passengers in the event of a flight cancellation. The regulation did not expressly confer a right to compensation for passengers whose flights had merely been delayed, as opposed to cancelled. The CJEU held that 'all [EU] acts must be interpreted in accordance with primary law as a whole, including the principle of equal treatment'. The principle of equal treatment requires that 'comparable situations must not be treated differently and that different situations must not be treated in the same way unless such treatment is objectively justified'. This meant that the passengers whose flights were delayed should be treated in the same way

[3] See Lenaerts, K. and Gutiérrez-Fons, J.A. (2010) 'Constitutional allocation of powers and general principles of EU law', *Common Market Law Review*, 47: 1629.

as passengers whose flights were cancelled and they should therefore be entitled to compensation (unless particular circumstances applied).

Example: General principles as the basis for a claim

Walker (Appellant) v. Innospec Ltd and others (Respondents) [2017] UKSC 47

Mr Walker brought a claim for discrimination. He argued that the Equality Act 2010, Sched.9, para.18 was incompatible with EU law and should be disapplied because it prevented his husband from receiving the same spouse's pension in the event of his death which would have been awarded to a female spouse.

The Supreme Court held that Mr Walker was entitled to a widower's pension for his husband in the same way as a heterosexual married man would have been entitled to a pension for his widow. The Equality Act 2010, Sched.9, para.18 which precluded Mr Walker from being treated in the same way as a heterosexual man contravened the general principle of non-discrimination and should be disapplied.

The general principles do not extend the scope of EU law. In the absence of EU legislation (for example a regulation or a directive) regulating a particular area, the general principles will not apply even if the EU has competence to act in that area. In that sense they can be thought of as parasitic. They do not apply where they cannot attach to an EU law or Member State law implementing EU law.

6.3 APPLICATION OF THE GENERAL PRINCIPLES IN HORIZONTAL SITUATIONS

As discussed at **2.3.2** and in **Chapter 5**, directives have been held by the CJEU not to have direct effect in horizontal situations (i.e. between private parties, for example a company and an employee). Instead, as a matter of EU law, a private party wishing to rely on a provision of a directive which has not been implemented or has been implemented incorrectly will either need to rely on the duty of consistent interpretation (also known as indirect effect or *Marleasing*), or alternatively bring a claim against the state in accordance with the principle in *Francovich*.

Where a directive implements certain general principles (for example non-discrimination) the CJEU has held that the general principle is applicable in horizontal situations, thereby allowing rights to be enforced against private parties (for example where an employee is enforcing their rights against a private employer). In other words, the fact that the general principle is implemented through a directive does not preclude this sort of claim. Examples are *Dansk Industri*, *Kücükdeveci* and *Mangold*. This is the approach which was followed in

Walker[4] and *Benkharbouche* (see the Court of Appeal's judgment at para.81). However, case law has considered the question of horizontal direct effect in relation to specific general principles as opposed to the general principles as a whole.

6.4 EXAMPLES OF THE GENERAL PRINCIPLES

The following is by no means a comprehensive list. It gives a flavour of some of the key general principles.

6.4.1 Proportionality

Proportionality can be summarised as follows: 'the content and form of the action must be in keeping with the aim pursued.'[5]

Proportionality acts as a check on the actions of the EU institutions. They must comply with the principle of proportionality when legislating and when taking action which affects individuals.

Proportionality also applies to the Member States when acting within the scope of EU law. For example, in Case 120/78 *Rewe-Zentral AG* v. *Bundesmonopolverwaltung für Branntwein (Cassis de Dijon)*, EU:C:1979:42, the CJEU held that minimum alcohol content requirements for spirits set out in German law were disproportionate. Labelling the alcohol was a less restrictive means of protecting the consumer and ensuring fair competition between producers.

For a discussion of proportionality as a principle governing the use of EU competence, see **8.5.2**.

6.4.2 Respect for fundamental rights

The respect for fundamental rights is an important general principle of EU law (see **7.6**).

[4] In *Walker*the Supreme Court decided that it was not relevant when non-discrimination became a general principle of EU law (in other words, it did not matter when the transposition deadline for the Framework Directive expired) because any contemporary denial to Mr Walker's husband of a spouse's pension, calculated on all the years of Mr Walker's service, would be incompatible with the Framework Directive. In so far as the Equalities Act 2010, Sched.9, para.18 authorises that, it must be (see para.74). This is a different approach from the one that would be adopted if a claimant was relying on the direct effect of a directive, where the time limit for implementation must have expired before a directive can be relied upon as having direct effect (see Table 5.1).

[5] See EUR-Lex – glossary of summaries, proportionality principle: **https://eur-lex.europa.eu/summary/glossary/proportionality.html?locale=en#:~:text=PROPORTIONALITY%20PRINCIPLE%20Like%20the%20principle%20of%20subsidiarity%2C%20the,necessary%20to%20achieve%20the%20objectives%20of%20the%20Treaties** (accessed 10 November 2020).

6.4.3 Equality

The principle of equality prevents comparable situations from being treated differently unless that difference is objectively justified (see, for example, the case of *Sturgeon* at **6.2**). It is also contrary to the principle of equal treatment for different situations to be treated in the same way unless such treatment is objectively justified. In Case C–550/07 P *Akzo Nobel*, EU:C:2010:512 the CJEU stated that:

> the principle of equal treatment is a general principle of European Union law, enshrined in Articles 20 and 21 of the Charter of Fundamental Rights of the European Union.

See also the relevant sections in **Appendix D**.

6.4.4 Legal certainty and protection of legitimate expectations

The principle of legal certainty requires that the law needs to be clear, understandable and predictable so that those whose actions are regulated by it can comply with it. It has particular importance in the commercial sphere where the ability to plan ahead is important for the allocation of business resources.[6] The protection of legitimate expectations is a specific expression of legal certainty, although the CJEU uses the concepts interchangeably.[7]

Legal certainty tends to be relied upon more frequently as an aid to interpretation rather than as the basis for a claim. However, an EU measure which breaches the principle of legal certainty will be invalid.[8]

An example of the CJEU invoking the principle of legal certainty is *Defrenne*. The case concerned equal pay between men and women. The Court held that the temporal effects of its judgment should be limited in order to preserve legal certainty, stating:

> important considerations of legal certainty affecting all the interests involved, both public and private, make it impossible in principle to reopen the question [of pay] as regards ... periods prior to the date of this judgment, except as regards those workers who have already brought proceedings or made an equivalent claim.

Limiting the effect of the judgment in this way is unusual. CJEU decisions generally take effect from the date on which the provision which is being interpreted entered into force. However, the CJEU limited the temporal effect of the judgment in *Defrenne*, applying the principle of legal certainty. It did so because many businesses would have suffered considerable financial hardship if the Court had not followed this exceptional course of action.

---

6 See, for example, Sharpston, E. (1990) 'Legitimate expectations and economic reality', 15 ELR 103. See also Kleinheisterkamp, J. (2018) 'Legal certainty, proportionality and pragmatism: Overriding mandatory laws in international arbitration', *International and Comparative Law Quarterly* 67(4), 903–30.

7 See Tridimas, T. (2007) *The General Principles of EU Law* (2nd edn: OUP, Oxford EU Law Library) at p.242.

8 Tridimas (2007), p.244.

The principle of legitimate expectations is one of the most frequently relied upon grounds of challenge before the CJEU.[9] The principle was summarised by the CJEU in Case 265/85 *Van den Bergh en Jurgens BV and Van Dijk Food Products (Lopik) BV* v. *Commission*, EU:C:1987:121. The Court stated that:

> any trader in regard to whom an institution has given rise to justified hopes may rely on the principle of the protection of legitimate expectation. On the other hand, if a prudent and discriminating trader could have foreseen the adoption of [an EU] measure likely to affect his interests, he cannot plead that principle if the measure is adopted.

Legitimate expectations has been the basis for invalidating a measure or the basis for an award of damages against EU institutions.[10] An important aspect of the principle of legitimate expectations is non-retroactivity of EU law, in particular in the context of criminal matters, where the prohibition is absolute.[11]

An example of a case based on legitimate expectations (among other grounds) is Case C–482/17 *Czech Republic* v. *Parliament and Council*, EU:C:2019:1035. The Czech Republic challenged Directive (EU) 2017/853. The directive had been brought in to limit civilians' access to firearms following terrorist attacks. The Czech Republic's challenge was based on the assertion that, *inter alia*, the ownership of firearms by Czech civilians was part of their cultural heritage and that the measures in the directive were incompatible with the principle of legitimate expectations because the requirements would lead to retroactive application and would be detrimental to the interests of the individuals concerned.

The CJEU disagreed. The plea in relation to legitimate expectations was unfounded. Legitimate expectations only applied where the person in question had been given 'precise assurances' by EU authorities and could not be pleaded where a 'prudent and alert economic operator [could] foresee that the adoption of an EU measure is likely to affect his or her interests'. The publication of the Directive in the Official Journal of the European Union (the 'OJ') meant that individuals should have foreseen that their authorisations to hold the specified weapons would be revoked.

6.4.5 Principles of effectiveness and equivalence

The principle of effectiveness, or effective judicial protection:

> obliges Member State courts to ensure that national remedies and procedural rules do not render claims based on EU law impossible in practice or excessively difficult to enforce.
> (Opinion of Advocate General Jääskinen, Case C–536/11 *Bundeswettbewerbsbehörde* v. *Donau Chemie AG*, EU:C:2013:67)

9 Tridimas (2007), p.251.
10 Tridimas (2007), p.251.
11 Tridimas (2007), pp.252–53.

The principle of effectiveness has been cited in a number of cases in the context of sex discrimination claims. In Case 14/83 *Von Colson* v. *Land Nordrhein-Westfalen*, EU:C:1984:153, the complainants made successful claims of sex discrimination in relation to job applications. They were awarded the cost of their train fares to their respective job interviews. The question referred to the CJEU was whether this level of compensation was consistent with the principle of effectiveness. The CJEU held:

> If a Member State chooses to penalize breaches of [the prohibition on sex discrimination] by the award of compensation, then in order to ensure that it is effective and that it has a deterrent effect, that compensation must in any event be adequate in relation to the damage sustained and must therefore amount to more than purely nominal compensation such as, for example, the reimbursement only of the expenses incurred in connection with the application.

The principle of effectiveness was also cited in Case C–213/89 *Factortame I (The Queen* v. *Secretary of State for Transport, ex parte Factortame Ltd*, EU:C:1990:257). The House of Lords made a reference to the CJEU. The House of Lords found that the appellants in the main proceedings would suffer irreparable damage if an interim injunction was not granted. However, the English courts had no power in national law to grant the injunction because of the common law rule that an interim injunction could not be granted against the Crown. The question referred was whether notwithstanding that rule of national law, English courts were required, under EU law, to grant an interim injunction against the Crown.

The CJEU held (at paras.20–21) that:

> any provision of a national legal system and any legislative, administrative or judicial practice which might impair the effectiveness of [EU] law by withholding from the national court having jurisdiction to apply such law the power to do everything necessary at the moment of its application to set aside national legislative provisions which might prevent, even temporarily, [EU] rules from having full force and effect are incompatible with those requirements, which are the very essence of [EU] law ... the full effectiveness of [EU] law would be just as much impaired if a rule of national law could prevent a court seised of a dispute governed by [EU] law from granting interim relief in order to ensure the full effectiveness of the judgment to be given on the existence of the rights claimed under [EU] law. It follows that a court which in those circumstances would grant interim relief, if it were not for a rule of national law, is obliged to set aside that rule.

The principle of equivalence is illustrated in the case of *Palmisani*. A claim to recover loss suffered due to late implementation of a directive was held to be comparable to a claim for non-contractual state liability. The CJEU stated that:

> [EU] law, as it stands at present, does not preclude a Member State from requiring any action for reparation of the loss or damage sustained as a result of the belated transposition of the Directive to be brought within a limitation period of one year from the date of its transposition into national law, provided that that procedural requirement is no less favourable than procedural requirements in respect of similar actions of a domestic nature.
>
> (Case C–261/95 *Palmisani* v. *Instituto Nazionale della Providenza Sociale (INPS)*, EU:C:1997:351)

CHAPTER 7

Key concepts: fundamental rights

7.1 OVERVIEW

Fundamental rights are general principles of EU law. They remain relevant after IPCD as aids to interpretation of retained EU law. As with other retained general principles of EU law they cannot be used as the basis for a claim after IPCD. The courts cannot disapply or quash domestic legislation (including retained EU law) on the basis that it conflicts with fundamental rights. Further, the courts cannot quash conduct or declare it otherwise unlawful on the basis of a breach of fundamental rights.

The Charter of Fundamental Rights will not apply in the UK's domestic legal system after IPCD. However, this does not mean that the rights reflected in the Charter are no longer protected in domestic law. Domestic legislation, including retained EU law and the ECHR as implemented through the Human Rights Act 1998 (HRA 1998), will protect rights after IPCD, albeit subject to certain exceptions.[1] Nonetheless, protections for fundamental rights in the UK will be weaker after IPCD because none of the remaining protections allows the courts to disapply primary legislation which does not comply with fundamental rights.[2] Prior to IPCD a court could disapply domestic legislation which breached fundamental rights where those rights formed part of EU law.

An understanding of how fundamental rights operated in the EU's legal system is crucial to making sense of how EUWA 2018 changes the operation of fundamental rights in UK law after IPCD. This is one of the most complex areas of EUWA 2018 and the effect of the changes it makes creates significant uncertainty.

---

1 For example, the rights which related to EU membership such as the right to vote and to stand as a candidate at elections to the European Parliament (Charter, Art.39) will be lost.

2 The courts are also precluded from disapplying retained direct principal EU legislation for HRA 1998 claims (EUWA 2018, Sched.8, para.30(1)). Retained direct principal EU legislation is to be treated as primary legislation for the purposes of HRA 1998.

7.2 BACKGROUND: FUNDAMENTAL RIGHTS AND HUMAN RIGHTS

There is often confusion about the rights protected in the EU legal system as compared with the Council of Europe's[3] European Convention on Human Rights (ECHR). The relationship between the Charter of Fundamental Rights and the ECHR is discussed at **7.16**. However, this short overview sets out the basic, high-level differences.

7.2.1 Difference between fundamental rights and human rights

The term 'fundamental rights' is used in the EU legal order to describe human rights. The EU's Fundamental Rights Agency describes the difference between fundamental rights and human rights in the following way:

> Traditionally, the term 'fundamental rights' is used in a constitutional setting whereas the term 'human rights' is used in international law. The two terms refer to similar substance as can be seen when comparing the content in the Charter of Fundamental Rights of the European Union with that of the European Convention on Human Rights.[4]

7.2.2 The Charter of Fundamental Rights and the European Convention on Human Rights

The Charter of Fundamental Rights is the EU's text on human rights and fundamental freedoms, adopted in 2000. The ECHR is an international treaty under which the member states of the Council of Europe undertake to protect fundamental civil and political rights for everyone within their jurisdiction. The ECHR was signed on 4 November 1950 in Rome and entered into force in 1953. Many of the rights set out in the Charter are based on equivalent rights in the ECHR. For further discussion, see **7.16**.

7.2.3 The European Court of Human Rights and the Court of Justice of the European Union

The European Court of Human Rights (ECtHR) is an international court set up in 1959. It sits in Strasbourg in France and is sometimes known as the 'Strasbourg Court'. It rules on individual or state applications alleging violations of the civil and political rights set out in the ECHR.

---

[3] The Council of Europe is separate from the EU. It was founded in the wake of the Second World War in 1949. Its aims are to promote human rights, democracy and the rule of law. It has 47 member states, 27 of which are member states of the EU. All the member states of the Council of Europe are signatories to the ECHR. For further information see: **www.coe.int/en/web/about-us/who-we-are** (accessed 10 November 2020).

[4] See European Union Agency for Fundamental Rights, Frequently Asked Questions: **https://fra.europa.eu/en/about-fundamental-rights/frequently-asked-questions** (accessed 10 November 2020).

The CJEU ensures compliance with EU law. It rules on the interpretation and application of the EU Treaties, including the Charter of Fundamental Rights. The CJEU sits in Luxembourg and is sometimes referred to as the 'Luxembourg Court'.

7.3 EU FUNDAMENTAL RIGHTS: GENERAL

The EU's founding treaties made no mention of fundamental rights. They were developed through the case law of the CJEU.[5]

The CJEU's 'discovery' of fundamental rights was a necessary step in introducing coherence in the relationship between EU and national law. As discussed in **Chapter 4**, the principle of the supremacy of EU law evolved for the same reason: to solve the question of how the EU and the domestic legal frameworks could interact within the EU legal order. The Member States' constitutional settlements and legal systems were underpinned by a respect for fundamental rights. Without corresponding rights in the EU's legal system, coherence as between the domestic and EU level would not have been possible. By reading fundamental rights protections into the EU Treaties, the CJEU avoided a clash between the EU and the Member States' legal orders which would have undermined the supremacy of EU law and through that the European project.[6]

Fundamental rights are general principles of EU law. They are applicable to the EU institutions. They also apply when the Member States are taking action which is regulated under the EU Treaties, including when they are implementing EU law. This is known as 'acting within the scope of Union law'. Fundamental rights are used as an aid to interpretation and also as the basis for legal challenges by individuals or the Member States. EU and domestic legislation which does not comply with fundamental rights is invalid.

7.4 EVOLUTION OF FUNDAMENTAL RIGHTS IN THE EU

The first case in which the CJEU referenced fundamental rights was Case 29/69 *Erich Stauder* v. *City of Ulm – Sozialamt*, EU:C:1969:57. The Court stated (at para.7) that fundamental rights were 'enshrined in the general principles of [EU] law and protected by the Court'.

---

[5] The first reference to fundamental rights in the treaties was in the Maastricht Treaty. Article F of Title 1 stated: 'The Union shall respect fundamental rights, as guaranteed by the European Convention for the Protection of Human Rights and Fundamental Freedoms signed in Rome on 4 November 1950 and as they result from the constitutional traditions common to the Member States, as general principles of [EU] law.'

[6] See Steiner, J. and Woods, L. (2010) *EU Law* (10th edn: OUP) at 6.3.1; and HM Government (2014) *Review of the Balance of Competences between the United Kingdom and the European Union: Fundamental Rights*, Chapter 2: **https://assets.publishing.service.gov.uk/government/uploads/system/uploads/attachment_data/file/334999/review-of-boc-between-uk-eu-fundamental-rights.pdf** (accessed 10 November 2020).

The potentially profound difficulty caused by the EU Treaties' silence on fundamental rights became clear in *Internationale Handelsgesellschaft mbH*. In this case there was a conflict between an EU regulation and a provision of the German constitution. The German Federal Constitutional Court made clear that if there was a conflict between fundamental rights in the German constitution and EU law then the provisions of the German constitution would take precedence over EU law. The CJEU's method of resolving the problem was to emphasise the EU's adherence to fundamental rights principles. It stated:

> respect for fundamental rights forms an integral part of the general principles of law protected by the Court of Justice. The protection of such rights, whilst inspired by the constitutional traditions common to the Member States must be ensured within the framework of the structure and objectives of the [Union].

In Case 4/73 *J. Nold, Kohlen- und Baustoffgroßhandlung* v. *Commission*, EU:C:1974:51, the CJEU first stated (at para.13) that international treaties for the protection of human rights on which the Member States had collaborated or to which they were signatories could 'supply guidelines which should be followed within the framework of [EU] law'.

7.5 CHARTER OF FUNDAMENTAL RIGHTS

The Charter was 'proclaimed' in December 2000. It brought together the fundamental rights recognised by the EU and made them more visible.

One of the key policy reasons for drafting the Charter was that it was perceived to be important that the EU institutions were constrained by the same principles which apply to the governments of the Member States.[7] Further, the competences conferred on the Union had been expanded into areas which were more likely to encroach on areas of fundamental rights.[8]

The Charter became legally binding when the Lisbon Treaty came into force in 2009.

The statements of the CJEU on the status of fundamental rights in the EU's legal order were codified in the TEU, Art.6(3):

---

[7] See the evidence given to Parliament by former UK Attorney General Lord Goldsmith QC, European Scrutiny Committee, *The Application of the EU Charter of Fundamental Rights in the UK: A State of Confusion* (HC 2013–14, 979). This policy aim appears to have been successful. In its 2018 'Report on the application of the EU Charter of Fundamental Rights', the European Commission states that: 'A culture of fundamental rights has gradually developed in the EU institutions. Policy makers are increasingly aware of the importance of ensuring that their policies are Charter compliant', section 4, p.17: **https://op.europa.eu/en/publication-detail/-/publication/784b02a4-a1f2-11e9-9d01-01aa75ed71a1/language-en** (accessed 10 November 2020).

[8] See Steiner, J. and Woods, L. (2010) *EU Law* (10th edn: OUP) at 6.3.1.

> Fundamental rights, as guaranteed by the European Convention for the Protection of Human Rights and Fundamental Freedoms and as they result from the constitutional traditions common to the Member States, shall constitute general principles of the Union's law.

7.6 RELATIONSHIP BETWEEN THE CHARTER AND THE GENERAL PRINCIPLES

The TEU, Art.6(3) states that fundamental rights are general principles of EU law. The Charter codifies those general principles which are fundamental rights. The Charter and the general principles are therefore intended to have the same meaning and scope and are often referred to interchangeably.[9] They are both part of the primary law of the EU.

7.7 AIM AND STATUS OF THE CHARTER

The aim of the Charter as set out in the preamble was to make fundamental rights more visible. The Charter was given the same status as the EU Treaties (see the TEU, Art.6(1)).

The Charter does not extend the competences of the EU (see the TEU, Art.6(1)). This is also confirmed in the Charter, Art.51(2). It states:

> The Charter does not extend the field of application of Union law beyond the powers of the Union or establish any new power or task for the Union, or modify powers and tasks as defined in the Treaties.

The Charter cannot be used as the basis for legislation. However, some of the legal bases in the TFEU reflect rights which also exist in the Charter (see, for example, the TFEU, Art.16(1) and the Charter, Art.8 in relation to data protection, and the TFEU, Art.19(1) and the Charter, Art.21 in relation to non-discrimination).

7.8 STRUCTURE OF THE CHARTER

The Charter contains six substantive titles. These are:

- dignity
- freedoms
- equality
- solidarity
- citizens' rights
- justice.

[9] See HM Government (2014) *Review of the Balance of Competences between the United Kingdom and the European Union: Fundamental Rights*, para.3.39 **https://assets.publishing.service.gov.uk/government/uploads/system/uploads/attachment_data/file/334999/review-of-boc-between-uk-eu-fundamental-rights.pdf** (accessed 10 November 2020).

The seventh title on general provisions explains how the Charter should be interpreted and applied. The Charter is also accompanied by Explanations. The Explanations are essential to a proper understanding of the Charter as they set out the sources and limits of the rights it contains. The EU Treaties, and the Charter itself, provide that 'due regard' must be had to the Explanations when interpreting the Charter (see the Charter, Art.52(7) and the TEU, Art.6(1)).

7.9 GENERAL PROVISIONS

The general provisions explain how the Charter is to be interpreted.

7.9.1 Article 51

Article 51 sets out the scope of application of the Charter: that it applies to the EU's institutions and to the Member States when acting within the scope of EU law. It also confirms that the Charter does not extend EU competence.

7.9.2 Article 52

Article 52 deals with the scope and interpretation of rights and principles. It states that:

- limitations on the exercise of the rights and freedoms set out in the Charter must be provided by law and respect the essence of those rights and freedoms. Limitations may only be made if they are proportionate and meet objectives of general interest recognised by the EU or the need to protect the rights and freedoms of others;[10]
- where rights in the Charter are provided for in the EU Treaties they are subject to the conditions and limits set down in the Treaties;[11]
- where the rights in the Charter correspond to rights in the ECHR the meaning and scope of those rights should be the same as in the ECHR, although the EU is not prevented from providing more extensive protections;[12]

[10] See the Charter, Art.52(1); it reflects cases such as Case C–356/12 *Glatzel*, EU:C:2014:350, paras.49–72 which confirm that the rights set out in the Charter are not absolute (except where they correspond to absolute rights in the ECHR). Instead, they may be limited where the restrictions in question correspond to objectives of general interest pursued by the EU and do not constitute a disproportionate and unreasonable interference which undermines the substance of those rights. For further detail see the Charter Explanations.

[11] See Art.52(2), the effect of which is that where rights in the Charter mirror the rights reflected in the treaties then they have the same meaning. In other words, the rights in the Charter should be read consistently with the source of the right.

[12] See Art.52(3); for further detail, see the Charter Explanations. This paragraph confirms that the rights in the Charter should be read in light of the source of the right.

- rights which stem from the constitutional traditions of the Member States should be interpreted in harmony with those traditions;[13]
- the principles set out in the Charter[14] can be implemented by the EU institutions in legislation or executive action and by the Member States when implementing EU law. The principles can only be used for interpreting the legislation which implements them or ruling on the legality of that legislation;[15]
- full account should be taken of national laws and practices as specified in the Charter;[16]
- the CJEU and the courts in the Member States must have due regard to the Charter Explanations.[17]

7.9.3 Article 53

Article 53 guarantees that nothing in the Charter will be interpreted as restricting or adversely affecting human rights and fundamental freedoms as recognised by EU law, international law and international agreements to which the EU or all the Member States are party, including the ECHR.

7.9.4 Article 54

Article 54 provides a safeguard against abuse of the Charter rights. It states that nothing in the Charter can be interpreted as implying any right to engage in activities aimed at destroying rights or freedoms recognised in the Charter or at limiting them beyond the extent envisaged by the Charter.

7.10 DIFFERENCE BETWEEN RIGHTS AND PRINCIPLES IN THE CHARTER

Some of the 'rights' set out in the Charter are in fact principles rather than rights. It is not always easy to distinguish between rights and principles. While some of the articles of the Charter are identified as being principles, there is no list of which of the articles reflect rights, and which reflect principles.[18]

---

13 See Art.52(4); as with para.(3), para.(4) states that the relevant rights should be read consistently with their source.

14 These should not be confused with the general principles of EU law, which include fundamental rights and have the status of primary law in the EU legislative order.

15 See Art.52(5); for further discussion see **7.10**.

16 See Art.52(6). The Charter Explanations state that para.(6) refers to the articles in the Charter which make reference to national laws and practices. Examples include Art.9 (right to marry and found a family) and Art.10(2) (right to conscientious objection). For further detail see **Appendix D**.

17 See Art.52(7).

18 See Costa, M. and Peers, S. (2020) *Steiner & Woods EU Law* (14th edn: OUP) at 6.4.2.

Principles are distinct from the civil and political rights which are protected under the ECHR. Principles stem from 'new social and economic rights' which are not justiciable in the same way as the rights under the ECHR. Instead, they inform policy making.[19]

The principles only give rise to rights where they are implemented in EU or national law. They can also be used to interpret the law which implements them.[20] However, the extent to which principles can be relied upon as the basis for challenging the legislation which implements them is questionable. For example, the CJEU found in *Glatzel*, paras.74–79 that the principle in Art.26 (integration of persons with disabilities) was insufficiently precise to be enforceable.

7.11 DID THE CHARTER APPLY IN THE UK?

There has been some confusion as to whether the UK had an 'opt-out' from the Charter by virtue of a protocol to the EU Treaties entitled 'Protocol (no 30) on the application of the Charter of Fundamental Rights of the European Union to Poland and to the United Kingdom'. The Protocol did not disapply the Charter in relation to the UK and Poland; rather it clarified the shared understanding of all Member States as to certain aspects of the application of the Charter at the request of Poland and the UK. The application of the Charter to the UK was confirmed by the CJEU in Joined Cases C–411/10 and C–493/10 *NS* v. *Secretary of State for the Home Department*, EU:C:2011:865. The CJEU stated (at para.119) that the Protocol 'does not call into question the applicability of the Charter in the United Kingdom'.

7.12 DOES THE CHARTER HAVE DIRECT EFFECT?

Some of the fundamental rights in the Charter have been held to have direct effect. They have been used to disapply conflicting domestic law. Examples include the *ERT* case (see **7.14**), *Benkharbouche* (see **4.5.1**) and *Walker* (see **6.2**). These fundamental rights apply in horizontal situations (i.e. between private parties) as well as vertically (against the state). However, this is by no means the case for all of the articles in the Charter. For further detail see **Appendix D**.

7.13 APPLICATION OF THE CHARTER TO THE EU INSTITUTIONS

The Charter applies to the EU institutions in the following ways:

---

[19] See also European Union Committee, *The Treaty of Lisbon: An Impact Assessment* (HL 2007–08, 62-I) at 5.17.

[20] Ibid.

- When the EU is legislating: secondary EU legislation which does not comply with the fundamental rights set out in the Charter is invalid. However, the CJEU will not set aside provisions of the EU Treaties on the grounds that they conflict with the Charter:

Example

Joined Cases C–293/12 and C–594/12 Digital Rights Ireland Ltd and Seitlinger, EU:C:2014:238

The CJEU held that a directive enabling the retention of data processed on the internet or on mobile phone networks for the purposes of investigating serious crime and terrorism was invalid.

EU legislation was required to lay down clear and precise rules and minimum safeguards to ensure that individuals had sufficient guarantees to protect their personal data from the risk of abuse, unlawful use and access. Under the legislation the interference with the fundamental right to data protection (Charter, Art.8(1)) and respect for private life (Charter, Art.7) was insufficiently circumscribed. Collection and use of the data was not limited to what was strictly necessary. The legislation did not contain adequate safeguards.

By adopting the directive, the EU legislature had exceeded the limits imposed by compliance with the principle of proportionality in light of the Charter, Arts.7, 8 and 52(1). The legislation was therefore invalid.

- When the EU institutions are taking action:

Example

Case C–185/95 P Baustahlgewebe, EU:C:1998:608

Baustahlgewebe was a company that made steel mesh products. Following investigations by the European Commission it was fined for price fixing. It appealed the fine on the basis that the Court of First Instance (now the General Court) had infringed the general principle of EU law requiring prompt determination of judicial proceedings.

The CJEU held that fundamental rights applied in this context. The Court noted that the ECHR, Art.6(1) provides that everyone is entitled to a fair and public hearing within a reasonable time. The general principle of EU law that everyone is entitled to a fair legal process is inspired by those fundamental rights. In particular, the right to legal process within a reasonable period is applicable in the context of proceedings brought against a Commission decision imposing fines on an undertaking for infringement of competition law (see paras.20–21).

Example

Case C–619/18 Commission v. Poland, EU:C:2019:531

The European Commission can rely on the Charter in infringement proceedings against the Member States. In this case, the Commission referred Poland to the CJEU on the basis that the new Polish law on the Supreme Court breached the TEU, Art.19(1) read in combination with the Charter, Art.47. The Polish law on the retirement of judges was incompatible with EU law because it undermined the principle of judicial independence.

- When interpreting the EU Treaties and secondary legislation:

Example

Case C–212/13 Rynes, EU:C:2014:2428

The CJEU considered the scope of the exemption from the 1995 Data Protection Directive for processing of personal data in purely personal or household contexts. The question before the Court was whether a CCTV camera which was used to protect the family home but which also filmed part of the street opposite fell within the exemption. The CJEU ruled that the exemption did not apply and therefore that the processing was regulated by the directive. The Court stated that the directive had to be interpreted in light of the fundamental rights set out in the Charter – in particular the right to privacy. Therefore, the exemption in the directive needed to be construed narrowly (see para.29).

Example

Case C–311/18 Data Protection Commissioner v. Facebook Ireland and Maximillian Schrems [Schrems II], EU:C:2020:559

This case concerned the validity of a Commission Decision (Commission Implementing Decision (EU) 2016/1250 (Privacy Shield)) enabling transfer of data from the EU to the US. The CJEU held that the decision was invalid on the basis that interception of the data by US intelligence services constituted a disproportionate interference with the rights of data subjects. Further, there was a lack of proper judicial redress. The Commission Decision was therefore incompatible with the relevant provisions of the GDPR, read in the light of the Charter.

7.14 APPLICATION OF THE CHARTER TO THE MEMBER STATES

The Charter also applies to the EU Member States when they act within the scope of EU law. The Charter therefore applies in the following ways:

- Where a Member State public body acts on the basis of an EU obligation:

Example

Case 5/88 Wachauf v. Germany, EU:C:1989:321

Fundamental rights apply when a Member State government department is distributing farming subsidies on the basis of an EU regulation (or under another provision of EU law).

- Where a Member State implements national legislation to give effect to a directive:

Example

Case C–20/00 Booker Aquaculture, EU:C:2003:397

A Member State is required to implement directives in a way which complies with EU law. The relevant domestic provisions which implemented the directive in question required diseased fish to be destroyed. That requirement engaged the right to property although it did not constitute a disproportionate interference with that right. The national scheme was therefore compatible with the fundamental right to property (see para.93 of the judgment).

- When a Member State derogates from EU law, in other words when a Member State relies on an exemption from EU law requirements (including when deciding whether to exercise a derogation in EU law):

Example

Case C–260/89 ERT, EU:C:1991:254

In this case, the CJEU held that EU law did not preclude conferring a television monopoly for reasons of a non-economic nature relating to the public interest. However, where a Member State wishes to rely on derogations which are likely to obstruct the exercise of the freedom to provide services, such justification must be interpreted in light of the general principles of EU law, in particular fundamental rights (see paras.41–45 of the judgment). The national rules in question could fall within the derogations only if they were compatible with fundamental rights.

Example

R (on the application of Zagorski) v. Secretary of State for Business, Innovation and Skills [2010] EWHC 3110 (Admin) (29 November 2010)

Ministers were acting within the scope of EU law when deciding whether to legislate to impose restrictions on the export of drugs which could be used as a preliminary to lethal injections for prisoners on death row. The question as to whether ministers were acting within the scope of Union law did not depend on whether they decided to legislate or not. Ministers were implementing Union law in deciding whether to impose a ban. That decision had to be made in accordance with fundamental rights (see para.70 of the judgment).

It can be unclear whether a Member State is acting within the scope of EU law. In Case C–206/13 *Cruciano Siragusa* v. *Regione Sicilia – Soprintendenza Beni Culturali e Ambientali di Palermo*, EU:C:2014:126, the CJEU stated that the following factors were relevant:

- Whether the legislation is intended to implement a provision of EU law.
- The nature of that legislation and whether it pursues objectives other than those covered by EU law. The legislation may fall outside the scope of EU law even if it is capable of indirectly affecting EU law.
- Whether there are specific rules of EU law on the matter or whether the domestic legislation is capable of affecting EU law.[21]

7.15 THE CHARTER IN THE DOMESTIC COURTS

The Charter is used in the following way in the domestic courts of the Member States:

- To interpret EU or national legislation:[22]

[21] See Case C–309/96 *Annibaldi* v. *Sindaco del Comune di Guidonia and Presidente Regione Lazio*, EU:C:1997:631, paras.21–23; Case C–40/11 *Yoshikazu Iida* v. *Stadt Ulm*, EU:C:2012:691, para.79; and Case C–87/12 *Ymeraga and Others*, EU:C:2013:291, para.41.

[22] The 2018 'Report on the application of the EU Charter of Fundamental Rights' stated that national courts in the EU made reference to the Charter during the course of 2018 in particular in the area of asylum and migration, data protection and judicial cooperation in criminal matters. The 2018 cases confirmed past patterns in relation to references to specific articles of the Charter. The right to an effective remedy and to a fair trial (Art.47) remained the Charter provisions most often referred to. National judges also referred to the right to the respect for private and family life (Art.7) and the right to protection of personal data (Art.8).

Example

The Rugby Football Union (Respondent) v. Consolidated Information Services Ltd (Formerly Viagogo Ltd) (In Liquidation) (Appellant) [2012] UKSC 55

The question before the Supreme Court was whether disclosing the names and addresses of individuals who had bought and sold tickets in breach of the Rugby Football Union (RFU)'s clear ticket policy was a disproportionate interference with their rights under the Charter, Art.8 (protection of personal data). This question fell within the scope of Union law.

The Court accepted that the assessment of proportionality involved balancing the rights of the RFU to its property rights as protected by the ECHR, Protocol No.1, Art.1 and intellectual property rights within the Charter, Art.17(2), against the right to privacy under ECHR, Art.8(1) and the Charter, Art.7 and the right to the protection of personal data under the Charter, Art.8.

In this case when weighing the impact of disclosure on individuals' right to privacy against the rights of the RFU in obtaining the information, the balance fell in favour of the RFU in obtaining the information.

- To check the legality of EU[23] or national law:

Example

In the *Schrems II* case (see **7.13**), the Irish High Court referred the question to the CJEU of whether the European Commission's standard contractual clauses which are annexed to a Commission Decision[24] can be used to send personal data outside the EU. Some of the questions explicitly referenced the Charter of Fundamental Rights. An extract from the reference is set out below:

> (4) Given the facts found by the High Court in relation to US law, if personal data is transferred from the European Union to the United States under [the SCC Decision] does this violate the rights of individuals under Articles 7 and/or 8 of the Charter?
>
> (5) Given the facts found by the High Court in relation to US law, if personal data is transferred from the European Union to the United States under [the SCC Decision]:
>
> (a) does the level of protection afforded by the United States respect the essence of an individual's right to a judicial remedy for breach of his or her data privacy rights guaranteed by Article 47 of the Charter?

- To give individuals direct access to a right:

23 Only the CJEU can declare an EU measure invalid. However, domestic courts can make a preliminary reference to the CJEU which results in the CJEU declaring the EU measure to be invalid.

24 Commission Decision 2010/87/EU of 5 February 2010 on standard contractual clauses for the transfer of personal data to processors established in third countries under Directive 95/46/EC of the European Parliament and of the Council [2010] OJ L39/5.

Example

Walker (Appellant) v. Innospec Ltd (Respondent) [2017] UKSC 47

Mr Walker relied on EU equality legislation to challenge UK law which enabled employers to pay same-sex partners lower pension benefits than those paid to heterosexual couples. The Supreme Court found that the UK legislation was invalid and must be disapplied as being contrary to the general principle of non-discrimination.[25]

7.16 RIGHTS IN THE CHARTER AND RIGHTS IN THE EUROPEAN CONVENTION ON HUMAN RIGHTS

Many of the rights set out in the Charter are based on equivalent rights in the ECHR. The Charter Explanations set out that where the rights in the Charter correspond to rights in the ECHR, the meaning and scope of those rights should be the same as in the ECHR, although the EU is not prevented from providing more extensive protections (see the Charter, Art.52(3)). This is discussed in more detail in relation to specific articles of the Charter in the right-by-right analysis at **Appendix D**.

Table 7.1 sets out some of the main differences between bringing a case based on the Charter as compared with under the ECHR as implemented in the UK through HRA 1998.

7.17 COMPARISON OF THE CHARTER AND THE EUROPEAN CONVENTION ON HUMAN RIGHTS

Although there is overlap between the Charter and the ECHR, there are some significant differences. These are explored in detail in the right-by-right analysis in **Appendix D**. However, a high-level explanation is set out in Table 7.1.

[25] The general principle of non-discrimination is set out in the Charter, Art.21. It is, however, worth noting that the judgment in *Walker* was decided on the basis of the general principle of non-discrimination and did not make reference to the Charter.

Table 7.1 Rights in the Charter compared with rights in the ECHR, as implemented in HRA 1998

Issue	Explanation
Scope of rights	Some rights in the Charter are wider in scope or more specific than under the ECHR. Examples are: • Charter, Art.8 (protection of personal data) has no direct equivalent in the ECHR • Charter, Art.47 (right to an effective remedy and a fair trial) is not limited to civil and criminal matters in the same way as the ECHR, Art.6
Remedies	Remedies under the Charter are more extensive than under HRA 1998 Primary legislation which is found to be incompatible with the Charter must be disapplied. Where primary legislation breaches HRA 1998, the remedy is a declaration of incompatibility (HRA 1998, s.4). The incompatible provision will have effect until Parliament amends or repeals it
Consistent interpretation	There is no material difference between the duty of consistent interpretation under HRA 1998, s.3[26] as compared with the duty of consistent interpretation in EU law
Rules of standing	The rules of standing are more generous under the Charter than under HRA 1998. HRA 1998 only allows a victim of a human rights violation to bring a claim against a public authority (see s.7(1)). Under the Charter, a claim can be brought if the person bringing the claim shows sufficient interest to proceed[27]
Damages	Damages for breaches under HRA 1998 are rare.[28] *Francovich* damages in EU law are more substantial[29]

[26] HRA 1998, s.3(1) states: 'So far as it is possible to do so, primary legislation and subordinate legislation must be read and given effect in a way which is compatible with the Convention rights.'

[27] Most claims under EU law were brought by way of judicial review. The standard for bringing a claim is sufficient interest under the Senior Courts Act 1981, s.31. See 'Briefing note on the Charter of Fundamental Rights of the European Union', Bingham Centre for the Rule of Law: **www.biicl.org/documents/1800_bingham_centre_eu_charter_briefing_-_final.pdf** (accessed 10 November 2020).

[28] See 'Human Rights Act 1998: overview', Practical Law UK, Practice Note 9-394-8040.

[29] See Lord Pannick's question to the minister in the debate on the EU (Withdrawal Bill) where he asked: 'Will he accept that the right to damages under the *Francovich* principle is more generous to claimants than the common law principle of judicial review under which you very rarely have a right to claim damages as you need to prove misfeasance in public office or something similar? Does he accept that *Francovich* is more generous?' UK Parliament, House of Lords Hansard – European Union (Withdrawal) Bill, 5 March 2018, vol.789, col.912: **https://hansard.parliament.uk/Lords/2018-03-05/debates/AE7EB742-4BCD-4D00-B43D-AD7ED9A21911/EuropeanUnion(Withdrawal)Bill** (accessed 10 November 2020).

CHAPTER 8

Key concepts: EU competence

8.1 OVERVIEW

EUWA 2018, s.6 directs UK courts and tribunals to have regard to the 'limits of EU competences' in interpreting retained EU law (see **Chapter 15**). This chapter explains the concept of EU competence which is not defined in the Act. In EU law, the term 'competence' is used to describe the EU's power to undertake specific actions. The EU Treaties limit both the existence and the exercise of EU competence. The question of whether the EU has competence to act can be a hotly contested issue as between the EU institutions themselves and between the Member States and the EU institutions. It is a question that goes to the division of power and to matters of sovereignty. This has led to litigation in the CJEU to establish the boundaries.

8.2 PRINCIPLE OF CONFERRAL

The TEU, Art.5(1) provides:

> The limits of Union competences are governed by the principle of conferral. The use of Union competences is governed by the principles of subsidiarity and proportionality.

The EU is a creation of its Member States. Its powers are those which the Member States have conferred on it, as set out in the EU Treaties. The EU Treaties provide the basis for, and set the limits of, what the EU can do. This is known as the principle of conferral.

Article 5(2) provides:

> Under the principle of conferral, the Union shall act only within the limits of the competences conferred upon it by the Member States in the Treaties to attain the objectives set out therein. Competences not conferred upon the Union in the Treaties remain with the Member States.

In practice, the question of whether something is within EU competence or within Member State competence is not always clear-cut. There has been a long-standing debate as to who ultimately decides the limits of EU competence – the CJEU or the highest court in a Member State. The CJEU maintains that it decides. However, in a case on the legality of the European Central Bank's Public Sector Purchase Programme, the German Federal Constitutional Court said that it was the court that decided the limits of EU competence for Germany.[1]

The UK perspective on this issue during membership of the EU was considered in *Pham* v. *Secretary of State for the Home Department* [2015] UKSC 19 (but a decision on the point was not needed on the facts of the case). Lord Mance said that it was ultimately for the domestic court to decide on the limits of EU competence in a way that was consistent with its domestic constitutional arrangements (see paras.84 and 90):

> In the present context, it is clearly very arguable that there are under the Treaties jurisdictional limits to European Union competence in relation to the grant or withdrawal by a Member State of national citizenship …
>
> A domestic court faces a particular dilemma if, in the face of the clear language of a Treaty and of associated declarations and decisions … the Court of Justice reaches a decision which oversteps jurisdictional limits which Member States have clearly set at the European Treaty level and which are reflected domestically in their constitutional arrangements. But, unless the Court of Justice has had conferred upon it under domestic law unlimited as well as unappealable power to determine and expand the scope of European law, irrespective of what the Member States clearly agreed, a domestic court must ultimately decide for itself what is consistent with its own domestic constitutional arrangements, including in the case of the [European Communities Act 1972] what jurisdictional limits exist under the European Treaties and upon the competence conferred on European institutions including the Court of Justice.

8.3 CATEGORIES OF EU COMPETENCE

The substantive areas of EU competence are set out in the TFEU, Arts.2–6. For example, the EU has competence in the area of the environment. The areas of competence fall into specific categories. The category of competence determines whether:

- only the EU can act in the area;
- there is a choice as to whether the EU acts or the Member States act;
- there is scope for both the EU and the Member States to act;
- only the Member States can act.

The main categories of competence are:

- exclusive EU competence;
- shared competence;
- supporting competence.

Table 8.1 shows into which categories various areas of competence fall.

---

[1] BVerfG, Judgment of the Second Senate of 5 May 2020 – 2 BvR 859/15.

Table 8.1 Categories of EU competence

Exclusive competence	Shared competence	Supporting competence
• Customs union • Competition rules for the internal market • Monetary policy for eurozone members • Conservation of marine biological resources • Common commercial policy • Conclusion of international agreements in specific circumstances	• Internal market • Social policy • Economic, social and territorial cohesion • Agriculture and fisheries • Environment • Consumer protection • Transport • Trans-European networks • Energy • Area of freedom, justice and security • Common safety concerns in public health matters	• Protection and improvement of human health • Industry • Culture • Tourism • Education, vocational training, youth and sport

8.3.1 Exclusive EU competence

In the areas where the EU has exclusive competence, only the EU may legislate and adopt legally binding acts. The Member States may only act in the area if they are authorised to do so by the EU or if they are required to implement EU acts in that area. Otherwise, it is unlawful for a Member State to act in an area of exclusive EU competence.

Examples

EU-only action

Only the EU can set tariff rates with third countries.

Member States authorised to act on behalf of the EU

Council Decision (EU) 2019/683 authorises the Member States to become parties, in the interest of the EU, to the Council of Europe Convention on an Integrated Safety, Security and Service Approach at Football Matches and Other Sports Events.

The EU cannot become party to the Convention because only states can be parties.

The Member States are therefore authorised to sign and ratify the Convention, acting in the interest of the Union, in respect of those parts of the Convention which fall under the exclusive competence of the EU.

Unlawful action by a Member State

Greece unilaterally submitted a proposal to the International Maritime Organization relating to maritime security. In C–45/07 *Commission* v. *Greece*, EU:C:2009:81, the Commission successfully brought infringement proceedings against Greece for acting in an area of exclusive EU competence.

8.3.2 Shared competence

In areas of shared competence, either the EU or the Member States may act. However, once the EU has acted, the Member States cannot do anything in that area that would conflict with or undermine EU action. The TFEU, Art.4(2) lists the principal areas of shared competence.

The TFEU, Art.2(2) says that the Member States shall 'exercise their competence to the extent that the Union has not exercised its competence'. Protocol (No 25) on the exercise of shared competence says:

> With reference to Article 2(2) of the Treaty on the Functioning of the European Union on shared competence, when the Union has taken action in a certain area, the scope of this exercise of competence only covers those elements governed by the Union act in question and therefore does not cover the whole area.

8.3.3 Supporting competence and related types of competence

- TFEU, Art.6 lists areas where the EU has competence to 'support, coordinate or supplement' the actions of the Member States. The Member States can still act in these areas even if the EU has acted.
- TFEU, Art.4(3) and (4) list areas where the exercise of EU competence 'shall not result in Member States being prevented from exercising theirs'. These areas are research, technological development and space, development cooperation and humanitarian aid.
- TFEU, Art.5 sets out the EU's competence to ensure coordination of Member State policies in specified areas (for example, social policy).

Example

The EU's European Development Fund provides development assistance to African, Caribbean and Pacific states and to EU Overseas Countries and Territories. The provision of EU funding via the Fund does not prevent a Member State from providing its own aid to the countries covered by the Fund.

8.3.4 *Sui generis* competence

The EU has competence to act in the area known as the Common Foreign and Security Policy (CFSP). The TEU, Art.24 says that the EU's competence in matters of the CFSP 'shall cover all areas of foreign policy and all questions relating to the Union's security'. An example of a CFSP decision is the decision to establish the European Union Integrated Border Management Assistance Mission in Libya.[2] CFSP competence exists alongside Member State competence in the area.

CFSP has a number of unique features that set it apart from other areas of EU competence. For example, decisions are taken by unanimity (with limited exceptions). For the purposes of categorising competence, CFSP can best be described as *sui generis*. Member States are not prevented from acting where the EU has acted. Their action must, however, be consistent with EU action. The TEU, Art.24(3) says that Member States must refrain from any action 'which is contrary to the interests of the Union or likely to impair its effectiveness as a cohesive force in international relations'. CFSP decisions do not form part of retained EU law (see **12.6**).

8.3.5 Competence to act internationally

The EU can act internationally on its own behalf (known as 'external competence'). This includes entering international agreements (TFEU, Art.216). The question of where competence lies often comes up in relation to international agreements which the EU is negotiating with third countries. If the subject matter of the agreement falls solely within the EU's exclusive competence, then the agreement has to be concluded by the EU alone, without the Member States[3] (known as an 'EU-only agreement'). However, if the agreement also contains provisions within the sole competence of the Member States, they also need to be parties. If the agreement is made up of a combination of provisions within exclusive EU competence and shared competence, then a policy decision needs to be taken as to whether the EU or the Member States will exercise the shared competence. If it is to be the Member States, then they will need to be parties to the agreement alongside the EU.

Where both the EU and the Member States are exercising competence, the resulting agreement with the third country or international organisation is referred to as a 'mixed agreement'.

This has a practical significance. An agreement between the EU and a third country can be concluded more quickly than an agreement between the EU, its Member States and a third country. This is because the latter needs to be ratified by

[2] Council Decision 2013/233/CFSP of 22 May 2013 on the European Union Integrated Border Management Assistance Mission in Libya (EUBAM Libya), as amended [2013] OJ L138/15.

[3] There are two qualifications to be aware of. If an international agreement which covers an area of exclusive EU competence allows only states to be parties, the EU can authorise Member States to enter the agreement on its behalf. The EU can authorise a Member State to act in an area of exclusive competence in its own right. For example, France has been authorised by the EU to negotiate an international agreement with the UK concerning the operation of the Channel Tunnel.

each Member State according to its own domestic procedures. This can be a time-consuming process.

Example

In Opinion 2/15, the Court of Justice had to consider the question of whether the EU had exclusive competence which would enable it to sign and conclude a free trade agreement with Singapore by itself, without the Member States as parties. The Court opined that, in the circumstances, the agreement could not be concluded by the EU alone.

8.4 AREAS OF EXCLUSIVE MEMBER STATE COMPETENCE

Areas of exclusive Member State competence are not listed in the EU Treaties. However, it follows from the principle of conferral that if a competence is not conferred on the EU, it remains with the Member States and the EU cannot act in that area. The TEU, Art.5(2) makes clear that 'Competences not conferred upon the Union in the Treaties remain with the Member States'.

The EU Treaties say expressly that national security remains the sole responsibility of each Member State (TEU, Art.4(2)).

8.5 PRINCIPLES GOVERNING THE USE OF EU COMPETENCE

8.5.1 Subsidiarity

The principle of subsidiarity limits how EU competence is exercised (TEU, Art.5). It requires that the EU should only act if:

- the proposed outcome cannot be sufficiently achieved by the Member States at national, regional or local level; and
- EU action would provide added value compared to action by the Member States.

The underlying idea is that powers should be exercised as close to the citizen as possible. The principle does not apply to areas which fall within the EU's exclusive competence. An EU legislative act can be challenged on the basis that it infringes the principle of subsidiarity. However, no challenge on this ground has been successful. The principle is unlikely to be of relevance in the interpretation of retained EU law.[4]

---

[4] Post-IPCD, it will not be possible to challenge retained EU law on the basis that the EU instrument from which it is derived was invalid for infringing the principle of subsidiarity (see **14.6**).

8.5.2 Proportionality

The TEU, Art.5(4) says:

> Under the principle of proportionality, the content and form of Union action shall not exceed what is necessary to achieve the objectives of the Treaties.

In Case C–493/17 *Weiss*, EU:C:2018:1000, the Court of Justice explained the principle of proportionality as follows:

> According to settled case-law of the Court, the principle of proportionality requires that acts of the EU institutions should be suitable for attaining the legitimate objectives pursued by the legislation at issue and should not go beyond what is necessary to achieve those objectives ...[5]

The principle is often summed up by the maxim 'don't use a sledgehammer to crack a nut'.

The Court has tended to allow EU institutions a broad discretion. For example, in Case C–343/09 *Afton Chemical*, EU:C:2010:419, it said:

> ... the European Union legislature must be allowed a broad discretion in an area which entails political, economic and social choices on its part, and in which it is called upon to undertake complex assessments. The legality of a measure adopted in that sphere can be affected only if the measure is manifestly inappropriate having regard to the objective which the competent institutions are seeking to pursue.

The principle applies not only to acts of the EU institutions but also to Member States when they are acting within the scope of EU law (for example implementing a directive).

The Court of Justice has consistently held that the principle of proportionality is one of the general principles of EU law (see further **6.4.1**). The principle is one that will be frequently encountered in retained EU case law. The principle remains relevant where a domestic court has to interpret retained EU law in accordance with retained general principles (see **Chapter 15**).

Examples: Proportionate and disproportionate measures from CJEU case law

Case C–453/03 ABNA, EU:C:2005:741

A directive required manufacturers of animal feed to inform customers of the exact composition of the feed so that any ingredients of potential concern in terms of food safety could be readily identified. The requirement was held to be disproportionate because it went beyond what was necessary to attain the objective of protecting animal and human health. The requirement infringed the economic interests of feed manufacturers who had invested in

[5] There is a debate as to whether there is an additional element – a consideration of whether the burden imposed by a measure is disproportionate to the benefits accrued. The Court's practice here has been inconsistent.

research and development and had an interest in protecting their exact feed formulations. A requirement to indicate the ranges of composition of each ingredient would be sufficient to enable identification of ingredients of potential concern.

Case C–183/95 Affish, EU:C:1997:373

The Commission inspected a small selection of establishments in Japan which prepared fish products for export and found that they did not meet the required EU standards. An EU decision was made to ban the import of all Japanese fish into the EU to protect public health. This blanket ban was challenged for being disproportionate. The Court said it was not feasible to check all Japanese fish factories and it was reasonable for the Commission to extrapolate from its findings in relation to a limited number of establishments to the country as a whole. The decision was found to be proportionate.

CHAPTER 9

EU law in the UK's legal system during EU membership

9.1 OVERVIEW

This chapter provides an overview of the most important provisions of the European Communities Act 1972. A knowledge of these provisions is fundamental to understanding how EUWA 2018 operates. The framework of ECA 1972 is the foundation of EUWA 2018. Wording from ECA 1972 is replicated in EUWA 2018. That is deliberate: it provides the necessary continuity of meaning as between EU law and retained EU law. This gives certainty to UK businesses, individuals, public bodies and other entities in terms of the law which applies to them after IPCD.

ECA 1972 gave effect to the UK's EU membership in domestic law. In the UK legal system, international law and domestic law operate in independent spheres. It was ECA 1972 which enabled EU law to become part of UK domestic law.

9.2 MAIN PROVISIONS OF ECA 1972

9.2.1 Section 1

Section 1 set out key definitions including the 'EU' and the 'Treaties'. The definition of the 'Treaties' included the TEU and the TFEU as well as the treaties which preceded those agreements, including the UK's accession agreement and a range of international agreements with third countries (see also **13.5**).

Section 1(3) contained a power to make Orders by which further treaties could be added to the definition of 'Treaties'. This had the effect of bringing those treaties within the scope of ECA 1972, s.2. This enabled the directly effective provisions of those treaties to become UK law by virtue of ECA 1972, s.2(1). Further, the powers under s.2(2) were available to implement them in domestic law, where necessary.

9.2.2 Section 2(1)

The manner in which EU law came into domestic law was considered in the case of *Miller* (*R (on the application of Miller and another) (Respondents)* v. *Secretary of*

State for Exiting the European Union (Appellant) [2017] UKSC 5). The Supreme Court confirmed that the source of EU law was not ECA 1972. Instead, ECA 1972 provided a 'conduit pipe' through which EU law passed into domestic law. ECA 1972, s.2(1) was the means through which EU law flowed into UK law. This is illustrated in the Explanatory Notes to EUWA 2018.

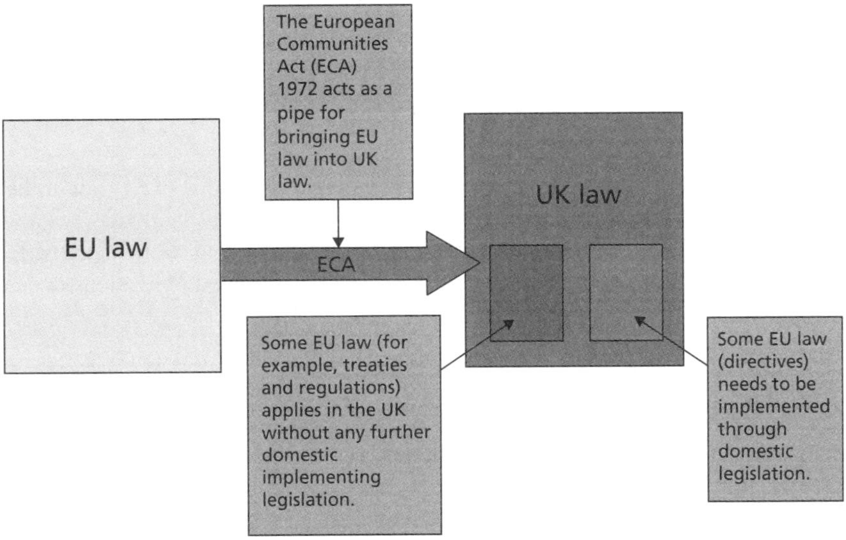

Figure 9.1 How EU law passes into domestic law

Note: The figure is adapted from the Explanatory Notes.

What flowed through s.2(1)?

Section 2(1) specified what flowed through the 'conduit pipe' as:

> All such rights, powers, liabilities, obligations and restrictions from time to time created or arising by or under the Treaties, and all such remedies and procedures from time to time provided for by or under the Treaties …

Figure 9.1 illustrates how rights, liabilities, etc. flowed through s.2(1). The rights, etc. were to be 'given legal effect' without the need for further implementing legislation. They were to be 'enforced, allowed and followed accordingly'. In other words, they became enforceable rights in the UK's domestic courts.

While s.2(1) used specific concepts (rights, obligations, etc.) it is not absolutely clear what this admitted through the conduit pipe in terms of EU law. For example, it is not clear how the general principles of EU law became enforceable in the UK courts. It is likely that they also flowed through s.2(1) as well as being implemented in the domestic secondary legislation which codified them, but there is nothing in ECA 1972 which explains this, neither are the authors aware of any case law on this point.

A further point to note is that a significant body of EU law was not given effect in the UK's domestic legal system. Rather, it operated at the international level. The prime example is CFSP decisions.

9.2.3 Section 2(2)

Section 2(2) conferred a broad power on ministers to implement EU law. Section 2(2) is divided into two subsections:

- Section 2(2)(a) enabled the relevant rights and obligations in EU law to be implemented in the UK.
- Section 2(2)(b) enabled the implementation of provisions which dealt with matters arising out of or related to the relevant rights and obligations under s.2(1).

Example: s.2(2)(a) and (b)

This is a fictional example, based on the remarks of the judge in the case of *Oakley Inc* v. *Animal Ltd* [2005] EWHC 210 (Ch) at para.130.

An EU directive required Member States to ban smoking in public places. In the UK, the directive could be implemented using s.2(2)(a). Section 2(2)(b) could be used to make provision for things which related to the smoking ban, such as creating a system of inspections to ensure compliance and provisions creating vicarious liability for publicans.

9.2.4 Section 2(4)

Section 2(4) set out that existing and future legislation (whether primary or secondary) had effect subject to the provisions of s.2, including s.2(1).[1] As discussed above, s.2(1) gave effect to directly applicable and directly effective EU rights and obligations in domestic law. The effect of s.2(4) was therefore that EU law took precedence over domestic law.[2]

In the case of *Factortame Ltd* v. *Secretary of State for Transport* [1990] 2 AC 85 Lord Bridge stated that the effect of ECA 1972, s.2(1) and (4) was that it was as if:

[1] Section 2(4) provided that 'any enactment passed or to be passed ... shall ... have effect subject to the foregoing provisions of this section'. The foregoing provisions included s.2(1), which gave effect to the rights and obligations in EU law in the domestic legal system.

[2] ECA 1972, s.2(1) and (4) gave effect to the supremacy of EU law for directly effective or directly applicable rights and obligations. However, there are other manifestations of supremacy such as the duty of consistent interpretation and *Francovich* damages which did not have an effect in domestic law through direct effect or direct applicability. Therefore, it is likely that a combination of ECA 1972, ss.2(1), (4) and 3(1) together gave effect to the supremacy of EU law in the UK legal system.

a section were incorporated in Part II of the [Merchant Shipping Act 1988] which in terms enacted that the provisions with respect to registration of British fishing vessels were to be without prejudice to the directly enforceable [EU] rights of nationals of any member state of the [EU].

9.2.5 Section 3

Section 3(1) provided that in proceedings in UK courts and tribunals, the meaning or effect of any of the 'Treaties', or the validity, meaning or effect of EU instruments were to be interpreted in accordance with the principles laid down by, and any relevant decisions of, the CJEU. An EU instrument was defined in Sched.1, Part 2 and included any instrument issued by an EU institution. This encompassed both EU legislation and the judgments of the CJEU.

Section 3(1) also provided that the question of the effect of EU law in the domestic legal system should be treated as a matter of law. This contrasts with the position which applies in the context of foreign law, which is generally treated as a question of fact, to be proved through evidence given in legal proceedings.

9.2.6 Schedule 2, para.1A

Schedule 2, para.1A enabled the UK to implement EU law so that references in domestic legislation were to that legislation as updated from time to time in EU law. These are known as ambulatory references. For an explanation as to how ambulatory references are dealt with in EUWA 2018 see **18.2.1**.

9.2.7 Schedule 1, Part 2

Schedule 1, Part 2 set out defined terms which applied to all domestic legislation through the Interpretation Act 1978, unless the contrary intention appeared. Examples included the definition of 'EU institution', 'EU obligation' and 'Enforceable EU right'.

9.3 AREAS OF COMPLEXITY

The functioning of ECA 1972 was not straightforward. One example is the apparent contradiction between the application of EU regulations under the TFEU, Art.288 and the manner in which EU law became domestic law through ECA 1972, s.2(1).

Under the TFEU, Art.288, regulations are 'directly applicable' and 'binding in their entirety'. This suggests that the whole of an EU instrument should take effect in domestic law. However, the wording of ECA 1972, s.2(1) made it clear that 'rights, obligations', etc. became part of domestic law. This suggests that the whole text was not available in domestic law – it was simply those parts which are properly described as rights, obligations, etc. which became part of the UK domestic legal system.

A further example of the complexity of the relationship between ECA 1972 and EU law is the operation of the supremacy of EU law. ECA 1972 did not state expressly how the supremacy of EU law worked in the UK legal system. While the UK courts have made it clear that supremacy attached to those parts of EU law which have direct effect (i.e. are sufficiently precise and unconditional to give rise to enforceable rights in domestic law), the duty of consistent interpretation and *Francovich* damages are manifestations of supremacy which involve no such test. In these areas it is arguable that supremacy applies more broadly than the narrower test of direct effect. See further **Chapters 4** and **5**.

EUWA 2018 makes no attempts to solve these complexities although these complexities should not be exaggerated. The central policy, as evidenced by the replication in EUWA 2018 of text from ECA 1972, is continuity. Although the international, reciprocal nature of the rights and obligations does not survive the transformation into retained EU law, the general policy intention is that the law should be interpreted in the same way as before. See **Chapter 15**.

A further point to note is that some of the main structures of ECA 1972, in particular the concept of the 'conduit pipe' under s.2(1), are reproduced in EUWA 2018. At the time of writing, it is not known whether a future free trade agreement with the EU will be concluded and if it is, how it will be implemented. However, in implementing the Withdrawal Agreement (EUWA 2018, s.7A) and the EEA EFTA Separation Agreement and the Swiss Citizens' Rights Agreement (EUWA 2018, s.7B) as well as the interpretation of those agreements (s.7C), some of the core architecture of ECA 1972 is retained. For example, ss.7A and 7B both create 'conduit pipes' in relation to the rights and obligations under the respective agreements in exactly the same terms as ECA 1972, s.2(1). Section 7A states:

> (1) Subsection (2) applies to –
>
> (a) all such rights, powers, liabilities, obligations and restrictions from time to time created or arising by or under the withdrawal agreement, and
> (b) all such remedies and procedures from time to time provided for by or under the withdrawal agreement,
>
> as in accordance with the withdrawal agreement are without further enactment to be given legal effect or used in the United Kingdom.
>
> (2) The rights, powers, liabilities, obligations, restrictions, remedies and procedures concerned are to be –
>
> (a) recognised and available in domestic law, and
> (b) enforced, allowed and followed accordingly.

Appendix B traces the replication of the wording of ECA 1972, s.2(1) through EUWA 2018. The reliance on the structure created by ECA 1972, s.2(1) emphasises the theme of continuity in interpretation.

The other point of interest is that rights and obligations in the Withdrawal Agreement have supremacy over UK domestic law, irrespective of whether the domestic law in question pre-dates IPCD or is enacted subsequently. This is achieved through s.7A(3), which is based on ECA 1972, s.2(4). It states that every enactment (including an enactment in EUWA 2018 itself) is to be read and has effect subject to s.7A(2). The drafting of ECA 1972, s.7A(2) mirrors s.2(1). These provisions in EUWA 2018 implement the obligation in the Withdrawal Agreement, Art.4(1) which states that the Withdrawal Agreement and the provisions of EU law made applicable by the Withdrawal Agreement should produce 'in the United Kingdom the same legal effects as those which they produce within the Union and its Member States'. See also **Chapter 20**.

CHAPTER 10

UK exit from the EU

10.1 OVERVIEW

This chapter provides a timeline setting out the key milestones on the road to the UK's withdrawal from the EU[1] and an explanation of the transition (or implementation) period that followed immediately after exit.

10.2 TIMELINE

Table 10.1 Key milestones on the road to the UK's withdrawal from the EU

	2013
23 January	Prime Minister David Cameron gives a speech at Bloomberg. He sets out plans to renegotiate the UK's relations with the EU and to put the renegotiated package to the British people in an in-out referendum
	2015
14 April	The Conservative Party manifesto for the 2015 General Election includes a commitment to hold an in-out referendum on the UK's membership of the EU before the end of 2017
10 November	Prime Minister David Cameron writes to the President of the European Council, Donald Tusk, setting out the four areas in which he is seeking to renegotiate the terms of the UK's membership of the EU: economic governance, competitiveness, sovereignty and immigration
17 December	The European Union Referendum Act 2015 receives Royal Assent. It provides for the holding of a referendum in the UK and Gibraltar on whether the UK should remain a member of the EU
	2016
23 June	The referendum takes place. The question is: 'Should the United Kingdom remain a member of the European Union or leave the European Union?'

[1] Adapted from Walker, N. (9 October 2020) *Brexit Timeline: Events Leading up to the UK's Exit from the EU*, House of Commons Library Briefing Paper, Number 7960. Contains Parliamentary information licensed under the Open Parliament Licence v3.0 available at **https://www.parliament.uk/site-information/copyright/open-parliament-licence/?dm_t=0,0,0,0,0**.

24 June	The referendum result is announced. There is a majority in favour of leaving the EU The results are: Remain: 16,141,241 (48.1%) Leave: 17,410,742 (51.9%) The turnout is 72% of registered voters Prime Minister David Cameron announces his resignation
13 July	Theresa May becomes Prime Minister
2017	
17 January	Prime Minister Theresa May gives a speech at Lancaster House setting out her priorities in the Brexit negotiations
24 January	The Supreme Court holds in *Miller*[2] that the government cannot rely on the Royal Prerogative to give notice of the UK's intention to withdraw from the EU
2 February	The government publishes a White Paper: *The United Kingdom's exit from, and new partnership with, the European Union*
16 March	The European Union (Notification of Withdrawal) Act 2017 comes into force. It gives the Prime Minister the power to notify the UK's intention to withdraw from the EU under the TEU, Art.50
29 March	Prime Minister Theresa May sends the TEU, Art.50 notification to the President of the European Council
30 March	The government publishes a White Paper: *Legislating for the United Kingdom's withdrawal from the European Union*
18 April	A General Election is called for 8 June 2017
29 April	The European Council adopts guidelines to define the framework for negotiations under the TEU, Art.50
22 May	The Council authorises the opening of negotiations with the UK and adopts the EU's negotiating mandate
8–9 June	The General Election takes place No party has an overall majority. The Conservatives are the largest single party. Theresa May goes to the Queen and announces that she is forming a government
19 June	EU exit negotiations begin
13 July	The European Union (Withdrawal) Bill is introduced
22 July	Prime Minister Theresa May gives a speech in Florence setting out her view of the UK's future in Europe. The speech includes a proposal for a two-year transition period
13 November	The government announces its intention to bring forward a Bill to implement the Withdrawal Agreement in domestic law
8 December	UK and EU negotiators publish a Joint Report on progress during Phase 1 of negotiations (covering citizens' rights, Northern Ireland and the financial settlement)

[2] *R (on the application of Miller) (Respondents)* v. *Secretary of State for Exiting the European Union (Appellant) (No.2)* [2016] EWHC 2768 (Admin).

15 December	The European Council decides that there has been sufficient progress in the negotiations to move to Phase 2 relating to the transition and framework for the future relationship. It adopts guidelines for Phase 2
	2018
29 January	The Council adopts a supplementary negotiating mandate
28 February	The draft Withdrawal Agreement is published
19 March	An amended draft of the Withdrawal Agreement is published
26 June	The European Union (Withdrawal) Act receives Royal Assent. Section 13 of the Act says that Parliament must approve the Withdrawal Agreement before it can be ratified (the so-called 'meaningful vote')
12 July	The government publishes a White Paper: *The future relationship between the United Kingdom and the European Union*
14 November	The UK and EU negotiators reach an agreement in principle on the Withdrawal Agreement
25 November	The European Council endorses the Withdrawal Agreement and approves the Political Declaration setting out the framework for the future relationship between the EU and the UK
10 December	In the *Wightman* case, the Court of Justice holds that a Member State may unilaterally revoke its notification of an intention to withdraw under the TEU, Art.50
12 December	Theresa May wins a vote of no confidence held among Conservative MPs
13 December	The European Council adopts conclusions on Brexit
	2019
15 January	The meaningful vote takes place. The government loses the vote by 230 votes
16 January	The government wins a vote of no confidence in the House of Commons
21 January	Prime Minister Theresa May presents a new approach to the negotiations in the House of Commons
29 January	A majority in the House of Commons indicates that it is against leaving the EU with no deal and it is against the Northern Ireland backstop
26 February	Prime Minister Theresa May commits to giving MPs a vote on delaying the UK's exit from the EU or ruling out no deal if the government loses the second meaningful vote
12 March	The second meaningful vote takes place. The government loses by a majority of 149
20 March	Prime Minister Theresa May writes to the President of the European Council to request an extension to the Art.50 notice period to 30 June
21 March	The European Council agrees to an extension to 22 May if the Withdrawal Agreement is approved the following week by the House of Commons. If it is not approved, it agrees an extension to 12 April 2019
27 March	Indicative votes are held in the House of Commons on a series of different approaches to Brexit. None achieves a majority
5 April	Prime Minister Theresa May requests an extension to 30 June 2019
10 April	The UK and EU agree an extension until 31 October 2019 but with the possibility of the date being brought forward if the Withdrawal Agreement is ratified before that date

23 May	The UK votes in the European Parliament elections
24 May	Theresa May announces that she will resign as leader of the Conservative Party on 7 June
23 July	Boris Johnson is voted leader of the Conservative Party
24 July	Boris Johnson takes over as Prime Minister
9 September	The European Union (Withdrawal) (No.2) Act 2019 receives Royal Assent Parliament is 'prorogued'. The prorogation is later found to be unlawful by the Supreme Court
24 September	In *Miller 2*, the Supreme Court decides unanimously that the decision to advise Her Majesty to prorogue Parliament is unlawful
17 October	A new Brexit deal is announced at the October European Council
21 October	The European Union (Withdrawal Agreement) Bill is introduced
22 October	The Bill passes its second reading but a programme motion setting the timetable to debate the Bill is defeated. Prime Minister Boris Johnson announces he will pause the passage of the Bill
28 October	The European Council agrees to an extension to the Art.50 notice period until 31 January 2020
30 October	The government introduces the Early Parliamentary General Election Bill, setting the date for a General Election as 12 December
12 December	General Election. The Conservative party wins a majority
19 December	The European Union (Withdrawal Agreement) Bill is introduced
2020	
23 January	The European Union (Withdrawal Agreement) Act receives Royal Assent
24 January	The Withdrawal Agreement is signed by the UK and EU
29 January	The European Parliament gives its consent to the conclusion of the Withdrawal Agreement
30 January	The Council adopts a decision to conclude the Withdrawal Agreement
31 January	The UK leaves the EU The Withdrawal Agreement comes into force The transition period begins

10.3 IMPLEMENTATION OR TRANSITION PERIOD

The UK's membership of the EU formally came to an end on 31 January 2020. Although the UK ceased to be an EU Member State on that date, EU law continued to apply to the UK, subject to limited exceptions, for the duration of the 'transition period' which began immediately after exit.

The transition period is also known as the 'implementation period'. The terms are interchangeable. The Withdrawal Agreement, Art.126 which establishes the concept refers to a 'transition or implementation period'. All other references in that Agreement are to a 'transition period'. EUWA 2018, as amended by EU(WA)A 2020, uses the term 'implementation period'.

The UK government's original intention had been that the Withdrawal Agreement and an agreement on the future relationship between the UK and EU would be negotiated in parallel and that the future relationship agreement would come into force as soon as the UK's EU membership came to an end.

The EU, however, took the view that EU law did not permit the negotiation of the future relationship agreement until the UK had ceased to be a Member State. This meant there would be a gap between the UK leaving the EU and the future relationship being negotiated and coming into force.

The UK and EU therefore agreed that there would be a time-limited period following exit during which the UK was no longer a Member State but EU law still applied to it, thereby ensuring continuity and legal certainty while the new relationship was negotiated. The thinking was that not only would this transition period give the UK and EU time to negotiate the future relationship, but businesses would have time to prepare for that new relationship without having to adapt to a new, temporary set of rules for the period between EU membership coming to an end and the future relationship taking effect.

The then Prime Minister Theresa May explained the purpose of the transition period in this way in her 'Florence speech':[3]

> But the fact is that, at [the point of exit], neither the UK – nor the EU and its Members [sic] States – will be in a position to implement smoothly many of the detailed arrangements that will underpin this new relationship we seek.
>
> Neither is the European Union legally able to conclude an agreement with the UK as an external partner while it is itself still part of the European Union.
>
> And such an agreement on the future partnership will require the appropriate legal ratification, which would take time.
>
> It is also the case that people and businesses – both in the UK and in the EU – would benefit from a period to adjust to the new arrangements in a smooth and orderly way.
>
> As I said in my speech at Lancaster House a period of implementation would be in our mutual interest. That is why I am proposing that there should be such a period after the UK leaves the EU.
>
> Clearly people, businesses and public services should only have to plan for one set of changes in the relationship between the UK and the EU.
>
> So during the implementation period access to one another's markets should continue on current terms and Britain also should continue to take part in existing security measures. And I know businesses, in particular, would welcome the certainty this would provide.
>
> The framework for this strictly time-limited period, which can be agreed under Article 50, would be the existing structure of EU rules and regulations.

The Withdrawal Agreement, Part 4 provides for a transition or implementation period. The key features of the transition period are as follows:

- It is time-limited.

  The transition period runs from the date of entry into force of the Withdrawal Agreement to 31 December 2020. The Withdrawal Agreement provides that it

[3] PM's Florence speech: a new era of cooperation and partnership between the UK and the EU, 22 September 2017: **www.gov.uk/government/speeches/pms-florence-speech-a-new-era-of-cooperation-and-partnership-between-the-uk-and-the-eu** (accessed 10 November 2020).

can be extended once for up to two years if agreed by the Joint Committee. A decision to extend had to be taken by 1 July 2020. The European Union (Withdrawal Agreement) Act 2020 prevented a UK minister from agreeing to an extension in the Joint Committee.

- EU law applies to the UK for the duration of the transition period, subject to limited exceptions.

  UK citizens are able to vote in European Parliament elections, for example. The UK's opt-ins, opt-outs and special arrangements in relation to justice and home affairs (JHA), the Schengen rules and monetary union continue to apply (except that the UK will not be able to opt in to any new JHA measures). Any new EU law which comes into effect or requires implementation during the transition period applies to the UK.

- The UK has no voting rights in the Council, no Commissioner, no members of the CJEU and no members of the European Parliament.
- The UK contributes to the EU budget and receives funding from EU programmes.
- Obligations in international agreements concluded by the EU, or by the EU and its Member States, with third countries continue to bind the UK.[4]
- The UK can opt to disapply a decision in the field of the CFSP for 'vital and stated reasons of national policy'.
- The UK can negotiate, sign and ratify new international agreements of its own provided they do not come into force until after the end of the transition period.
- The CJEU continues to have jurisdiction.

The implementation of the transition period in domestic law by EU(WA)A 2020 is discussed at **20.2**. Retained EU law comes into effect immediately after the end of the transition period.

[4] The EU notified the other parties to those agreements that the UK should be treated as if it were a member state for the purposes of those agreements during the transition period.

Table 10.2 Application of EU law to the UK

	UK is a Member State	**EU law applies to the UK**
UK membership of the EU		
1 January 1973–31 January 2020	✓	✓
		(Subject to special arrangements, e.g. the JHA opt-in)
Transition period		
31 January 2020–31 December 2020	✗	✓
		(Subject to limited exceptions)
Post-transition		
31 December 2020 onwards	✗	✗
		(Subject to EU law made applicable by the Withdrawal Agreement, e.g. under the Ireland/Northern Ireland Protocol)

CHAPTER 11

Retained EU law: EU-derived domestic legislation

11.1 OVERVIEW

Retained EU law is a new and unique concept in domestic law. As explained in **Chapter 1**, EUWA 2018 created retained EU law to make sure that there was a functioning statute book after EU law ceased to apply to the UK, and to provide legal certainty and continuity to individuals, public bodies and businesses. This was achieved by adopting an approach that meant that 'as a general rule, the same rules and laws [would] apply on the day after the UK [left] the EU as before'.[1]

At Second Reading of the European Union (Withdrawal) Bill, the Secretary of State for Exiting the European Union said that the Bill's task was to 'rebuild United Kingdom law in a way that makes sense outside the European Union'. He continued with the following description of retained EU law:

> ... the first step the Bill takes is to preserve all the domestic law we have made to implement our EU obligations. That mainly means preserving thousands of statutory instruments that have been made under the European Communities Act with subjects ranging from aeroplane noise to zoo licensing. It also extends to preserving any other domestic law that fulfils our European Union obligations or otherwise relates to the European Union.
>
> Equally, the Bill converts European Union law – principally EU Regulations – all 12,000 of them – into domestic law on exit day. It also ensures that rights in the EU treaties that are directly effective – that is, rights that are sufficiently clear, precise and unconditional that they can be relied on in court by an individual – continue to be available in UK law ...
>
> ... the Bill ensures that any question as to the meaning of retained EU law is to be decided on in UK courts in accordance with the Court of Justice's case law and retained general principles of European Union law as they stood on exit day.
>
> (HC Deb 7 September 2017, vol.628, col.345)

[1] Explanatory Notes, para.24. The Explanatory Notes relate to EUWA 2018 which received Royal Assent on 26 June 2018. At that point, no transition period had been agreed. The working assumption was that EU law would cease to apply on the day that the UK left the EU. EU(WA)A 2020 subsequently amended EUWA 2018 to replace references to 'exit day' with references to 'IP completion day'.

This chapter looks at the definition of retained EU law in EUWA 2018. In broad terms, retained EU law is composed of EU-derived domestic legislation, direct EU legislation and EU rights and obligations saved by EUWA 2018, s.4, all as interpreted in accordance with retained case law and retained general principles. **Chapters 11** to **15** consider each element in turn.

This chapter focuses on the first category of retained EU law that appears in EUWA 2018 – EU-derived domestic legislation. EU-derived domestic legislation is, in essence, domestic legislation which was made to implement EU obligations. EUWA 2018 preserves this body of law, with certain exceptions. The main consequences which flow from law being categorised as EU-derived domestic legislation are also explained.

11.2 DEFINITION OF RETAINED EU LAW

Chapter 1 explained the rationale for the creation of retained EU law. **Chapters 2** to **9** covered the underlying concepts of EU law and ECA 1972 necessary to an understanding of the operation of retained EU law. We now turn to the provisions of EUWA 2018.

EUWA 2018, s.6(7) defines 'retained EU law' as follows:

> 'retained EU law' means anything which, on or after IP completion day, continues to be, or forms part of, domestic law by virtue of section 2, 3 or 4 or subsection (3) or (6) above (as that body of law is added to or otherwise modified by or under this Act or by other domestic law from time to time)

Figure 11.1 illustrates the components which make up retained EU law.

Retained EU law		
EU-derived domestic legislation	Direct EU legislation	All other EU rights and obligations saved by EUWA 2018, s.4
interpreted in accordance with retained case law and retained general principles		

Figure 11.1 Components of retained EU law

We shall consider each component, beginning with EU-derived domestic legislation.

11.3 EU-DERIVED DOMESTIC LEGISLATION

The concept of EU-derived domestic legislation is introduced in EUWA 2018, s.1B in the context of the transition or implementation period. The operation of

EU-derived domestic legislation in that period is discussed at **20.2**. This chapter focuses on EU-derived domestic legislation after the end of the transition period.

In broad terms, EU-derived domestic legislation refers to the domestic legislation that was made to give effect to the UK's obligations under EU law. A large quantity of this domestic legislation was made under ECA 1972. As the Explanatory Notes say:

> If the ECA were repealed and no further action was taken, all of the secondary legislation which has been made under it would fall away and cease to be part of the UK statute book, leaving significant gaps.

However, as will be explained, secondary legislation made under ECA 1972 is only one element of EU-derived domestic legislation.

The Explanatory Notes refer to EU-derived legislation as 'preserved legislation' while other elements of retained EU law are referred to as 'converted legislation'. This reflects the fact that EU-derived domestic legislation has always been domestic law. It continues as domestic law after the end of the transition period but is 're-badged'. In accordance with the 'continuity' policy behind EUWA 2018, EU-derived domestic legislation is preserved. It may then be modified using the s.8 deficiencies-correcting power (see **Chapter 17**).

When considering s.2 which saves EU-derived domestic legislation and the definition of EU derived domestic legislation in s.1B(7), there are two important 'signposts' to look out for – 'so far as' and 'as it has effect', discussed at **11.5**.

11.4 STATUS OF DIRECTIVES

Directives are not saved by s.2 and do not form part of retained EU law. While this might appear to be significant, the position in EUWA 2018 reflects the status that directives had in domestic law during the UK's EU membership. Directives did not become part of domestic law. Instead, they were implemented in UK law. Directives are not drafted in such a way as to enable them to regulate a particular activity (although some provisions may be sufficiently clear, precise and unconditional to confer rights on individuals which they can enforce directly in the courts of the Member States – this is known as direct effect). Therefore, a directive might be thought of as an instruction to a Member State to legislate for a particular outcome. The outcome is brought about by the domestic legislation implementing the directive. In not incorporating directives into domestic law, EUWA 2018 is therefore doing no more than replicating the position which pertained when the UK was an EU Member State.

The role which directives had in domestic law during the UK's EU membership persists (albeit subject to exceptions). The duty of consistent interpretation or *Marleasing*[2] principle remains post-IPCD. The direct effect of directives continues,

2 This is the leading case on consistent interpretation. See *Marleasing*.

although its application is limited. The recitals in directives continue to be relevant to the interpretation of the legislation which implemented them.

In terms of the duty of consistent interpretation, there are several provisions which point to its relevance post-IPCD. EU-derived domestic legislation continues to have effect in domestic law 'as it has effect in domestic law immediately before IP completion day' (EUWA 2018, s.2(1)). This provision creates continuity. EU-derived domestic legislation should be read in the same way as it was pre-IPCD. This includes being read in light of the directive which it implemented, in accordance with the duty of consistent interpretation.

A further provision which ensures that the duty of consistent interpretation continues to apply in domestic law post-IPCD is EUWA 2018, s.6(3). It ensures that the case law of the CJEU including *Marleasing* applies (so far as relevant) when considering the 'meaning or effect' of retained EU law.

In addition, the continuing application of the principle of the supremacy of EU law in s.5(2) is relevant to the interpretation of retained EU law. As discussed at **5.11**, the duty of consistent interpretation is one of the manifestations of the supremacy of EU law.

The recitals in directives continue to be relevant to the interpretation of EU-derived domestic legislation because of the formulation 'as it has effect' in EUWA 2018, s.2(1). In addition, as discussed above, s.6(3) provides that, as a general rule, the meaning or effect of retained EU law (including EU-derived domestic legislation) should continue to be interpreted in accordance with retained case law. This includes CJEU case law which confirms the role of recitals in interpreting EU law (see **3.2** and **Chapter 15**).[3]

The concept of direct effect is important in terms of what happens to rights in directives post-IPCD. Where a directive was not implemented or was implemented incorrectly by the UK, directly effective rights in that directive were capable of being relied upon by individuals in the domestic courts to enforce their rights under EU law. These directly effective rights in directives will be saved through EUWA 2018, s.4 provided that they are 'of a kind' which has been recognised by the CJEU or a domestic court or tribunal in a case decided before IPCD (see **13.6** and **13.7**).

11.5 WHAT IS EU-DERIVED DOMESTIC LEGISLATION?

EUWA 2018, s.2(1) provides:

> EU-derived domestic legislation, as it has effect in domestic law immediately before IP completion day, continues to have effect in domestic law on and after IP completion day.

[3] The Explanatory Notes cite Joined Cases C–424/10 and C–425/10 *Ziolkowski and others* v. *Land Berlin*, EU:C:2011:866, paras.37, 42 and 43. The Explanatory Notes (at footnote 20, p.17) set out that: 'the Court relied on recitals to ascertain the purpose of the Citizenship Directive, and the structured nature of the rights contained in it.'

In essence, this provision preserves, in domestic law, domestic legislation which was made to implement EU obligations.

'EU-derived domestic legislation' is defined in EUWA 2018, s.1B(7):

> (7) In this Act 'EU-derived domestic legislation' means any enactment so far as –
>
> (a) made under section 2(2) of, or paragraph 1A of Schedule 2 to, the European Communities Act 1972 ...

'any enactment so far as'

It is important to pay attention to the term 'enactment' and the phrase 'so far as'. The term 'enactment' means an enactment 'whenever passed or made' and is defined broadly (see EUWA 2018, s.20(1) and **14.3.1**).

The use of the phrase 'so far as' in EUWA 2018, s.1B(7) indicates that where, for example, an Act contains 40 sections, only 10 of which implement EU obligations, it is only those 10 provisions that count as 'EU-derived domestic legislation' and not the Act as a whole. Although the principle is easy to state, identifying and separating out the relevant provisions in practice is likely to prove more difficult.[4]

'made under section 2(2) of ... [ECA 1972]'

This is the most straightforward category to comprehend and identify. It covers any provision of subordinate legislation made using the power in ECA 1972, s.2(2) (see **9.2.3**). The statutory powers under which subordinate legislation is made can be identified from the preamble to the instrument. Subordinate legislation in this category needs to be expressly preserved. It would otherwise fall away when the parent Act under which it was made, ECA 1972, was repealed. (For the position during the implementation period of legislation made under ECA 1972, s.2(2), see **20.2**.)

Example

The Energy Efficiency (Refrigerators and Freezers) Regulations 1997 (SI 1997/1941) were made under ECA 1972, s.2(2).

The preamble says:

> The Secretary of State, being a Minister designated for the purposes of section 2(2)(a) of the European Communities Act 1972 in relation to measures relating to energy efficiency and performance requirements for household products, in exercise of the powers

[4] See the exchange between Lord Keen of Elie and Baroness Taylor of Bolton (HL Deb 20 February 2018, vol.789, col.672): **https://hansard.parliament.uk/lords/2018-02-28/debates/4DBF014C-1181-4968-B725-F095E3D3B6E6/EuropeanUnion(Withdrawal)Bill** (accessed 10 November 2020).

> conferred by section 2(2) of that Act and of all other powers enabling him in that behalf, hereby makes the following Regulations:

'made under ... paragraph 1A of Schedule 2 to, [ECA 1972]'

ECA 1972, Sched.2, para.1A contained a power to specify that a reference to an EU instrument in subordinate legislation automatically included any amendments made by the EU to that instrument (so-called 'ambulatory effect': see **18.2.1**). This allowed cross-references to EU law in domestic implementing legislation to be kept up to date with the latest EU iteration of that law without the need to go through the process of amending the reference in the domestic implementing legislation.

Example

The Cosmetic Products Enforcement Regulations 2013 (SI 2013/1478) provide that the term 'the EU Cosmetics Regulation' used in the 2013 Regulations is to mean:

> Regulation (EC) No 1223/2009 of the European Parliament and of the Council on cosmetic products (recast), as amended from time to time.

The preamble says:

> The Secretary of State makes these Regulations in exercise of the powers conferred by section 2(2) of, as read with paragraph 1A of Schedule 2 to, the European Communities Act 1972.

EUWA 2018, s.1B(7) continues:

> (b) passed or made, or operating, for a purpose mentioned in section 2(2)(a) or (b) of [ECA 1972]

'passed ... for a purpose mentioned in section 2(2)(a) or [2(2)](b) of [ECA 1972]'

This category captures:

- provisions of Acts of Parliament that were passed to give effect to EU obligations or to deal with matters arising out of, or related to, EU obligations.

At first sight, this category might seem redundant because an Act of Parliament will remain part of domestic law regardless of the UK's withdrawal from the EU and the repeal of ECA 1972. However, categorisation of legislation as EU-derived domestic legislation does have consequences beyond preservation (see **11.7**).

The definition of 'retained EU law' in s.6(7) includes anything which continues to be domestic law 'by virtue of section 2'. There has been some debate as to whether Acts of Parliament which implement EU obligations constitute

EU-derived domestic legislation *by virtue* of s.2 (for the reason that they would remain part of domestic law regardless of s.2). However, s.20(6) makes it clear that:

> references to anything which continues to be domestic law by virtue of section 2 include references to anything to which subsection (1) of that section applies which continues to be domestic law on or after IP completion day (whether or not it would have done so irrespective of that section).

In other words, s.20(6) clarifies that an Act of Parliament which implements EU obligations is counted as 'domestic legislation by virtue of section 2' even though it would have remained domestic legislation in any event.

Legislation falling into this category is not entirely straightforward to identify. There is no central, authoritative record that one can consult to check whether a particular provision of an Act was passed to give effect to an EU obligation. It will not necessarily be apparent on the face of an Act that a particular provision is intended to implement an EU obligation. In some cases, there will be Explanatory Notes which assist. The Cabinet Office 'Guide to Making Legislation', first published in 2013, said that where a Bill was intended to implement EU obligations, the Explanatory Notes on the Bill should:

> include in the form of an annex a set of 'transposition notes', illustrating how the Government intends to transpose the main elements of the directive(s) into UK law.

However, transposition notes do not exist for every relevant Act and they are not always easy to track down.

Example

The Pollution Prevention and Control Act 1999 was passed to make provision to implement an EU directive, among other things.

This is apparent from the long title of the Act:

> An Act to make provision for implementing Council Directive 96/61/EC and for otherwise preventing and controlling pollution; to make provision about certain expired or expiring disposal or waste management licences; and for connected purposes.

'made ... for a purpose mentioned in section 2(2)(a) or [2(2)](b) of [ECA 1972]

This category covers:

- provisions of subordinate legislation made to give effect to EU obligations or to deal with matters arising out of, or related to, EU obligations, using a statutory power *other than* ECA 1972, s.2(2).

Where secondary legislation has been made to implement EU obligations, there should be a transposition note annexed to the Explanatory Memorandum which sets out how all the main elements of the directive have been transposed.

Example

The Part-Time Workers (Prevention of Less Favourable Treatment) Regulations 2000 (SI 2000/1551) implementing Directive 97/81/EC were made under the Employment Relations Act 1999, s.19.

'operating, for a purpose mentioned in section 2(2)(a) or [2(2)](b) of [ECA 1972]'

This category covers provisions of legislation which have the effect of implementing EU obligations (or which deal with matters arising out of, or related to, EU obligations) regardless of whether they were originally made or passed for that purpose. This would be the case, for example, where the UK had made legislation on a particular topic which preceded the exercise of EU competence in that area. If the EU subsequently adopted a directive in that area and the pre-existing UK legislation already achieved the outcome required by the directive, no new implementing legislation would need to be made to fulfil the EU obligations. It is not straightforward to identify whether legislation falls into this category.

Example

Existing consumer protection legislation in the UK already addressed some areas which were later covered by the Unfair Commercial Practices Directive (Directive 2005/29/EC).

EUWA 2018, s.1B(7) continues:

> (c) relating to –
>
> (i) anything which falls within paragraph (a) or (b), or
> (ii) any rights, powers, liabilities, obligations, restrictions, remedies or procedures which are recognised and available in domestic law by virtue of section 2(1) of [ECA 1972]

This is a broad category which catches provisions in domestic legislation which are linked to, but do not fall within, the categories in s.1B(7)(a) or (b) discussed above. It also catches enactments linked to rights, etc. which flowed through the ECA 1972, s.2(1) conduit pipe.

EUWA 2018, s.1B(7) concludes:

> (d) relating otherwise to the EU or the EEA,
> [...]

This is a broad, 'sweep-up' category, catching provisions of domestic law 'which relate in some way' (Explanatory Notes, p.21) to the EU and EEA.

There is no definitive list of what comes within this category and, pending any judicial decisions on the point, no straightforward way of identifying whether a particular piece of legislation is caught.

Example

The example given in the Explanatory Notes is an Act of Parliament which contains cross-references to a definition in an EU instrument.

'as it has effect'

The phrase 'as it has effect' in EUWA 2018, s.2(1) serves to catch legislation which has been passed or made before IPCD but has not come into force.[5] It also acts to preserve legislation as it was interpreted by the courts. In other words, where the courts read in certain words to achieve compliance with EU law or disapplied certain provisions because they were incompatible with EU law, that effect still applies.

Example

In *P (Appellant)* v. *Commissioner of Police of the Metropolis (Respondent)* [2017] UKSC 65, the Supreme Court read the words in italics below into the Equality Act 2010, s.42(1) in order to achieve compatibility with Council Directive 2000/78/EC:

(1) For the purposes of this Part, holding the office of constable is to be treated as employment –

(a) by the chief officer, in respect of any act done by the chief officer *or (so far as such acts fall within the scope of the Framework Directive) by persons conducting a misconduct meeting or misconduct hearing* in relation to a constable or appointment to the office of constable;

(b) by the responsible authority, in respect of any act done by the authority in relation to a constable or appointment to the office of constable.

The Supreme Court emphasised that:

> this conforming interpretation has to be understood broadly: the court is not amending the legislation, and the italicised words are not to be treated as though they had been enacted ...The italicised words are merely intended to indicate how section 42(1) should be interpreted in a case such as the present, in order to avoid a violation of EU law.

Comment: The effect of the phrase 'as it has effect in domestic law immediately before IP completion day' in EUWA 2018, s.2(1) is that the Equality Act 2010, s.42(1) continues to

[5] Note that the position is different in relation to EU direct legislation which refers to legislation which is operative immediately before IPCD. See **12.5**.

have effect in domestic law taking into account the above interpretation of the Supreme Court. The phrase also reinforces EUWA 2018, s.6(3) which requires courts, among other things, to interpret retained EU law in accordance with retained domestic case law as it had effect immediately before IPCD (subject to certain qualifications). See **Chapter 15**.

'IP completion day'

IP completion day means 31 December 2020 at 11.00 p.m. This could have been changed by a minister in subordinate legislation but only to take into account any changes to EU summertime arrangements.

11.6 EXCLUSIONS

Enactments contained in the following legislation are excluded from the definition of 'EU-derived domestic legislation' (s.1B(7)):

- ECA 1972;
- EUWA 2018;
- regulations made under EUWA 2018;
- EU(WA)A 2020;
- regulations made under EU(WA)A 2020.

This means, for example, that ECA 1972, s.2(2) which provided a power to implement an EU obligation does not become part of EU-derived domestic legislation.

It is important to note that EU-derived legislation is preserved subject to s.5 (Exceptions to savings and incorporation) and Sched.1 (Further provision about exceptions to savings and incorporation) (see **Chapter 14**), and s.5A (Savings and incorporation: supplementary). Section 5A was inserted into EUWA 2018 by EU(WA)A 2020, s.25. It provides that the temporary status of EU law during the transition period does not prevent it from having effect at the end of that period as retained EU law.

11.7 CONSEQUENCES OF FALLING WITHIN THE CATEGORY OF EU-DERIVED DOMESTIC LEGISLATION

Various consequences flow from an enactment being categorised as EU-derived domestic legislation. For example:

- It is clear that the subordinate legislation made under ECA 1972, s.2(2) remains in force even after ECA 1972 itself (the parent Act) is repealed.
- The courts have to interpret EU-derived domestic legislation in the way set out in EUWA 2018, s.6.
- The power in EUWA 2018, s.8 is available to make good any 'deficiencies'.

CHAPTER 12

Retained EU law: direct EU legislation

Retained EU law		
EU-derived domestic legislation	Direct EU legislation	All other EU rights and obligations saved by EUWA 2018, s.4
interpreted in accordance with retained case law and retained general principles		

Figure 12.1 Direct EU legislation as a component of retained EU law

12.1 OVERVIEW

This chapter focuses on the second category of retained EU law that appears in EUWA 2018 – direct EU legislation. EUWA 2018, s.3 saves direct EU legislation, such as EU regulations, and turns it into UK domestic law at the end of the transition period. This ensures that EU legislation which applied directly in UK law without the need for specific implementing measures (beyond ECA 1972, s.2(1)) continues to have effect in UK law after the transition period.

The incorporation of direct EU legislation into domestic law is key to achieving the policy of continuity after IPCD. If EUWA 2018 did not incorporate direct EU legislation into domestic law, it would cease to have effect at the end of the transition period.

The end of the application of direct EU legislation in the absence of s.3 would occur for the principal reason that direct EU legislation only applies to EU Member States. The end of the application of direct EU legislation is also reflected in domestic law through the removal of the conduit pipe created by ECA 1972, s.2(1).

12.2 AREAS OF COMPLEXITY

There is an interesting technical question about how direct EU legislation worked in UK domestic law during the UK's membership of the EU. Under the TFEU, Art.288, regulations are 'binding in [their] entirety' and 'directly applicable in all

Member States'. This suggests that the entire text of the regulations applies in the Member States (including in the UK during its membership of the EU or during the transition period). However, the idea that the entire text of EU regulations has the force of law in the UK is not consistent with ECA 1972, s.2(1), which gave effect to EU regulations in UK law. Section 2(1) states that it is the 'rights, powers, liabilities, obligations' etc. which have legal effect and are recognised and available in UK law. This suggests that only those parts of the text which are rights, powers, etc. became part of UK domestic law.

The drafting of EUWA 2018, s.3 sidesteps any arguments that it only saves 'rights, powers, liabilities, obligations', etc. (and thus not the whole text of direct EU legislation). It does so by avoiding references to ECA 1972, s.2(1) in the provisions relating to saving and incorporation. Instead, EUWA 2018, s.3(1) states that direct EU legislation 'forms part of domestic law'.

12.3 STATUS OF RECITALS TO DIRECT EU LEGISLATION

The intention of s.3 is that the text of direct EU legislation forms part of UK law on and after IPCD. The Explanatory Notes to EUWA 2018 make it clear that this includes the recitals (see Explanatory Notes, para.83).

It is likely that the recitals never actually became part of domestic law during the UK's EU membership. Recitals have interpretative value. Therefore, it is arguable that they did not flow through ECA 1972, s.2(1) because they are not rights or obligations, etc. As set out above, EUWA 2018 gets around the issue of whether the whole text of the regulation or merely the rights, obligations, etc. became part of UK law during EU membership by bringing the whole text of the regulation into domestic law.[1] Therefore, the recitals are also brought into domestic law through s.3.

12.4 DEFINITION OF DIRECT EU LEGISLATION

EUWA 2018, s.3 provides:

> (1) Direct EU legislation, so far as operative immediately before IP completion day, forms part of domestic law on and after IP completion day.
>
> (2) In this Act 'direct EU legislation' means –
>
> (a) any EU regulation, EU decision or EU tertiary legislation, as it has effect in EU law immediately before IP completion day and so far as –

Direct EU legislation comprises EU regulations, EU decisions and EU tertiary legislation, subject to exceptions. 'Retained direct EU legislation' is defined in EUWA 2018, s.20(1).

1 This is achieved by the reference to 'as it has effect in EU law' and 'direct EU legislation . . . forms part of domestic law'.

12.4.1 EU regulations

As discussed in **Chapter 2**, regulations are legally binding acts. The TFEU, Art.288 states that they are 'binding in [their] entirety and directly applicable in all Member States'. This means that regulations become enforceable law in the Member States without the need for national implementing legislation. In the UK, ECA 1972, s.2(1) enabled this to happen. The Supreme Court explained this process in the case of *Miller*:

> the 1972 Act gives effect to EU law, it is not itself the originating source of that law. It is ... the 'conduit pipe' by which EU law is introduced into domestic law.

In practice, the functioning of regulations is more intricate. Regulations often combine provisions which create such rights and obligations, together with other provisions which are drafted like directives. For example, Art.15 of Regulation 2020/741 of 25 May 2020 on minimum requirements for water reuse requires Member States to lay down rules on penalties which apply to infringements of the regulation. Article 15 reads like a directive and will have to be implemented in domestic law by Member States. Within the scheme of EUWA 2018, those parts of regulations which have been implemented in domestic law will be saved under s.2 (see **Chapter 11**).

12.4.2 EU decisions

The reference to decisions encompasses decisions within the meaning of the TFEU, Art.288 and decisions made under former Art.34(2)(c) of the TEU as it applied before the Lisbon Treaty.[2]

Decisions within the meaning of the TFEU, Art.288 are binding in their entirety. A decision which specifies those to whom it is addressed is binding only on the addressees (for example, an EU Member State or an individual company). However, much like regulations, decisions are something of a hybrid. Some do not need implementing legislation. Others require implementation in Member State law in order to give effect to them (see, for example, *Hansa Fleisch*). This means that some decisions will be saved under s.3; the domestic legislation which implements others will be saved under s.2. It is also possible that it will not be clear from the decision in question whether it should have been implemented in domestic law or not. A decision might therefore fall partly within s.2 (where it has been implemented), partly within s.3 (where it did not require implementation) or in s.4 (where implementation has not taken place and the provisions in question contain rights, obligations, etc.). For further detail see **Chapter 13**.

[2] The TFEU, Art.288 refers to the institutions adopting regulations, directives, decisions, etc. However, there are EU bodies which are not institutions under the TEU, Art.13 (see **2.7**). One example is the European Securities and Markets Authority. Where decisions are not saved under EUWA 2018, s.3 this should not make a material difference because the relevant rights, obligations, etc. will be swept up by EUWA 2018, s.4 (see **Chapter 13**).

EUWA 2018 does not preclude arguments after IPCD that an unimplemented or an incorrectly implemented provision in a decision has direct effect, notwithstanding the fact that this argument has not been made before IPCD. This is in contrast to arguments about the direct effect of directives, where such arguments can only be made where the relevant rights are 'of a kind' recognised by the CJEU or by a UK court or tribunal prior to IPCD (see s.4(2)(b) and **13.6**). For an overview of direct effect after IPCD, see **Appendix A**.

Decisions in the context of justice and home affairs (JHA)

The decisions which EUWA 2018 saves also include decisions under former Art.34(2)(c) of the Treaty on European Union (see the definition of 'EU decision' in EUWA 2018, s.20(1)). Decisions under former Art.34(2)(c) did not have direct effect in the law of Member States. Former Art.34(2)(c) was a legal basis for decisions in the field of police and judicial cooperation in criminal matters prior to the coming into force of the Lisbon Treaty. An example of this sort of instrument is the Council Decision 2008/976/JHA on the European Judicial Network. The European Judicial Network facilitates judicial cooperation between EU countries, particularly in actions to combat serious crime, and to enable appropriate communication and information sharing with contact points and judicial authorities in other EU countries. The decision has been revoked using the s.8 deficiencies-correcting power (see **Chapter 17**).[3]

12.4.3 EU tertiary legislation

EUWA 2018 defines EU tertiary legislation in s.20(1). Tertiary legislation is similar to UK secondary legislation in that it is a form of delegated legislation. It consists of 'delegated acts' and 'implementing acts' which may take the form of regulations, directives or decisions. Tertiary legislation in the form of delegated acts can be used to supplement or amend certain elements of the parent legislation. Tertiary legislation in the form of implementing acts is used where uniform conditions are needed to implement a legally binding act (see also **2.4**).

Tertiary legislation which is in the form of a directive is not saved, in keeping with the rest of EUWA 2018. But where the power to make tertiary legislation comes from a directive and it is made in the form of a regulation or a decision, that regulation or decision will be saved under s.3.[4]

---

[3] See the Law Enforcement and Security (Amendment) (EU Exit) Regulations 2019 (SI 2019/742).

[4] See the definition of EU tertiary legislation in EUWA 2018, s.20(1) which includes any provision made under an EU directive by virtue of the TFEU, Arts.290 or 291(2), or former Art.202 of the Treaty establishing the European Community.

Example

Directive (EU) 2016/680 on the protection of natural persons regarding processing of personal data connected with criminal offences or the execution of penalties, and on the free movement of such data enables the European Commission to make a decision that a third country ensures an adequate level of protection of personal data (an 'adequacy decision'). This enables a free flow of data from the EU to the country in question.

After IPCD, the directive will not be saved. However, any adequacy decisions made under the directive would be saved.[5]

12.5 ANALYSIS OF KEY PHRASES

'so far as operative immediately before IP completion day' (s.3(1))

This provision ensures that only direct EU legislation which is 'operative' in UK law immediately before IPCD is saved under s.3. The term 'operative' has a specific meaning explained below.

'forms part of domestic law' (s.3(1))

This provision gives effect to the policy of continuity by ensuring that direct EU legislation does not fall away once the UK leaves the EU.

'as it has effect in EU law' (s.3(2)(a))

This reference avoids having to get into the detail of how direct EU legislation becomes domestic law. The drafting is different from that of EUWA 2018, s.2, which uses the phrase 'as it has effect in domestic law'. Section 3 sidesteps the question as to whether the whole text of direct EU legislation came into domestic law via ECA 1972, s.2(1) or whether just the rights and obligations, etc. were brought in. It is arguable that the text of direct EU legislation did not become part of domestic law during the UK's EU membership. However, there is no direct authority on this point and the TFEU, Art.288 (as well as Case 43/71 *Politi s.a.s.* v. *Ministry for Finance of the Italian Republic*, EU:C:1971:122) suggests that the entire text of direct EU legislation should be available in domestic law. The reference to 'as it has effect in EU law' avoids this problem.

This provision is also important in terms of the interpretation of the direct EU legislation which is saved through s.3. Where recitals or case law gave a particular meaning to the instrument in question, that interpretation is intended to survive. Where using foreign language versions of the instrument to interpret it is helpful in

5 At the time of writing no adequacy decisions have been made under this particular directive.

elucidating its meaning, that approach can continue. The legislative background will also potentially be relevant, as was the case when the UK was an EU Member State (see **3.2.2**). Further, any amendments to the legislation prior to IPCD also remain after IPCD. In other words, this is a 'signpost' pointing the reader of the statute towards continuity: the intention is that the law should mean the same after IPCD as it did before.

'so far as' (s.3(2)(a))

These are limiting words and refer to the conditions in s.3(2) (and are repeated throughout s.3(2)). In other words, direct EU legislation is subject to a number of qualifications or exclusions.

12.6 QUALIFICATIONS OR EXCLUSIONS

EUWA 2018, s.3(2)(a) continues:

> (ai) it is applicable to and in the United Kingdom by virtue of Part 4 of the withdrawal agreement,
> (bi) it neither has effect nor is to have effect by virtue of section 7A or 7B,
> (i) it is not an exempt EU instrument (for which see section 20(1) and Schedule 6), and
> ...
> (iii) its effect is not reproduced in an enactment to which section 2(1) applies

'(ai) it is applicable to and in the United Kingdom by virtue of Part 4 of the withdrawal agreement'

This provision ensures that only the law which applies in the UK during the transition period is saved from IPCD.

Part 4 of the Withdrawal Agreement deals with the transition period. It provided that EU law continued to apply to the UK as if it was an EU Member State for the duration of the transition period despite the UK's departure from the EU on 31 January 2020 (see **10.3** and **20.2**). Section 3(2)(a)(ai) ensures that the EU regulations, decisions or tertiary legislation which applied to the UK during the transition become retained EU law at the end of the transition period.

However, not all provisions of EU law applied to the UK automatically during the transition period. For example, in the area of JHA, the UK could not opt in to new JHA measures (except those amending measures which it was already participating in).[6] Those new measures would not be converted into domestic law at the end of the transition period. Section 3(2)(a)(ai) ensures that only the measures which applied to the UK during the transition period are saved.

---

6 See the Withdrawal Agreement, Art.127(5).

'(bi) it neither has effect nor is to have effect by virtue of section 7A or 7B'

'by virtue of section 7A [General implementation of remainder of withdrawal agreement]'

This is an exception to the incorporation of direct EU legislation. It is needed because s.7A implements parts of 'relevant separation agreement law' which includes provisions of EU law made applicable by the Withdrawal Agreement (other than provisions relating to the transition period). The exception is required because the provisions of the Withdrawal Agreement operate differently from retained EU law.

EUWA 2018, s.7A acts in the same way as ECA 1972, s.2(1) functioned during the UK's EU membership. ECA 1972, s.2(1) allowed EU law to apply directly in UK law without the need for further implementing provisions. In the same way, s.7A allows provisions of the Withdrawal Agreement (where they create rights, powers, liabilities, etc.) to apply directly in UK law. They also apply in a dynamic fashion (note the wording 'from time to time created or arising under the withdrawal agreement').[7]

Relevant separation agreement law is also fundamentally different from retained EU law because it implements international commitments between the UK and the EU. Retained EU law, however, is confined to areas where there are no reciprocal relationships with the EU (although it cannot be excluded that this position may change if there is a future trading arrangement secured as between the UK and the EU, depending on how that treaty is implemented). The relevant standards are saved but the rights and obligations which existed between Member States are no longer there. See also **20.3**.

'by virtue of section 7B [General implementation of EEA EFTA Separation Agreement and Swiss Citizens' Rights Agreement]'

This exception to the incorporation of direct EU legislation allows for the implementation of the EEA EFTA Separation Agreement and Swiss Citizens' Rights Agreement. In the same way as s.7A, s.7B sets up a conduit pipe similar to that under ECA 1972, s.2(1), allowing provisions of those agreements to flow directly into UK law.

'(i) it is not an exempt EU instrument (for which see section 20(1) and Schedule 6)'

Schedule 6 as originally enacted ensured that EUWA 2018 did not go wider than the application of EU law to the UK and save instruments (or parts of instruments)

[7] The reference to 'from time to time … arising', etc. is needed because in limited areas there will be dynamic alignment with EU law after IPCD, for example in the field of coordination of social security systems for the purposes of Part 2, Title III of the Withdrawal Agreement.

which did not apply to the UK prior to its departure from the EU (see Explanatory Notes, para.84). Certain instruments did not apply to the UK during EU membership because of the opt-ins, opt-outs or special arrangements in the Schengen Protocol (Protocol No 19) or the Justice and Home Affairs Protocol (Protocol No 21) as well as measures relating to the eurozone (Protocol No 15).

The amendments to Sched.6 made by EU(WA)A 2020 reflect the fact that these instruments are filtered out and do not apply to the UK during the transition period as agreed in the Withdrawal Agreement, Art.127(1)(a).

The instruments listed under Sched.6, para.2 relate to the Common Foreign and Security Policy: see **8.3.4**. CFSP decisions[8] made under the TEU were excluded from coming through the conduit pipe under ECA 1972, s.2(1). This was done by excluding the CFSP section of the TEU from the definition of 'Treaties' in ECA 1972. As these decisions did not come through the conduit pipe when the UK was a Member State, they are not made part of retained EU law, consistent with the policy of continuity.

There is an unresolved debate as to whether these CFSP measures are decisions within the scope of the TFEU, Art.288. The drafting ensures that even if they do fall within the scope of Art.288, they will be exempt instruments.

'(iii) its effect is not reproduced in an enactment to which section 2(1) applies'

At a high level, the point of s.3(2)(a)(iii) is to avoid duplication on the statute book. The saving of the text of direct EU legislation (see **12.2**) is subject to s.3(2)(a)(iii). This means that where provisions in EU-derived domestic legislation mirror provisions in direct EU legislation, s.3(2)(a)(iii) operates to exclude those provisions from saving and incorporation through s.3, and ensures that they are instead saved only through the operation of s.2.

The precise meaning of s.3(2)(a)(iii) is not clear. It is arguable that it excludes from the saving and incorporation of direct EU legislation those provisions which functioned like directives. As discussed above, certain provisions of direct EU legislation actually function much more like directives than regulations. For example, an EU regulation might allow Member States to create an exception to a rule in the regulation. These provisions of regulations will have been implemented in UK domestic law during EU membership. The effect of s.3(2)(a)(iii) may therefore be to ensure that only the domestic legislation saved under s.2 remains part of UK domestic law. The instruction to Member States to draft that legislation, by contrast, does not become part of UK domestic law under s.3. This avoids duplication on the statute book because it would be confusing to keep both the instruction to legislate and the legislation itself as retained EU law. However, a narrower reading of the

[8] An example of a CFSP decision is Council Decision (CFSP) 2018/1788 of 19 November 2018 in support of the South-Eastern and Eastern Europe Clearinghouse for the Control of Small Arms and Light Weapons (SEESAC) for the implementation of the Regional Roadmap on combating illicit arms trafficking in the Western Balkans [2018] OJ L293/11.

scope of s.3(2)(a)(iii) might suggest that s.3(2)(a)(iii) is only relevant where the effect of the provisions in EU-derived domestic legislation and direct EU legislation is exactly the same.

EUWA 2018, s.3(2)(b) provides:

> (b) any Annex to the EEA agreement, as it has effect in EU law immediately before IP completion day and so far as –
>
> (ai) it is applicable to and in the United Kingdom by virtue of Part 4 of the withdrawal agreement,
> (bi) it neither has effect nor is to have effect by virtue of section 7A or 7B,
> (i) it refers to, or contains adaptations of, anything falling within paragraph (a), and
> (ii) its effect is not reproduced in an enactment to which section 2(1) applies, or

'(b) any Annex to the EEA agreement, as it has effect in EU law immediately before IP completion day'

The Annexes to the EEA Agreement set out which EU regulations, decisions and tertiary legislation apply to the EEA states. They also set out any adaptations to those instruments which are required in an EEA context.

Example

Regulation (EU) 524/2013 creates an online dispute resolution (ODR) platform at EU level. Consumers and traders can use the platform to resolve disputes in relation to a product or service which they have bought anywhere in the EU.

Regulation (EU) 524/2013 applies to the EEA as set out in an Annex to the EEA Agreement. The Annex makes adaptations to the Regulation.

Extract from Annex XIX (Consumer protection) to the EEA Agreement:

> Regulation (EU) No 524/2013 of the European Parliament and of the Council of 21 May 2013 on online dispute resolution for consumer disputes and amending Regulation (EC) No 2006/2004 and Directive 2009/22/EC (OJ L 165, 18.6.2013, p. 1).
>
> The provisions of the Regulation shall, for the purposes of this [the EEA] Agreement, be read with the following adaptations:
>
> (a) As regards the EFTA States, the ODR platform referred to in Article 5 of the Regulation shall be accessible within 40 working days from the entry into force of Decision of the EEA Joint Committee No 194/2016 of 23 September 2016.
> (b) The ODR platform shall be accessible in all the languages referred to in Article 129(1) of the EEA Agreement.[9]

---

[9] Article 129(1) states: '1. This Agreement is drawn up in a single original in the Danish, Dutch, English, Finnish, French, German, Greek, Icelandic, Italian, Norwegian, Portuguese, Spanish and Swedish languages, each of these texts being equally authentic.'

During the UK's EU membership and during the transition period, the EEA Agreement was one of the 'Treaties' by virtue of ECA 1972, s.1. This meant that its provisions could apply in the UK through the conduit pipe of ECA 1972, s.2(1) (see **Chapter 9**).

In order to ensure continuity, the text of the Annexes to the EEA Agreement which contain adaptations to direct EU legislation are retained under s.3. This is subject to the deficiencies-correcting power in s.8.

'and so far as –

(ai) it is applicable to and in the United Kingdom by virtue of Part 4 of the withdrawal agreement,
(bi) it neither has effect nor is to have effect by virtue of section 7A or 7B'

Under s.3(2)(b)(ai) and (bi), the saving of the text of the Annexes to the EEA Agreement is subject to some further conditions.

Where the adaptations relate to instruments which do not apply to the UK during the transition period,[10] these are not incorporated under s.3 on IPCD. Further, where the EEA EFTA Separation Agreement provides for ongoing cooperation in particular areas, those provisions override the saving and incorporation under s.3.

'(i) it refers to, or contains adaptations of, anything falling within paragraph (a), and
(ii) its effect is not reproduced in an enactment to which section 2(1) applies'

Section 3(2)(b)(i) ensures that only adaptations of instruments which are saved through s.3 are retained. The reason for this is clear: the adaptations on their own would be meaningless if the instrument which they adapted was not itself saved.

Where any adaptations of the Annexes to the EEA Agreement have been implemented in domestic law those will be saved under s.2 rather than under s.3. This is the effect of s.3(2)(b)(ii).

EUWA 2018, s.3(2)(c) provides:

(c) Protocol 1 to the EEA agreement (which contains horizontal adaptations that apply in relation to EU instruments referred to in the Annexes to that agreement), as it has effect in EU law immediately before IP completion day and so far as –

(i) it is applicable to and in the United Kingdom by virtue of Part 4 of the withdrawal agreement, and
(ii) it neither has effect nor is to have effect by virtue of section 7A or 7B.

Protocol 1 to the EEA Agreement contains 'horizontal' adaptations to EU instruments which make provision for how those instruments should apply in the EEA states.

[10] The Withdrawal Agreement, Part 4 deals with the transition period.

Example: Horizontal adaptation

6. PUBLICATION OF INFORMATION

(a) Where, according to an act referred to, an [EU] Member State is to publish certain information on facts, procedures and the like, also the EFTA States shall, under the Agreement, publish the relevant information in a corresponding manner.

(b) Where, according to an act referred to, facts, procedures, reports and the like are to be published in the Official Journal of the European [Union], the corresponding information regarding the EFTA States shall be published in a separate EEA section* thereof.

Section 3(2)(c) saves the horizontal adaptations into UK domestic law. This means that the Annexes saved through s.3(2)(b) are interpreted in the same way after IPCD, thus ensuring continuity.

The saving only applies where the horizontal adaptations were applicable to the UK during the transition period and is subject to the provisions which implement the Withdrawal Agreement or the EEA EFTA Separation Agreement. This is the effect of s.3(2)(c)(i) and (ii).

EUWA 2018, s.3(3) provides:

(3) For the purposes of this Act, any direct EU legislation is operative immediately before IP completion day if –

(a) in the case of anything which comes into force at a particular time and is stated to apply from a later time, it is in force and applies immediately before IP completion day,

(b) in the case of a decision which specifies to whom it is addressed, it has been notified to that person before IP completion day, and

(c) in any other case, it is in force immediately before IP completion day.

Section 3(1) states that direct EU legislation is incorporated into domestic law 'so far as operative immediately before IP completion day'. Section 3(3) defines what 'operative' means.

The way in which the applicability of EU legislation is expressed in EU law is not uniform, hence the length of the definition. There is also scope for misunderstanding, especially for UK lawyers. The concept of entry into force does not mean the same thing in EU law as it does in UK national law. If a legislative instrument is in force in the UK then it has legal effect – it can be enforced through the courts. In EU law, a measure which enters into force may not actually apply – or have legal effect – until a later date. In EU terms, 'entry into force' indicates that the measure has legal existence in the EU legal order but it is not necessarily the date on which the measure takes effect. For example, a regulation may specify a date after entry into force as the date of applicability from which the measure produces rights and obligations and can be enforced in the courts. This gap between the entry into force date and the date of application allows those who will be affected by the measure time to prepare for compliance with the new requirements.

As a general rule, statements setting out the date of applicability of the relevant EU legislative instrument will be at the end of the instrument. Some instruments do not set out the date from which they enter into force. Where these instruments have general application (for example EU regulations) they will come into force (in the sense of having legal effect) on the 20th day following their publication in the Official Journal. Decisions addressed to particular parties (such as a specified Member State) take effect when they are notified to those parties.

Some EU legislation will have certain provisions which apply from one point in time and other provisions which apply from a later date. For example, an EU regulation might be divided into two parts. Part one imposes obligations on businesses relating to health and safety from June 2020. Part two imposes further obligations from June 2021. Whether the obligations from June 2021 apply in domestic law after IPCD depends on how the EU instrument deals with the issue of application. If the instrument as a whole applies (i.e. is enforceable or 'operative') before IPCD, then the obligations imposed from June 2021 will be binding in UK law from that date. However, if only part one of the instrument applies before IPCD and part two only applies after IPCD, then only part one of the instrument will be saved as direct EU legislation. See also 'Staggered application dates'.

When considering this provision, it is worth bearing in mind the aim of the 'snapshot'. Only EU legislation which had legal effect in UK law before IPCD is captured by the 'snapshot'. The effect of that legislation is saved, including the effect of obligations in that legislation which only become binding at a date falling after IPCD.

'(a) in the case of anything which comes into force at a particular time and is stated to apply from a later time, it is in force and applies immediately before IP completion day'

In s.3(3)(a) we see one of the ways in which the applicability of EU legislation is described. Some EU instruments enter into force at a particular time but do not apply (or in other words have legal effect) until a later time. The drafting here provides that only those instruments which apply (or have legal effect) immediately before IPCD are incorporated by s.3. Those which have merely entered into force but do not yet apply are not incorporated under this limb.

Example

The Regulation on minimum requirements for water reuse comes into force on the 20th day following its publication in the OJ. It was published in the OJ on 5 June 2020. It will therefore be 'in force' immediately before IPCD. However, it does not 'apply' until 26 June 2023. This means that it will not both be 'in force' and 'apply' within the meaning of s.3(3)(a). This instrument is therefore not 'operative' immediately before IPCD and will not be saved through s.3.

5.6.20 | EN | Official Journal of the European Union | L 177/32

REGULATION (EU) 2020/741 OF THE EUROPEAN PARLIAMENT AND OF THE COUNCIL

of 25 May 2020

on minimum requirements for water reuse

Article 16

Entry into force and application

This Regulation shall enter into force on the twentieth day following that of its publication in the *Official Journal of the European Union.*

It shall apply from 26 June 2023.

This Regulation shall be binding in its entirety and directly applicable in all Member States.

Done at Brussels, 25 May 2020.

'(b) in the case of a decision which specifies to whom it is addressed, it has been notified to that person before IP completion day, and'

EU decisions apply (or are legally binding) when they are notified to the person to whom they are addressed (s.3(3)(b)).

'(c) in any other case, it is in force immediately before IP completion day.'

This final provision in s.3(3)(c) reflects the fact that some EU legislation does not specify both an entry into force date and an applicability date.

If a legislative act, within the meaning of the TFEU, Art.289(3),[11] specifies an entry into force date but no separate date of application, it enters into force (i.e. takes effect) on the date specified as the entry into force date. If it does not specify an entry into force date or a date of application, it will have legal effect on the 20th day following its publication in the OJ (TFEU, Art.297(1)). This is also the case for particular non-legislative acts, i.e. those adopted in the form of regulations, directives which are addressed to all Member States and decisions which do not specify to whom they are addressed (TFEU, Art.297(2)). The difference between legislative and non-legislative acts is explained at **2.4.1**.

For the purposes of s.3(3)(c), the date from which the measure has legal effect will be the relevant date in terms of considering whether it is 'operative' immediately before IPCD.

[11] The TFEU, Art.289(3) says: 'Legal acts adopted by legislative procedure shall constitute legislative acts.'

Example

In accordance with the TFEU, Art.297(2), this instrument comes into force (i.e. has legal effect) on the day following its publication in the OJ. It is a non-legislative act and a decision which does not specify to whom it is addressed.

This instrument will be 'operative' immediately before IPCD.

18.12.2019 | EN | Official Journal of the European Union | L 328/89

COMMISSION IMPLEMENTING DECISION (EU) 2019/2167

of 17 December 2019

approving the Network Strategy Plan for the air traffic management network functions of the single European sky for the period 2020-2029

Article 2

This Decision shall enter into force on the day following its publication in the *Official Journal of the European Union.*

Done at Brussels, 17 December 2019.

For the Commission
The President
Ursula VON DER LEYEN

Staggered application dates

There is particular difficulty where an instrument has staggered application dates. Section 3(3) may operate so as to save only part of an instrument where parts of that instrument apply before IPCD and parts apply after IPCD.

The extracts set out below are taken from Regulation (EU) 2020/1056 of 15 July 2020 on electronic freight transport information.

31.7.2020 EN Official Journal of the European Union L 249/33

REGULATION (EU) 2020/1056 OF THE EUROPEAN PARLIAMENT AND OF THE COUNCIL

of 15 July 2020

on electronic freight transport information

Article 18

Entry into force and application

1. This Regulation shall enter into force on the twentieth day following that of its publication in the *Official Journal of the European Union.*
2. It shall apply from 21 August 2024.
3. However, Article 2(2), Article 5(4), Article 7, Article 8, Article 9(2) and Article 10(2) shall apply from the date of entry into force of this Regulation.

This Regulation shall be binding in its entirety and directly applicable in all Member States.

Done at Brussels, 15 July 2020.

This regulation has separate entry into force and application dates. Certain articles are specified as applying from the date of entry into force (see Art.18(3)). The regulation was published in the OJ on 31 July 2020 and entered into force on the 20th day following publication. The provisions listed in Art.18(3) will therefore be 'operative' before IPCD and will be saved through s.3. However, the bulk of the regulation only applies from August 2024 (see Art.18(2)). The bulk of the regulation will therefore not be 'operative' on IPCD and will not be saved into domestic law. It is likely that this regulation will be revoked using the powers under s.8, unless the regulation can work in domestic law on the basis of the few articles which are saved and incorporated through s.3.

Some instruments may apply in their entirety but state particular dates by which certain actions have to be taken (for example a reduction in emissions of harmful chemicals may be set for a date which falls several years after IPCD). The fact that an instrument sets out future dates by which action needs to be taken does not prevent it from being saved if the instrument as a whole has a date of application which is pre-IPCD. It will then be within the meaning of 'operative' in s.3(1).

EUWA 2018, s.3(4) provides:

(4) This section –

(a) brings into domestic law any direct EU legislation only in the form of the English language version of that legislation, and

> (b) does not apply to any such legislation for which there is no such version,
>
> but paragraph (a) does not affect the use of the other language versions of that legislation for the purposes of interpreting it.

This provision ensures that only the English language versions of direct EU legislation are saved as UK domestic law. This is for reasons of practicality. Amending the different language versions would be a significant task and unnecessary. However, the provision clarifies that other language versions of the EU legislation can still be considered by UK domestic courts in interpreting retained direct EU legislation. It is possible that there are instruments in force dating from before the UK's accession to the EU which were not translated into English. If this is the case then the rights and obligations in those instruments may be saved by virtue of s.4.

EUWA 2018, s.3(5) provides:

> (5) This section is subject to section 5 and Schedule 1 (exceptions to savings and incorporation) and section 5A (savings and incorporation: supplementary).

This subsection states that the savings in s.3 are subject to s.5 and Sched.1 (see **Chapter 14**) and s.5A. Section 5A was inserted into EUWA 2018 by EU(WA)A 2020, s.25. It provides that the temporary status of EU law during the transition period does not prevent it from having effect at the end of that period as retained EU law.

CHAPTER 13

Retained EU law: all other EU rights and obligations

Retained EU law		
EU-derived domestic legislation	Direct EU legislation	All other EU rights and obligations saved by EUWA 2018, s.4
interpreted in accordance with retained case law and retained general principles		

Figure 13.1 All other EU rights, etc. as a component of retained EU law

13.1 OVERVIEW

This chapter considers the third category of retained EU law which is referred to in EUWA 2018 by the rather unwieldy term 'anything which is retained EU law by virtue of section 4' (EUWA 2018, s.20(7)). Section 4 acts as a 'safety net'. This chapter explains what is caught by s.4.

As explained in **Chapter 1**, the aim of EUWA 2018 was to ensure continuity and legal certainty once EU law ceased to apply to the UK. The chosen method was to convert EU laws into UK law and to preserve the laws that were made in the UK to implement EU obligations, unless and until Parliament or the devolved legislatures, as appropriate, decided to make changes. The policy was to ensure that wherever possible, the same laws would apply from the end of the transition period as had applied before that point. This meant ensuring that all such laws continued to apply, as a starting point.

It was clearly not feasible to list every law that would be preserved or converted. Instead, EUWA 2018 takes the approach of preserving or converting laws by category:

- Section 2 deals with domestic law which was made to implement EU obligations.
- Section 3 deals with direct EU legislation.

However, that does not cover everything. Section 4 was needed in order to catch everything else.

The wording of s.4(1) accordingly tracks the wording of ECA 1972, s.2(1), the original conduit pipe through which EU rights, etc.[1] flowed into domestic law (see **9.2.2** and **Appendix B**). It provides that any rights, etc. which were recognised immediately before IPCD by virtue of ECA 1972, s.2(1) continue to be recognised on and after IPCD. This is subject to the exceptions in s.4(2).

However, tracking the wording of ECA 1972, s.2(1) does not give absolute clarity as to everything that is caught by s.4. That is because it is not clear what ECA 1972, s.2(1) admitted through the conduit pipe in terms of EU law (see **Chapter 9**). For example, it is clear that s.4(1) saves directly effective rights in the TEU and TFEU. The position in relation to the general principles is less straightforward (see **13.5.4**).

Despite the stated policy intention that s.4 should act as a 'sweeper provision' which suggests it should catch anything not caught by ss.2 or 3 (unless expressly excluded), there appears to be some overlap as far as rights in directives are concerned between what is saved under s.2 and what is saved under s.4. The drafting of s.4 also raises an issue as to which directly effective rights in directives are saved.

13.2 EUWA 2018, S.4: GENERAL

EUWA 2018, s.4 provides:

> (1) Any rights, powers, liabilities, obligations, restrictions, remedies and procedures which, immediately before IP completion day –
>
> (a) are recognised and available in domestic law by virtue of section 2(1) of the European Communities Act 1972, and
> (b) are enforced, allowed and followed accordingly,
>
> continue on and after IP completion day to be recognised and available in domestic law (and to be enforced, allowed and followed accordingly).
>
> (2) Subsection (1) does not apply to any rights, powers, liabilities, obligations, restrictions, remedies or procedures so far as they –
>
> (a) form part of domestic law by virtue of section 3,
> (aa) are, or are to be, recognised and available in domestic law (and enforced, allowed and followed accordingly) by virtue of section 7A or 7B, or
> (b) arise under an EU directive (including as applied by the EEA agreement) and are not of a kind recognised by the European Court or any court or tribunal in the United Kingdom in a case decided before IP completion day (whether or not as an essential part of the decision in the case).
>
> (3) This section is subject to section 5 and Schedule 1 (exceptions to savings and incorporation) and section 5A (savings and incorporation: supplementary).

[1] In this chapter, rights, etc. refers to rights, powers, liabilities, obligations, restrictions, remedies and procedures. References to a UK court include references to a tribunal.

In its evidence to the House of Lords Select Committee on the Constitution, the government described EUWA 2018, s.4 as a 'sweeper' provision which would ensure that, as a starting point, all rights, etc. that were available in domestic law as a result of ECA 1972, s.2(1) would continue to be available in domestic law after exit.[2] The idea behind s.4 is to make sure that, in achieving the Act's overall aim of saving and continuing all EU law that applied in the UK before IPCD, nothing is inadvertently left out.

Section 4(1) comprehensively sweeps up any rights, etc. which came through the ECA 1972, s.2(1) conduit pipe but it has to be read subject to s.4(2). That section operates to exclude particular rights, etc. from the savings provision in s.4(1).

13.3 EUWA 2018, S.4(1)

Given the policy intention behind EUWA 2018, s.4, it is not surprising that it mirrors the wording of ECA 1972, s.2(1). It is instructive to look back at how s.2(1), as originally enacted, operated.[3] Section 2(1) brought into the domestic legal system, on an ongoing basis, all provisions of EU law that, as a result of the UK's membership of the EU, had to be given legal effect in the domestic legal order without further enactment by the UK.

13.3.1 Direct applicability and direct effect

In the context of s.4, it is useful to consider the terms 'directly applicable' and 'directly effective'. The two are often used interchangeably but it aids understanding to draw a distinction between them. A provision of EU law is *directly applicable* if it takes effect in the national legal order without the need for transposition by the Member State. For example, the TFEU, Art.288 provides that an EU regulation is directly applicable in all Member States.

A provision of EU law has *direct effect* if it is sufficiently clear, precise and unconditional to be invoked and relied on by individuals in EU courts or in national courts without the need for any implementing measures. A directive is not directly applicable because it requires implementation in domestic law. However, a specific provision of a directive may have direct effect. Provisions of a regulation are directly applicable but they are not necessarily directly effective (see, for example, Case C–403/98 *Azienda Agricola Monte Arcosu* v. *Regione Autonoma della Sardegna*, EU:C:2001:6, paras.26 and 29). Section 2(1) brought both directly applicable and directly effective rights, etc. into domestic law. See further **5.2**.

2 Select Committee on the Constitution, *European Union (Withdrawal) Bill* (HL 2017–19, 69), para.30. The evidence was given before the transition period had been agreed.

3 For a fuller explanation, see **Chapter 9**.

13.4 IDENTIFYING S.4 RIGHTS, ETC.

Although it is clear conceptually that rights, etc. which came through the conduit pipe of ECA 1972, s.2(1) continue (unless specifically excluded), it is less clear what those specific rights, etc. actually are. There is no definitive list in the Act or elsewhere. Identifying exactly what is saved by s.4 is not straightforward. The rights, etc. may be found in many places such as the TEU, the TFEU, international agreements to which the EU is a party, the general principles and directives.

The Explanatory Notes put the emphasis on rights and, as rights are the most significant aspect of what is saved by s.4, this commentary takes the same approach. However, it is also the case that powers, liabilities, obligations, restrictions, remedies and procedures may also be saved under s.4. An example of each of these categories is given in Table 13.1.

Table 13.1 Examples of a right, power, liability, obligation, restriction, remedy and procedure

	Example	Source
Right	Right to equal pay	TFEU, Art.157
Power	Decision-making powers bestowed on the Board of Governors of the European Schools in educational, budgetary and administrative matters	Convention defining the Statute of the European Schools
Liability	State liability in damages	CJEU case law: *Francovich*
Obligation	Obligation on a company to pay men and women equally for equal work	TFEU, Art.157
Restriction	Prohibition on customs duties on import and exports	TFEU, Art.30
Remedy	Damages for a sufficiently serious breach of EU law by the state[4]	CJEU case law: *Francovich*
Procedure	Procedure for requesting assistance[5]	Agreement between the European Union and Japan on mutual legal assistance in criminal matters

The Explanatory Notes, para.93 state that where directly effective rights, etc. are retained under s.4, it is the right, etc. that is retained, not the text of the article itself. See discussion at **5.2**.

[4] Note that although the remedy is saved under s.4, a right to damages in accordance with the rule in *Francovich* is subsequently disapplied by Sched.1, para.4.

[5] The rights, etc. in this agreement are saved by s.4 but the Law Enforcement and Security (Amendment) (EU Exit) Regulations 2019 (SI 2019/742) made under EUWA 2018, s.8 (among other powers) stops the rights, etc. from being recognised and available in domestic law (see **Chapter 17**).

13.5 RIGHTS

A particular challenge will be identifying whether a right comes within the scope of s.4 and is therefore available for an individual to rely on. It is instructive to refer back to the exact wording of ECA 1972, s.2(1). It made clear that it was the rights, etc. 'from time to time created or arising by or under the Treaties' which came through the conduit pipe. The rights we are concerned with for the purposes of s.4 therefore have to be in the 'Treaties' or in instruments made under the 'Treaties'.

The definition of 'Treaties' (or 'EU Treaties') in ECA 1972, s.1(2) comprised treaties listed by name and treaties described by type. The named 'Treaties' included:

- the constitutive EU treaties, i.e. the TEU and the TFEU;
- the Euratom Treaty;
- the EEA Agreement.

The treaties included by type were:

- treaties entered into by the EU with the Member States (known as 'mixed agreements');
- treaties entered into by the EU without the Member States (known as 'EU-only agreements');
- treaties entered into by the UK which are ancillary to the EU treaties (known as 'UK-only agreements').

EU-only agreements automatically came within the definition of 'Treaties'. However, for mixed agreements and UK-only agreements to come within the definition, they had to be added (or 'specified') by an Order in Council made under ECA 1972, s.1(3). For example, the European Union (Definition of Treaties) (Partnership and Cooperation Agreement) (Turkmenistan) Order 2018 (SI 2018/1071) added the Partnership and Cooperation Agreement between the European Communities and their Member States, of the one part, and the Republic of Turkmenistan, of the other part, to the definition of 'Treaties'.

It is difficult to put an exact figure on how many treaties came within the definition of 'Treaties' in ECA 1972 and are therefore potentially relevant for the purposes of EUWA 2018, s.4(1). There is neither a definitive list of the agreements within the definition of 'Treaties' in ECA 1972 nor a definitive list of the directly effective rights, etc. in those agreements, in EUWA 2018 or elsewhere. The Treaties Office Database of the European External Action Service lists over 1,000 agreements which involve the EU but not all of these will necessarily come within the definition of 'Treaties' in ECA 1972. For example, the database includes agreements in the area of the CFSP. ECA 1972 expressly excludes such agreements from the definition of 'Treaties'.

By no means is it the case that all the international agreements within the definition of 'Treaties' contain directly effective rights. The proportion that does so is likely to be small. However, the lack of a definitive list of relevant treaties let alone a list of directly effective rights in those treaties makes it difficult to ascertain with certainty what rights are saved and therefore may be relied on.

13.5.1 Constitutive EU treaties

It is convenient to consider the constitutive EU treaties separately from the rest. EUWA 2018 does not provide a definitive list of articles in the TEU and TFEU which come within the scope of s.4(1). The Explanatory Notes set out a non-exhaustive list of the articles in the TFEU which the government considers to have direct effect. Examples given include the TFEU, Art.18 (non-discrimination on ground of nationality) and Art.157 (equal pay).

Where there is existing CJEU case law to the effect that a particular treaty article has direct effect, it will be evident that the right in that article has been saved (subject to the possibility of being 'extinguished' by regulations made under EUWA 2018, s.8: see **Chapter 17**). The Act does not appear to close off the possibility of a claimant seeking to argue from first principles that a specific treaty article has always had direct effect and is therefore saved under s.4 even in the absence of any retained case law that has expressly found the article to have direct effect (compare this to the case of directly effective rights in directives discussed at **13.6**).

A right in a treaty article which has direct effect is saved in domestic law even though the TFEU and TEU no longer apply to the UK. A number of these rights will no longer make sense without that framework.

In these cases, the 'deficiencies-correcting power' in EUWA 2018, s.8 is available to 'extinguish' the right or make some other suitable alteration (**Chapter 17**).

Example

The right to vote in the UK in elections to the European Parliament is saved by s.4 but is no longer relevant. The European Parliamentary Elections Etc. (Repeal, Revocation, Amendment and Saving Provisions) (United Kingdom and Gibraltar) (EU Exit) Regulations 2018 (SI 2018/1310) 'extinguish' the right.

13.5.2 Other treaties

As explained at **8.3.5**, the EU has competence to act externally and to enter into international agreements with third countries (non-EU states) or international organisations, within the limits of its competence. Rights in international agreements to which the EU is a party or to which the EU and its Member States are parties are capable of having direct effect. The test in EU law for determining whether a provision in an international agreement has direct effect is slightly different from the better-known test that applies to directives. To determine whether a right in an international agreement has direct effect, the CJEU considers not only whether the provisions are clear, precise and unconditional but also whether the 'nature and broad logic' of the international agreement precludes direct effect (see Joined Cases C–659/13 and C–34/14 *C&J Clark International*, EU:C:2016:74, para.84).

Example

In *Simutenkov*, the CJEU found an article in the EU-Russia Partnership and Cooperation Agreement to have direct effect. The article provides that Russian nationals employed in the territory of a Member State should not be discriminated against as regards working conditions, remuneration or dismissal, as compared to the Member State's own nationals.

In the last few years, it has become more commonplace for the EU to include provisions in its bilateral trade agreements which make clear that the agreement is not intended to have direct effect.

Example

The EU-Canada Comprehensive Economic and Trade Agreement, Art.30.6, para.1 says:

> Nothing in this Agreement shall be construed as conferring rights or imposing obligations on persons other than those created between the Parties under public international law, nor as permitting this Agreement to be directly invoked in the domestic legal systems of the Parties.

From IPCD, EU-only agreements cease to apply to the UK (although the UK might seek to accede in its own right). The UK and the EU have agreed that mixed agreements which are classified as bilateral (i.e. an agreement between the EU and its Member States on the one hand, and a third country on the other) also cease to apply to the UK. The government has been engaged in a programme to put in place arrangements with third countries to replicate the effects of the current arrangements.[6] The UK remains bound by mixed multilateral agreements to which it is a party in its own right, e.g. the United Nations Convention on the Law of the Sea.

However, EUWA 2018, s.4 may save directly effective rights, etc. even though the international agreement from which they originate has fallen away and the rights and obligations in that agreement no longer exist in international law. A number of these rights will no longer make sense in the new context. Where this is the case, these directly effective rights may be 'extinguished' using the s.8 deficiencies-correcting power.

---

[6] See Fella, S. (2019) *UK Replacement of the EU's External Agreements after Brexit*, House of Commons Library Briefing Paper, Number 8370, 19 September.

For an example of how rights in international agreements have been dealt with using this power, see the Immigration, Nationality and Asylum (EU Exit) Regulations 2019 (SI 2019/745), reg.55. It takes a generic approach by 'extinguishing' all rights in a named agreement (e.g. the Convention determining the state responsible for examining applications for asylum lodged in one of the Member States of the European Communities) which would otherwise be caught by EUWA 2018, s.4, as opposed to identifying specific rights, etc. in the agreement and 'turning them off' individually.

EUWA 2018 does not appear to close off the possibility of a claimant seeking to argue from first principles that a specific article in an international agreement has always had direct effect and is therefore saved under s.4 even in the absence of any retained case law that has expressly found the article to have direct effect (compare this to the case of directly effective rights in directives discussed at **13.6**).

13.5.3 Directives

It is not only rights, etc. in treaties that may come within the scope of s.4. Rights, etc. in instruments made under the EU Treaties (such as directives) may also be in scope.

The approach in EUWA 2018 is not to save EU directives per se but to save the domestic legislation which implements those directives (see **11.4**). If the UK has fully and correctly implemented all the EU directives it was required to implement before IPCD, then all relevant rights will have been saved by EUWA 2018, s.2. However, if the UK failed to implement a directive containing directly effective rights or implemented such a directive incorrectly, the rights which an individual should have benefited from will not have been given effect in domestic law and will therefore not be saved by s.2. The extent to which these rights are saved by s.4 is discussed at **13.6**.

13.5.4 General principles

It is clear from EUWA 2018 that the general principles have been converted into domestic law. For example, s.6 refers to 'retained general principles' in the context of the interpretation of retained EU law (see **15.7**) and Sched.1, para.3 removes the right to bring a claim for failure to comply with the general principles (see **Appendix C**). However, how this happens is not made express.

General principles may be saved through the instruments that 'codify' them which are retained through EUWA 2018, ss.2 and 3. If they are not saved in this way, they must be saved by s.4. Section 4(1) saves the rights, etc. under ECA 1972, s.2(1) (i.e. rights, etc. 'from time to time created or arising by or under the Treaties' which came through the conduit pipe), subject to s.4(2). The general principles are difficult to place with precision within that description. They are referred to in the EU Treaties and in the CJEU's case law. They are part of the 'unwritten' law of the EU.[7]

13.6 EUWA 2018, S.4(2)

Section 4(2) prevents certain rights, etc. from being saved.

Section 4(2)(a) prevents rights, etc. from being saved under s.4 if they already form part of domestic law because they are incorporated into domestic law under EUWA 2018, s.3 as retained direct EU legislation. Without this carve-out, rights, etc. would be saved both under s.3 and under s.4 which would cause duplication.

Section 4(2)(aa) prevents rights, etc. from being saved under s.4 if they come into domestic law under s.7A (General implementation of the remainder of withdrawal agreement) or s.7B (General implementation of EEA EFTA and Swiss agreements) (see **20.3**).

Section 4(2)(b) prevents directly effective rights which arise from an EU directive from being converted into domestic law unless they are 'of a kind' recognised by the CJEU or a UK court before IPCD. This requires some unpacking.

As explained at **13.5.3**, if the UK has fully and correctly implemented all the EU directives it was required to implement before IPCD, then all relevant rights, etc. will have been saved by EUWA 2018, s.2. However, if the UK failed to implement a directive containing directly effective rights or implemented such a directive incorrectly, the rights, etc. which an individual should have benefited from will not have been given effect in domestic law and will therefore not be saved by s.2.

Section 4(1)(b) goes some way towards making sure that those directly effective rights which were not implemented fully or properly are still available. The effect of s.4(1)(b) is to save all directly effective rights but only if those rights are 'of a kind' recognised by the CJEU or UK court as being directly effective before IPCD.

It is not entirely clear what is meant by 'of a kind'.[8] The Explanatory Notes take a narrow interpretation:

> The reference in subsection (2)(b) to rights 'of a kind' is intended to ensure that rights are retained if they are of a similar kind to those so recognised. So rights arising under a particular directive that have been recognised by a court before exit day as having direct effect, could be relied upon by other individuals who are not parties to that case, in circumstances which the directive is intended to address.

This suggests that the 'of a kind' formulation does no more than allow a claimant to rely on a right which has previously been found to have direct effect even though they were not party to the original case.

[7] See Costa, M. and Peers, S. (2020) *Steiner & Woods EU Law* (14th edn: OUP) at 6.2.4.

[8] See Select Committee on the Constitution, *European Union (Withdrawal) Bill* (HL 2017–19, 69), para.34.

A broader interpretation would be that one right is 'of a kind' with another if it exhibits the same characteristics that led the CJEU or a domestic court to find that the latter right had direct effect. Other possibilities are that a right is 'of a kind' with a recognised directly effective right if they are both drafted in the same style or if they have the same purpose (in the sense that a right not to be discriminated against on the ground of sex might be said to be 'of a kind' with a right not to be discriminated against on the ground of age). It remains to be seen how domestic courts will interpret the phrase.

The general rule is that only decisions of the CJEU or a UK court on the issue of direct effect which are made *before* IPCD are relevant. If, for example, the CJEU made a finding after IPCD that a right in a directive that was made before IPCD had direct effect *ab initio*, a claimant could not rely on that decision to argue that a right was of a kind recognised by the CJEU. There is an exception to this general rule in Sched.8, para.38. A right is saved if it is of a kind recognised by a UK court in a case decided after IPCD but begun before IPCD.

13.7 RIGHTS SAVED TWICE?

Where a right in a directive has been fully and properly implemented in domestic law and has been recognised by the CJEU as being directly effective, then that right will be saved under s.2 and under s.4. It has been noted that this could lead to a situation where there is a mismatch between the content of the right saved under s.2 and the content of the right as saved under s.4.[9] The Act does not expressly specify which form of the right would take precedence if this situation arose, potentially causing uncertainty. This might not be a common issue in practice. If there is potential for a significant degree of divergence in the content of the right, it may well not have direct effect in the first place. It is also possible that some general principles may be saved under s.2 and s.4.

13.8 EUWA 2018, S.4(3)

Section 4 is subject to EUWA 2018, s.5 (Exceptions to savings and incorporation), Sched.1 (Further provision about exceptions to savings and incorporation) (see **Chapter 14**) and s.5A (Savings and incorporation: supplementary). Section 5A was inserted into EUWA 2018 by EU(WA)A 2020, s.25. It provides that the temporary status of EU law during the transition period does not prevent it from having effect at the end of that period as retained EU law.

[9] See Select Committee on the Constitution, *European Union (Withdrawal) Bill* (HL 2017–19, 69), paras.35–36.

CHAPTER 14

Exceptions

14.1 OVERVIEW

Chapters 4 and **7** explain the principle of the supremacy of EU law and the Charter of Fundamental Rights as they applied during the UK's EU membership. These are the foundations on which EUWA 2018, s.5 is built. An understanding of how the supremacy of EU law and the Charter operated is a prerequisite for making sense of s.5.

Section 5 deals succinctly with the supremacy of EU law and the application of the Charter. It does not attempt to solve the underlying complexity of these topics. Instead, s.5 aims to 'signpost' how the application of these concepts has changed in UK law after IPCD, as well as what has been retained.

The heading of s.5, 'Exceptions to savings and incorporation' is arguably misleading. It is the case that the effect of s.5(1) is that 'post-IPCD'[1] domestic legislation will not be subject to EU rules on the supremacy of EU law. However, in order to keep 'stable' the parts of the statute book which stem from the time of the UK's EU membership (i.e. the majority) the principle of the supremacy of EU law continues to apply, albeit in a more limited fashion and subject to further exceptions such as the lack of the ability to use the general principles as the basis for a claim. However, the continuing application of the supremacy of EU law enables certain aspects to remain the same, such as the duty of consistent interpretation when considering the meaning of pre-IPCD domestic law which implements directives.

The removal of the Charter from domestic law creates uncertainty. This is because the 'sources' of the rights codified in the Charter remain. However, the Charter Explanations (see **7.8**) do not assist in explaining whether the sources of the rights are enforceable in UK domestic law or not. The table in **Appendix D** gives an overview of what the sources of the rights are and whether they might be enforceable in domestic law. This will become clearer as cases come to the courts.

1 Note that legislation which is passed or made *before* IPCD but which creates new domestic frameworks (for example in the area of trade) is not subject to the supremacy of EU law. This follows from the application of usual principles of statutory interpretation such as the doctrine of implied repeal and is also signposted at s.5(2). The principle of the supremacy of EU law continues so far as relevant. It would not be relevant to new domestic frameworks.

Another area of difficulty is that EUWA 2018 makes it clear that the case law which relates to the Charter is still relevant and such cases are to be read as if they referred to the underlying source of the right and not the Charter.

Section 5 is subject to relevant separation agreement law (see **Chapter 20**).

14.2 SUPREMACY OF EU LAW

Chapter 4 discusses how the supremacy of EU law applies in EU Member States. It also sets out how the principle of supremacy was implemented in the UK during the UK's period of EU membership. In order to understand how s.5 changes the principle of supremacy after the transition period, it is useful to recap on the main points about how supremacy operates in the EU system. They are as follows:

- The supremacy of EU law means that national law which conflicts with EU law must be disapplied in favour of EU law.
- Supremacy is necessary to ensure that EU law applies in the same way across the EU Member States.
- A domestic court faced with an apparent contradiction between EU law and national law will first try to read the provisions of national law so that they are compatible with EU law. The court may even go so far as to read further provisions into national law or 'read out' certain words in order to resolve the contradiction.
- If it is not possible to read national law so as to make it consistent with EU law then the domestic court will consider whether the conditions for direct effect have been met and if they have, the court will disapply domestic law which conflicts with EU law. The conditions for direct effect are:
  - the provision must be sufficiently clear and precise;
  - it must be unconditional, and leave no room for the exercise of discretion in implementation by Member States;
  - where the question before the court is whether a directive has direct effect, the challenge in question must be against a public body.

14.3 EUWA 2018, S.5(1)–(3)

Sections 5(1)–(3) provide:

> (1) The principle of the supremacy of EU law does not apply to any enactment or rule of law passed or made on or after IP completion day.
>
> (2) Accordingly, the principle of the supremacy of EU law continues to apply on or after IP completion day so far as relevant to the interpretation, disapplication or quashing of any enactment or rule of law passed or made before IP completion day.
>
> (3) Subsection (1) does not prevent the principle of the supremacy of EU law from applying to a modification made on or after IP completion day of any enactment or rule of law passed or made before IP completion day if the application of the principle is consistent with the intention of the modification.

These provisions have been relatively controversial.[2] This chapter now sets out the aims of these provisions and considers the problems which commentators and Parliamentary Committees have highlighted.

Section 5(1) and (2) should be read together. They are intended to make a relatively simple proposition: after IPCD, the normal rules of implied repeal apply.[3] New Acts of Parliament take precedence over all earlier legislation.[4] However, domestic legislation which pre-dates IPCD should still be read as it would have been prior to IPCD.

The purpose behind this proposition is twofold:

- The first goal is to retain the legal hierarchy which existed prior to IPCD for the legislation which belongs to that era. This ensures continuity in terms of how that legislation sits within the statute book and interacts with other legislation.
- The second goal reflects the policy that retained EU law should not be entrenched but is intended to be able to be repealed over time by new domestic legislation.

Section 5(3) ensures that the hierarchy which existed prior to IPCD does not automatically change if that was not the intention behind modifications which have been made.

Domestic legislation which brings in new 'post-Brexit' frameworks – for example the Immigration and Social Security Co-ordination (EU Withdrawal) Act 2020 and the Agriculture Act 2020 – takes precedence over earlier conflicting legislation, irrespective of the latter's origin (i.e. EU or domestic).

14.3.1 Detailed commentary: s.5(1) and (2)

'The principle of the supremacy of EU law'

The House of Lords Select Committee on the Constitution has remarked that this wording sits uncomfortably in legislation which deals with a position where EU law no longer applies in the UK.[5] While this argument is understandable, it could be said to move too far in the direction of regarding the body of retained EU law as purely domestic law. It ignores the origins of retained EU law. Given the Act's aim of

2 See, for example, Select Committee on the Constitution, *European Union (Withdrawal) Bill* (HL 2017–19, 69).

3 The doctrine of implied repeal means that where there is a conflict between the two, a more recent Act of Parliament repeals a previous Act of Parliament by implication.

4 The normal rules of implied repeal include the rule that constitutional statutes such as the Bill of Rights 1688 or the Human Rights Act 1998 are not subject to implied repeal and can only be repealed with express language.

5 See, for example, Select Committee on the Constitution, *European Union (Withdrawal) Bill* (HL 2017–19, 69), para.89: 'We consider that the notion of maintaining the supremacy principle following exit amounts to a fundamental flaw at the heart of the Bill. We do not consider that clause 5 clearly operates to bestow supremacy on retained EU law once exit day arrives. The supremacy of EU law will cease to apply when the UK leaves the EU and Parliament repeals the ECA. Retained EU law, being domestic law, cannot benefit from the principle of the supremacy of EU law.'

achieving continuity, the inclusion of the supremacy of EU law helps to ensure that retained EU law keeps the same meaning after IPCD as before. Supremacy is part of the 'snapshot'.

The emphasis on preserving retained EU law as it was before (in so far as possible) is repeated throughout the core provisions of EUWA 2018. It is also apparent from the Explanatory Notes and statements made by ministers as the European Union (Withdrawal) Bill made its way through Parliament. As discussed at **Chapter 15**, retained EU law is to be interpreted in accordance with the retained case law of the domestic courts and the CJEU, having regard to the limits of EU competences (see EUWA 2018, s.6(3)). The Explanatory Notes to EUWA 2018 explain (at para.111) that this means:

> taking a purposive approach to interpretation where the meaning of the measure is unclear (i.e. considering the purpose of the law from looking at other relevant materials such as the treaty legal base for a measure, its recitals and preambles, and the travaux preparatoires (working papers) leading to the adoption of the measure). It also means applying an interpretation that renders the provision of EU law compatible with the treaties and general principles of EU law.

All this points towards retained EU law as being designed so as to keep as much as possible of its previous character, unless and until Parliament or the devolved legislatures, as the case may be, decide otherwise. Thus keeping the concept of the supremacy of EU law ensures that the reader understands that the law in question retains its original, EU characteristics.

It is, however, also worth pointing out that the supremacy of EU law is only partially retained. A key aspect of supremacy, the operation of the direct effect of directives, is curtailed. *Francovich* damages are removed, and the general principles are no longer available as the basis for a claim or for disapplying conflicting legislation. This points to an important aspect of EUWA 2018, which is that it is aimed at preserving the interpretation of retained EU law as it was before, but largely removes its 'teeth' by dispensing with some of the main methods of enforcing it.

'does not apply to any enactment or rule of law passed or made on or after IP completion day'

The effect of this provision is that supremacy does not apply to new domestic law. The doctrine of implied repeal is no longer subject to the supremacy of EU law.

Example

This is a fictional example.

After IPCD, the government brings forward new domestic legislation to change the requirements relating to the transportation of live animals. This is an area in which there are a number of EU regulations and decisions. This legislation has been retained as direct EU legislation under EUWA 2018, s.3. The new domestic legislation repeals a significant proportion of the direct EU legislation.

A few months after IPCD there is a conflict between some provisions of direct EU legislation which has not been repealed and new domestic legislation on the conditions in which live animals can be transported.

The supremacy of EU law has no bearing on the new domestic legislation. The normal rules of implied repeal apply. The conflicting provisions in retained direct EU legislation are impliedly repealed by the new domestic legislation. The relevant standards on the conditions in which live animals can be transported are therefore those set out in the new domestic legislation.

'enactment'

'Enactment' is defined in EUWA 2018, s.20(1) and includes enactments contained in a wide variety of legislation including Orders in Council, rules, regulations, schemes, warrants, byelaws or other instruments made under an Act as well as the legislation of the devolved administrations, including Acts of the Scottish Parliament (these are excluded from the definition of 'enactment' under the Interpretation Act 1978, Sched.1).

The definition of 'enactment' in EUWA 2018, s.20(1) also includes retained direct EU legislation (except in ss.1B or 7 or if there is a contrary intention).

The term 'enactment' has been interpreted to mean 'any provision, long or short, which achieves a distinct objective' (see *John Lyon's Charity* v. *London Sephardi Trust* [2017] EWCA Civ 846, [2017] PLSCS 140, 167 NLJ 7755 at [39]). The courts have clarified that the word enactment does not mean the same thing as 'Act' and that 'Act' means the whole Act, whereas a section or part of a section in an Act may be an enactment (see, for example, *Wakefield and District Light Railways Co* v. *Wakefield Corporation* [1907] 2 KB 256).

'rule of law'

It is clear from a ministerial statement[6] that 'rule of law' is intended to mean rule of common law. The Act therefore states that new rules of common law are no longer subject to the supremacy of EU law.

The House of Lords Constitution Committee criticised this drafting. It stated that it mischaracterised the common law which 'emerges and evolves'. This is in contrast with legislation, which takes effect at a particular time.[7] The difficulty for the legislative draftsman is clear, however. The scheme of EUWA 2018 works on the basis of what happens before, on or after IPCD. That does not sit well with the idea of concepts which emerge and evolve. Further, given that common law rules could be set aside in the event of a conflict with EU law, there is a potential need to refer back to this pre-IPCD hierarchy.

'Accordingly, the principle of the supremacy of EU law continues to apply on or after IP completion day so far as relevant to the interpretation, disapplication or quashing of any enactment or rule of law passed or made before IP completion day.'

The proposition in this provision is that the hierarchy created by the principle of the supremacy of EU law remains.

Section 5(2) preserves the following methods of resolving a conflict:

- consistent interpretation;
- disapplication (pre-IPCD primary legislation or common law); or
- quashing (pre-IPCD secondary legislation)

on the basis of the supremacy of EU law.

Example

This is a fictional example.

A regulation saved through EUWA 2018, s.3 as direct EU legislation sets out that ladders for domestic use should be no more than six metres tall. The UK's Domestic Ladders Act 2012 states that ladders for domestic use can be up to 10 metres tall.

6 See the statement of the Minister of State, Ministry of Justice that 'any rule of law ... is a reference in the Bill to common law rules' (HC Deb 21 November 2017, vol.631, col.896).

7 The Committee stated: 'This raises questions about the extent to which judges who articulate new common law rules or principles are in fact making new law or are declaring the common law as it has always been (whether or not it was previously so appreciated or articulated) and whether or not the supremacy principle would apply in such instances.' The Committee stated that it was 'difficult to say, in respect to any given rule or principle of common law, that it was made on a given date. As a result, the application of clause 5(2) to the common law is likely to be far from straightforward.' Select Committee on the Constitution, *European Union (Withdrawal) Bill* (HL 2017–19, 69).

Post-IPCD this matter is litigated. The judge finds that the maximum height of ladders for domestic use in the UK is six metres. The effect of s.5(2) is that the relevant provision of the Domestic Ladders Act 2012 should be disapplied in favour of the six metre limit for the height of ladders set out in the regulation.

It is important to note that the operation of the principle of the supremacy of EU law is subject to a number of exceptions. Table 14.1 gives an overview of the aspects of the supremacy of EU law which are retained and those which are lost.

'so far as relevant to the interpretation, [etc.]'

These words are an important limitation on the application of the principle of supremacy. Most significantly, they ensure that pre-IPCD legislation associated with the process of exiting the EU such as the Taxation (Cross-Border Trade) Act 2018 is not subject to the principle of the supremacy of EU law. The supremacy of EU law is not relevant to these Acts of Parliament because they are intended to create new, post-EU membership domestic frameworks.

Table 14.1 Overview: The aspects of supremacy which remain after IPCD and the aspects which are lost (note that this is subject to transitional provisions – see **18.3** and **Appendix C**)

Provision	Aspects of supremacy which survive	Aspects of supremacy which are lost
Treaty articles	Can still have direct effect Retained EU law must still be interpreted in accordance with the relevant legal basis in the EU Treaties[8]	The direct effect of certain treaty articles can be 'switched off' using the power in EUWA 2018, s.8
EU-derived domestic legislation	Must still be interpreted in accordance with the duty of consistent interpretation[9] Directly effective rights in directives which have not been implemented or which have been implemented incorrectly are still available if they are of a kind recognised by the CJEU or a UK court in a case decided before IPCD	New domestic legislation will have precedence over EU-derived domestic legislation in the event of a conflict in accordance with the doctrine of implied repeal

[8] This is achieved through the words 'as it has effect' in EUWA 2018, ss.2(1) and 3(2)(a). These words signpost that the interpretation of the relevant instruments should be as before. See also the Explanatory Notes at para.63 which cite *BECTU*, paras.36–38.

[9] Note that the fact that directives are not incorporated by EUWA 2018 does not mean that the duty

Provision	Aspects of supremacy which survive	Aspects of supremacy which are lost
Direct EU legislation	Direct EU legislation can still have precedence over conflicting pre-IPCD domestic legislation or rules of common law	New domestic legislation will have precedence over direct EU legislation. This would not have been the case before IPCD. Prior to IPCD, a conflict between direct EU legislation and domestic legislation would have resulted in the domestic legislation being disapplied
General principles	The general principles remain as an aid to interpretation. Retained EU law must be interpreted so as to give effect to the general principles	Can no longer be relied upon in order to disapply or quash any enactment or other rule of law which conflicts with the general principles. The actions of domestic authorities can no longer be quashed or otherwise declared unlawful on the basis that they conflict with the general principles
Francovich damages	N/A	*Francovich* damages do not survive after the end of the transition period

14.3.2 The relevance of supremacy

The House of Lords Select Committee on the Constitution in its report on the European Union (Withdrawal) Bill took the view that the effect of the supremacy of EU law could have been better expressed by stating that in a conflict between pre-exit domestic legislation and direct EU legislation (s.3) or the rights, etc. saved under s.4, the law saved under ss.3 and 4 should have the status of primary legislation deemed to be enacted on exit day. It would therefore take precedence over pre-exit domestic legislation.[10] The drawback of this approach is that it would have changed the character of retained EU law. The supremacy of EU law is a central principle. Removing it from retained EU law would have had potentially far-reaching consequences including calling into question the continued application of aspects of retained EU law which are manifestations of the supremacy of EU law such as direct effect, the duty of consistent interpretation (also known as indirect effect or *Marleasing*) and the continuing application of retained case law. This could have undermined the certainty which EUWA 2018 is intended to create.

---

of consistent interpretation does not apply. This is discussed in further detail at **11.4**. See also **4.5.1**.

[10] See Select Committee on the Constitution, *European Union (Withdrawal) Bill* (HL 2017–19, 69), p.29.

14.3.3 EUWA 2018, s.5(3): Effect of modifications

EUWA 2018, s.5(3) enables the principle of the supremacy of EU law to continue to apply even where changes are made to retained EU law. This provision mirrors similar drafting in s.6(6), which allows the relevant instruments to continue to be interpreted in accordance with the retained general principles of EU law and retained case law even when they have been amended, if that is the intention of the amendments.

This provision is necessary to displace the normal assumption that new domestic legislation will repeal retained EU law. The logic behinds its inclusion is that making changes to retained EU law should not change its meaning, if the intention of the drafter was to keep the meaning of the legislation as it was prior to IPCD. For example, if domestic regulations which implement a directive are normally interpreted consistently with the directive under the principle of consistent interpretation (which is an aspect of supremacy) then that interpretation should not change simply because some aspect of the provisions has been amended so that they work properly after IPCD if that was not the intention. Ascertaining the 'intention of a modification' is not a straightforward task and will depend on the context.

14.4 CHARTER OF FUNDAMENTAL RIGHTS

EUWA 2018, s.5(4) and (5) provide:

> (4) The Charter of Fundamental Rights is not part of domestic law on or after IP completion day.
>
> (5) Subsection (4) does not affect the retention in domestic law on or after IP completion day in accordance with this Act of any fundamental rights or principles which exist irrespective of the Charter (and references to the Charter in any case law are, so far as necessary for this purpose, to be read as if they were references to any corresponding retained fundamental rights or principles).

14.4.1 Overview

EUWA 2018, s.5(4) makes it clear that the Charter of Fundamental Rights is not retained in domestic law on or after IPCD.

Section 5(5) has the following effect:

- it clarifies that s.5(4) should not be interpreted as excluding fundamental rights or principles as codified in the Charter from the savings provisions;
- references in case law to the Charter are to be read as if they were references to the underlying fundamental rights or principles codified in the Charter.

Section 5(4) and (5) also needs to be read in light of Sched.1, para.3. The effect of this provision is that fundamental rights which are general principles can only be used as an aid to interpretation, not as the basis for a claim.

14.4.2 Why was the Charter not retained?

The government's position at the time that the European Union (Withdrawal) Bill was introduced was that the Charter only made pre-existing rights more visible. It did not create new rights, and therefore not retaining the Charter made no material difference. The Charter was merely packaging and labelling; the content had an existence independent of the Charter.

Even if the Charter did nothing more than codify rights which already existed in the EU's legal system, subs.(4) itself hints at the difficulty which the removal of the Charter causes. References to the Charter run through the case law which is being retained. That case law will have to be reinterpreted to refer to the underlying rights which will have to be uncovered (having been made less visible again by the removal of the Charter). The task of rediscovering the underlying fundamental rights may involve looking at the case law in a different way. It will also require an analysis of the source of the rights.

The difficulty caused in removing the Charter was debated during the passage of the Bill through the House of Commons.[11] The justification for not retaining the Charter was advanced as follows:

- The Charter applies to the EU institutions. It also applies to the Member States when they are acting 'within the scope of EU law' – in other words when conducting activities regulated by EU law.[12]
- Given that the UK was leaving the EU the government's position was that retaining the Charter in domestic law would be 'curious if not perverse'.[13]

This reasoning is problematic within the scheme of EUWA 2018. Elsewhere in the Act, whether a matter fell within the scope of EU law before IPCD is relevant to the interpretation of retained EU law (see EUWA 2018, s.6(3) as discussed in **Chapter 15**). The scope of EU law, as well as the concept of acting within its scope, are therefore important to achieving continuity in the meaning of retained EU law, thus providing legal certainty. It is also important in terms of ensuring that EU principles of interpretation and retained case law do not 'bleed' into the rest of the statute book but remain confined to informing the interpretation of retained EU law.

14.4.3 Effects of the removal of the Charter

The Joint Committee on Human Rights analysed the effects of the removal of the Charter when the European Union (Withdrawal) Bill was going through Parliament. In summary, the Committee concluded that:

- Some of the rights would be lost because they stem from EU membership (Arts.39–45).
- Charter rights based on the general principles will no longer be enforceable.

---

[11] See HC Deb 21 November 2017, vol.631, col.835.

[12] This includes acting within the scope of exemptions from EU law: see further **6.2**.

[13] HC Deb 21 November 2017, vol.631, col.862.

- Rights which are enforceable through HRA 1998 will still be available as the basis for a challenge but the remedies under HRA 1998 are weaker than those under the Charter and the rules of standing are more difficult to satisfy.
- Some of the Charter rights will be protected through equivalent measures in domestic law but they may be less comprehensive than the protections offered by the Charter.
- Some of the rights may be preserved through directly effective provisions of the EU treaties, but it is not always clear whether a particular treaty article has direct effect.
- Some of the Charter rights are based on provisions of international treaties which have not been incorporated in domestic law.[14]

Appendix D sets out an overview of each of the Charter rights and the effect of the removal of the Charter from domestic law on IPCD.

It is important to note the retained general principles will no longer be enforceable after IPCD. However, they may apply to the interpretation of retained EU law.

14.5 STATUS OF RETAINED EU LAW FOR THE PURPOSES OF THE HUMAN RIGHTS ACT 1998

As set out in **Chapter 16**, retained direct principal EU legislation (for example a regulation retained under EUWA 2018, s.3 such as the General Data Protection Regulation)[15] is to be treated as primary legislation for the purposes of HRA 1998 (see EUWA 2018, Sched.8, para.30(2)). This means that direct principal EU legislation cannot be disapplied or quashed if it is incompatible with the ECHR – it can only be subject to a declaration of incompatibility.

Retained direct minor EU legislation (for example a regulation which is tertiary legislation such as the Commission Delegated Regulation with regard to liquidity coverage requirement for Credit Institutions)[16] is to be treated as 'subordinate legislation' for the purposes of HRA 1998 (see EUWA 2018, Sched.8, para.30(3)), except where it amends primary legislation (where it will be treated as 'primary legislation'). Where such legislation is found to breach HRA 1998 a court may strike it down.

There is a question about the relationship between claims brought on the basis of a breach of HRA 1998 and the prohibition on challenges to the validity of retained EU law in Sched.1, para.1. If a challenge on the basis of HRA 1998 could be characterised as a challenge to the validity of retained EU law then it might be

---

[14] See Joint Committee on Human Rights, *Legislative Scrutiny: The EU (Withdrawal) Bill: A Right by Right Analysis* (HL HC 2017–19, HL Paper 70, HC 774).

[15] Regulation (EU) 2016/679 of 27 April 2016 on the protection of natural persons with regard to the processing of personal data and on the free movement of such data, and repealing Directive 95/46/EC (General Data Protection Regulation) [2016] OJ L119/1.

[16] See Commission Delegated Regulation (EU) 2015/61 of 10 October 2014 to supplement Regulation (EU) 575/2013 with regard to liquidity coverage requirement for Credit Institutions [2014] OJ L11/1.

argued that Sched.1, para.1 operates to prohibit such a challenge. However, it is clear from the parliamentary debates in the House of Commons (see **14.6.3**) and the wording of para.1 that the reference to challenges in that paragraph is intended to refer to challenges to retained EU law which raise questions as to the validity of an EU instrument on the grounds set out in the TFEU, Art.263.[17] Therefore, it is clear that challenges under HRA 1998 are not precluded by Sched.1, para.1.

14.6 EUWA 2018, SCHEDULE 1

14.6.1 Overview

EUWA 2018, Sched.1 is linked to s.5. It contains other important exceptions to the saving and incorporation of retained EU law. The function of Sched.1 is, broadly speaking, to remove certain types of challenges or remedies which were available under EU law. They include challenges to the validity of EU law, challenges based on the general principles of EU law and claims for *Francovich* damages.

It would be wrong to think that the effect of Sched.1 is somehow less significant because the provisions are contained in a schedule and not in the main provisions of the Act. The removal of the general principles of EU law as a ground for challenge is one of the most significant changes which EUWA 2018 creates.

In order to understand fully the impact of the changes in Sched.1, the earlier chapters of this work will assist. The manner in which challenges to the validity of EU law could be brought prior to IPCD, the role of the general principles and *Francovich* damages when the UK was a Member State will inform an understanding of Sched.1. As with many other provisions of EUWA 2018, Sched.1 operates on a complex foundation and references the relevant matters sparingly. It assumes that the reader of the statute has prior knowledge of these issues. Further, the concepts it deals with are not settled as a matter of EU law. Although the domestic courts are not permitted to 'discover' new general principles of EU law after IPCD (see Sched.1, para.2) there is no definitive list of general principles of EU law.

14.6.2 Challenges to the validity of retained EU law

Schedule 1, para.1 provides:

> 1(1) There is no right in domestic law on or after IP completion day to challenge any retained EU law on the basis that, immediately before IP completion day, an EU instrument was invalid.
>
> (2) Sub-paragraph (1) does not apply so far as –
>
> (a) the European Court has decided before IP completion day that the instrument is invalid, or

[17] Prior to the end of the transition period, a domestic case which raised a question of the validity of EU law would have had to have been referred to the CJEU by the UK court under the TFEU, Art.267 because only the CJEU can decide questions of validity of EU law.

(b) the challenge is of a kind described, or provided for, in regulations made by a Minister of the Crown.

(3) Regulations under sub-paragraph (2)(b) may (among other things) provide for a challenge which would otherwise have been against an EU institution to be against a public authority in the United Kingdom.

14.6.3 Detailed commentary

Schedule 1, para.1(1) states that retained EU law cannot be challenged on or after IPCD on the basis that an original EU instrument is invalid. The bases on which the CJEU can declare an EU instrument invalid are set out in Table 3.1. In summary they are as follows:

- Lack of competence (i.e. the EU does not have power to act in the relevant area). This is similar to the UK doctrine of *ultra vires*.
- Infringement of an essential procedural requirement.
- Infringement of the EU treaties or any rule of law relating to their application.
- Misuse of powers.

Only the CJEU is able to declare EU law invalid in the EU legal order. The rationale for Sched.1, para.1(1) is that it would be out of line with the theme of continuity for domestic courts to make rulings about such matters. These sorts of issues have never been for domestic courts to decide,[18] so it is consistent with the theme of continuity for these issues to remain outside the remit of the domestic courts.

The position in Sched.1, para.1(1) can be modified through regulations made under para.1(2)(b). Paragraph 1(2)(b) enables ministers to prescribe challenges to the validity of retained EU law of a kind described or provided for in regulations. This power has been exercised under the Challenges to Validity of EU Instruments (EU Exit) Regulations 2019 (SI 2019/673) (the 'Challenges to Validity Regulations'). These regulations make transitional provision in relation to cases brought in UK courts before IPCD which raised a question as to the validity of an EU law. While the UK was an EU Member State and during the transition period, a question of the validity of EU law which came up in a domestic case would have to have been referred by the domestic court to the CJEU. The Explanatory Memorandum to the Challenges to Validity Regulations says that the purpose of the regulations is to deal with an outcome where the UK leaves the EU without a withdrawal agreement, in which case, without the regulations, UK courts would be left:

[18] See the Solicitor General's comments in the House of Commons Debate on the European Union (Withdrawal) Bill (HC Deb 21 November 2017, vol.631, col.862). In response to an amendment seeking to delete sub-paragraph 1 he stated: 'How would our domestic courts approach the task of assessing challenges to the validity of converted law? That is a job that they have never had before. Who would defend those challenges? What remedies would be available to the courts? How could converted law that was found to be invalid be replaced?' (HC Deb 21 November 2017, vol.631, col.971).

> in a scenario where they might be unable to proceed with a ruling in a domestic case in the absence of a ruling on the validity of an EU instrument; the judgment of the CJEU would not be binding or applicable in the UK and no court in the UK would have the necessary jurisdiction in place of the CJEU to be able to provide a ruling on validity.

To ensure that this category of cases was not left in limbo, the Challenges to Validity Regulations provide for the UK court to take a decision on the validity of the EU instrument in question, something it would not have been able to do when the UK was a Member State. The regulations cover cases brought before IPCD where a reference on the question of validity has already been made to the CJEU as well as cases brought before IPCD which raised a question of validity of an EU instrument but where a reference had not yet been made to the CJEU.

The Challenges to Validity Regulations now need to be read in light of the Withdrawal Agreement. The Withdrawal Agreement confers jurisdiction on the CJEU to hear references from UK courts which are pending before IPCD.[19] Where the challenge is pending before the CJEU, the Challenges to Validity Regulations will not be relevant[20] and the case will proceed to judgment by the CJEU. The domestic courts will therefore only have jurisdiction to deal with a validity challenge where the action has been brought before IPCD but the preliminary reference has not yet been made.

Other than where the transitional provisions created by the Challenges to Validity Regulations apply, the general position after IPCD will be that a validity challenge to an EU instrument will not be permitted. Where an EU instrument could have been challenged on the basis that it infringed fundamental rights, for example a challenge similar to those in the *Schrems I and II* cases,[21] this challenge is no longer possible and alternative means of challenge will need to be found. As the Explanatory Memorandum to the Challenges to Validity Regulations says (at 2.8):

> … if after exit[22] the CJEU declares an EU law to be invalid and disapplies it across the EU27, the retained domestic version of that EU law would remain on the UK statute book.

'Sub-paragraph (1) does not apply so far as –

(a) the [CJEU] has decided before IP completion day that the instrument is invalid'

This provision ensures that the past CJEU case law on invalidity is preserved in UK law. It reflects the policy of continuity. It means that instruments which were

---

[19] See the Withdrawal Agreement, Art.86. A case is pending before the CJEU where the document initiating the proceedings has been registered by the registry of the Court of Justice or the General Court.

[20] This is because the Withdrawal Agreement has precedence over domestic law (see the Withdrawal Agreement, Art.4 and EUWA 2018, s.7A).

[21] See Case C–362/14 *Maximillian Schrems* v. *Data Protection Commissioner*, EU:C:2015:650 and Case C–311/18 *Data Protection Commissioner* v. *Facebook Ireland and Maximillian Schrems*, EU:C:2019:1145. In these cases two successive EU decisions which allowed the transfer of personal data to the US were declared invalid by the CJEU on the basis that they breached the fundamental right to data protection and the right to a judicial remedy (the Charter, Arts.7, 8 and 47).

[22] This should be read as a reference to IPCD.

declared by the CJEU to be invalid remain invalid and are not revived after IPCD. For example, the decisions which allowed transfers of personal data to the United States which were invalidated under the *Schrems I and II* cases remain invalid after IPCD.

'(b) the challenge is of a kind described, or provided for, in regulations made by a Minister of the Crown.'

The Challenges to Validity Regulations have been made under this power.

This power can be used more extensively: para.1(3) enables a minister to provide that the relevant challenge can be brought against a domestic public authority. At the time of writing, no such provision has been made.

14.7 GENERAL PRINCIPLES OF EU LAW

Schedule 1, paras.2 and 3 provide:

> 2 No general principle of EU law is part of domestic law on or after IP completion day if it was not recognised as a general principle of EU law by the European Court in a case decided before IP completion day (whether or not as an essential part of the decision in the case).
>
> 3(1) There is no right of action in domestic law on or after IP completion day based on a failure to comply with any of the general principles of EU law.
>
> (2) No court or tribunal or other public authority may, on or after IP completion day –
>
> (a) disapply or quash any enactment or other rule of law, or
> (b) quash any conduct or otherwise decide that it is unlawful,
>
> because it is incompatible with any of the general principles of EU law.

14.7.1 Overview

The removal of general principles of EU law as the basis for a claim in Sched.1, para.3(1) is significant. The use of the general principles of EU law to disapply conflicting provisions of national law is an important aspect of the functioning of EU law. While HRA 1998 may provide an alternative route of challenge after IPCD, the rules on standing for HRA 1998 cases are narrower than under EU law. Under EU law, national provisions which conflict with general principles can be disapplied even if they are in an Act of Parliament. Under HRA 1998, the court is not able to disapply Acts of Parliament. Where provisions of an Act of Parliament are found to be in breach of HRA 1998, the courts are able to make a declaration of incompatibility, but the relevant provisions cannot be disapplied.

Schedule 1, para.2 is less significant. It precludes the domestic courts from 'discovering' new general principles of EU law after IPCD. However, although the list of general principles is not definitive or fully agreed it is relatively rare for the CJEU to discover new general principles of EU law.

14.7.2 Development of general principles

Paragraph 2 is intended to stop the development of retained EU law in the context of the general principles. This is consistent with the 'continuity' theme in EUWA 2018, the purpose of which is to ensure legal certainty after IPCD. However, the overarching goal is that over time retained EU law should be repealed and replaced.[23]

It is relatively unlikely that new general principles would be discovered by the domestic courts in any event.

The drafting here is arguably somewhat strained. As discussed above, the scheme of timing in EUWA 2018, which differentiates between 'before' and 'on or after' IPCD does not necessarily sit well with legal concepts which evolve and are 'discovered'.[24] The general principles evolve rather than apply from a particular point in time. However, this is a signpost to the courts that retained EU law is not intended to be developed as a parallel form of EU law. Instead its function is to hold the position while new mechanisms can be found to regulate activity in the UK.

14.7.3 Claims based on the general principles

'general principles of EU law'

This term is not defined in the legislation. This is the same approach as has been taken in relation to the 'principle of supremacy of EU law'. The general principles are complex. There is no agreed list of general principles (for a fuller discussion see **Chapter 6**). EUWA 2018 is not intended to solve these complexities. It merely points in as succinct a way as possible to the role that the general principles of EU law should play in domestic law after IPCD.

In terms of the role that the general principles play in EU law, they are as follows:

- As an aid to interpretation: EU law and domestic law which implements EU obligations must be interpreted so as not to conflict with the general principles of EU law.
- As the basis for a challenge to action by the EU institutions, whether legislative or administrative, as well as a challenge to inaction on the part of the EU institutions.
- As the means of challenging legislative or administrative action by a Member State where the action is performed in the context of a right or an obligation

[23] See the Explanatory Notes at para.10: 'The principal purpose of the Act is to provide a functioning statute book on the day the UK leaves the EU. As a general rule, the same rules and laws will apply on the day after exit as on the day before. It will then be for Parliament and, where appropriate, the devolved legislatures to make any future changes.'

[24] Of course, the general principles only apply at the point at which the EU has legislated in a particular area, but that does not mean that a general principle in question only came into existence at the point at which it was recognised by the CJEU.

arising from EU law. In other words, where the Member State is acting within the scope of Union law.

Paragraph 3(1) makes it clear that challenges based on a failure to comply with the general principles of EU law are no longer permitted after the transition period comes to an end (although it is important to note that this is subject to transitional provisions as discussed at **18.3** and **Appendix C**). This means that had the circumstances in the *Walker* case (see **6.2**) arisen after IPCD, the effect of para.3(1) is that this sort of challenge would no longer be capable of being brought.

That is not to say that the legislation reverts to its pre-challenge form. The effect of the *Walker* case is not undone after IPCD. Someone in Mr Walker's position would be able to bring a challenge after IPCD on the basis that the law is as established in *Walker*. In other words, the court would not need to disapply the offending provisions of the Equality Act 2010 a second time. In a similar situation, the court would simply apply the law as established in *Walker*, relying on the words 'as it has effect in domestic law' in EUWA 2018, s.2(1). The words 'in accordance with any retained case law' in s.6(3)(a) would also be relevant as well as the transitional provisions in Sched.8, para.39(6) (see **Appendix C**).

The effect of EUWA 2018, Sched.1, para.3(1) and (2) is to ensure that there is clarity about the role of the general principles in domestic law. There is no right to disapply or quash any enactment or other rule of law based on the fact that it is incompatible with any of the general principles of EU law. No conduct may be quashed or deemed unlawful because it is incompatible with any of the general principles of EU law.

Example

This is a fictional example.

After IPCD, a public body is responsible for distributing farming subsidies under an EU regulation saved under EUWA 2018, s.3.

A case is brought on the basis that the regime for applying time limits under the regulation should be interpreted in accordance with the general principle of proportionality and that farmers should therefore not lose a subsidy on the basis of an unavoidable delay in submitting the relevant paperwork.

Analysis: This case is permitted after IPCD because it is about using the principle of proportionality to interpret the scheme.

A challenge is brought under the same regulation after IPCD on the basis that the public body acted disproportionately by refusing the farmers their subsidies and that the decision to refuse subsidies should be quashed on the basis that it was incompatible with the general principle of proportionality.

Analysis: This type of challenge is not permissible after IPCD under Sched.1, para.3(1). Further, the court may not quash the decision or otherwise decide that it is unlawful on the basis that it breaches the principle of proportionality (see Sched.1, para.3(2)).

Comment: In some cases, the distinction between interpreting retained EU law in light of the general principles and challenging action on the basis of the general principles may be relatively nuanced. In other cases the difference may be more substantial, and the effect of para.3(1) and (2) will be to deprive a potential claimant of a cause of action or a remedy after IPCD which may have existed before IPCD.

14.8 *FRANCOVICH* DAMAGES

Schedule 1, para.4 provides:

> 4 There is no right in domestic law on or after IP completion day to damages in accordance with the rule in *Francovich.*

The rule in *Francovich* enables an individual to seek a remedy for a failure by a Member State to implement, or correctly apply, provisions of EU law. *Francovich* is discussed in more detail at **5.12**.

Paragraph 4 removes the right to seek damages in accordance with the rule in *Francovich.* The government's rationale for removing this right as set out during the passage of the Bill was that *Francovich* damages were not relevant once the UK had left the EU.[25] *Francovich* damages were linked to EU membership and its obligations. Once those obligations no longer applied then this cause of action should no longer be available.

The removal of *Francovich* damages should be read in light of the specific transitional and saving provisions in Sched.8 to the Act, as discussed at **Appendix C**.

14.9 INTERPRETATION

Schedule 1, para.5 provides:

> 5(1) References in section 5 and this Schedule to the principle of the supremacy of EU law, the Charter of Fundamental Rights, any general principle of EU law or the rule in *Francovich* are to be read as references to that principle, Charter or rule so far as it would otherwise continue to be, or form part of, domestic law on or after IP completion day by virtue of section 2, 3, 4 or 6(3) or (6) and otherwise in accordance with this Act.
>
> (2) Accordingly (among other things) the references to the principle of the supremacy of EU law in section 5(2) and (3) do not include anything which would bring into domestic law any modification of EU law which is adopted or notified, comes into force or only applies on or after IP completion day.

The Explanatory Notes to EUWA 2018 (at para.216) state:

[25] The Advocate General for Scotland stated that the rationale for removing the right was that: 'it is related to a breach of European Union law, and it would not be appropriate to continue … after we have left the European Union' (HL Deb 5 March 2018, vol.789, col.977).

> Paragraph 5 clarifies that references in section 6 and this Schedule to the principle of supremacy of EU law, the Charter of Fundamental Rights, any general principle of EU law or the rule in *Francovich* are to be read as references to that principle, Charter or rule as they stand at exit day, not as they will operate in EU law in the future.

The reference to 'exit day' in the Explanatory Notes should now be understood as referring to IPCD.

14.10 TRANSITIONAL PROVISIONS

An Act will often contain transitional provisions or confer power to make transitional provisions by delegated legislation. Transitional provisions set out detailed aspects of how the transition from the old law to the new is intended to work. Schedule 8, Part 4 contains important transitional provisions which relate to s.5 and Sched.1. Note that these provisions are subject to relevant separation agreement law, specific provision made by regulations under EUWA 2018, s.23(6) (power to make transitional, transitory or saving provision) and EU(WA)A 2020, s.41(5) (transitional, transitory or saving provision).

14.10.1 EUWA 2018, Sched.8, para.39(1)

Schedule 8, para.39(1) provides that the following are extinguished on or after IPCD (even where the relevant event giving rise to the cause of action occurred before IPCD):

- The right to challenge the validity of retained EU law on the basis that an EU instrument was invalid.
- The effect of the Charter of Fundamental rights in domestic law.
- Challenges[26] based on the general principles of EU law.
- *Francovich* damages.

The actual position is not as stark as this, as set out in **Appendix C**.

[26] Under EUWA 2018, s.6(3), the general principles apply as an aid to interpretation.

CHAPTER 15

Interpretation of retained EU law

Retained EU law		
EU-derived domestic legislation	Direct EU legislation	All other EU rights and obligations saved by EUWA 2018, s.4
interpreted in accordance with retained case law and retained general principles		

Figure 15.1 Interpretation of retained EU law

15.1 OVERVIEW

This chapter covers EUWA 2018, s.6. It explains how retained EU law is to be interpreted by UK courts[1] and the circumstances in which a decision of the CJEU[2] binds a UK court when it is interpreting retained EU law. It also looks at the status of CJEU decisions made on or after IPCD.

In general terms, pre-IPCD decisions of the CJEU bind UK courts when interpreting retained EU law whereas post-IPCD decisions of the CJEU do not. UK courts may, however, have regard to post-IPCD CJEU judgments where they are relevant.

The White Paper said (at para.2.14):

> ... for as long as [retained EU law] remains on the UK statute book, it is essential that there is a common understanding of what that law means. The Government believes that this is best achieved by providing for continuity in how that law is interpreted before and after exit day.

If retained EU law has not been modified on or after IPCD, it must be interpreted in accordance with relevant 'retained case law' (which includes relevant CJEU case law) and the 'retained general principles' (EUWA 2018, s.6(3)). The concepts of retained case law and retained general principles are discussed at **15.6** and **15.7**.

1 References to UK courts in this chapter include tribunals, unless otherwise indicated.

2 EUWA 2018 uses the term 'European Court' to refer to the CJEU.

The courts must also have regard, among other things, to the limits of EU competences as they stood immediately before IPCD (see **15.8**). This means that the principle of conferral (discussed at **8.2**) is relevant to the interpretation of retained EU law.

If retained EU law has been modified, it can be interpreted in accordance with retained case law and the retained general principles if that is the intention behind the modification. In the absence of an express indication as to what the intention is, it will be for the court to decide. The determination of the intention behind a modification will have a direct bearing on how the retained EU law in question is interpreted, which could in turn lead to the case having a different outcome.

The Supreme Court and the High Court of Justiciary may depart from CJEU case law. At the time of writing, draft regulations have been laid before Parliament which would allow the Court of Appeal of England and Wales and equivalent courts to do so too.

15.2 GENERAL RULE

EUWA 2018, s.6 deals with the interpretation of retained EU law by UK courts. In broad terms, it sets out the circumstances in which a decision of the CJEU binds a UK court when it is interpreting retained EU law. Section 6 is best understood by drawing a dividing line between CJEU decisions made before IPCD and CJEU decisions made on or after IPCD. The general rule (which is subject to qualifications) is that pre-IPCD decisions of the CJEU bind UK courts whereas post-IPCD decisions of the CJEU do not.

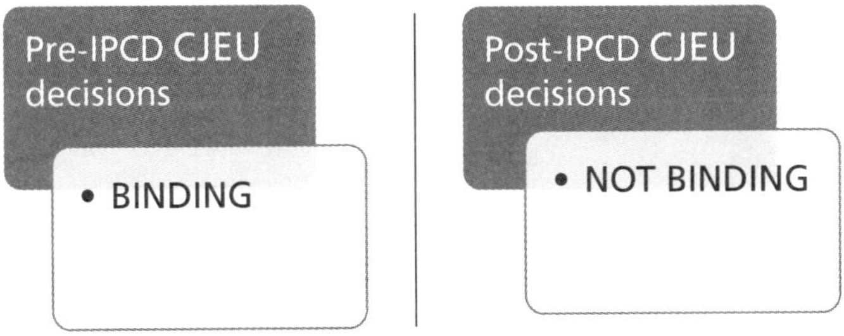

Figure 15.2 General rule as to when CJEU decisions bind UK courts

15.2.1 CJEU decisions made post-IPCD

Section 6(1) provides that a UK court is not bound by decisions made by the CJEU post-IPCD (nor is it bound by principles laid down by the CJEU post-IPCD). In addition, a UK court cannot refer a matter to the CJEU post-IPCD. These are not, however, blanket rules. Section 6(6A) says that s.6(1) is subject to relevant separation agreement law (explained in **Chapter 20**). EUWA 2018, s.7A and directly applicable or directly effective provisions of the Withdrawal Agreement are part of relevant separation agreement law. The Withdrawal Agreement provides that a UK court may make a reference to the CJEU in relation to the citizens' rights part of that Agreement for up to eight years from IPCD. Section 7A provides that any enactment is to be read and has effect subject to the rights, etc. in the Withdrawal Agreement. As a result, s.6(1) does not prevent a reference being made by the UK courts to the CJEU in relation to citizens' rights.

The Withdrawal Agreement also provides that the CJEU shall continue to have jurisdiction in any cases brought by or against the UK before the end of the transition period. CJEU judgments handed down in these cases after the end of the transition period bind the UK and UK courts (see the Withdrawal Agreement, Arts.86 and 89). Section 6(1) does not prevent this from happening.

Section 6(2) establishes the general rule that UK courts 'may' have regard to a decision of the CJEU made post-IPCD so far as it is 'relevant' to the matter in hand. When the European Union (Withdrawal) Bill was introduced, the text said that a UK court could have regard to a post-IPCD decision if it considered it *appropriate* to do so. However, senior members of the judiciary were concerned that this formulation did not provide sufficient guidance for judges. The House of Lords Select Committee on the Constitution also expressed concerns that this formulation might involve judges in political controversy.[3] The clause was amended accordingly.

In addition to CJEU decisions, s.6(2) says that courts may choose to have regard to 'anything done' by the CJEU post-IPCD. However, beyond decisions of that court and principles laid down by it, it is not obvious what other action of the CJEU might be of potential relevance. However, s.6(2) also provides that courts may have regard to anything done post-IPCD by another EU entity or the EU so far as it is relevant. This is broad enough to include, for example, explanatory memoranda or guidance relating to EU law published by the European Commission.

Section 6(2) is not strictly necessary in order to allow the courts to have regard to CJEU decisions post-IPCD. This was acknowledged when the Bill was going through Parliament. The Secretary of State for Exiting the European Union said of what became s.6(2):

> UK courts will ... be able to take those post-exit judgments into account when making their decisions, if they consider it appropriate to do so, as they can, of course, with judgments of courts from other jurisdictions – common law, around the Commonwealth and elsewhere.[4]

Under s.6(2), courts may consider post-IPCD CJEU case law in relation to any matter before them, not just matters of retained EU law, if they consider it relevant.

The general rule in s.6(2) is subject to the qualifications in s.6(3)–(6), explained below. It is also subject to relevant separation agreement law by virtue of s.6(6A).

---

3 See Select Committee on the Constitution, *European Union (Withdrawal) Bill* (HL 2017–19, 69), paras.132–42.

4 HC Deb 14 November 2017, vol.631, col.278. Note that 'appropriate' later became 'relevant'.

15.2.2 CJEU decisions made pre-IPCD

The general effect of EUWA 2018, s.6, so far as CJEU case law is concerned, is that a court must interpret retained EU law in accordance with principles laid down by, and decisions made by, the CJEU up to the end of the transition period.

More specifically, s.6(3) provides:

> Any question as to the validity, meaning or effect of any retained EU law is to be decided, so far as that law is unmodified on or after IP completion day and so far as they are relevant to it –
>
> (a) in accordance with any retained case law and any retained general principles of EU law, and
>
> (b) having regard (among other things) to the limits, immediately before IP completion day, of EU competences.

Section 6(3) requires some unpacking.

15.3 UNMODIFIED RETAINED EU LAW

For the purpose of interpreting retained EU law, there is a distinction between retained EU law which has been modified and retained EU law which has not. The term 'modified' is explained at **15.6.1**. Note that it is a question of whether the retained EU law has been modified by domestic law, not a question of whether the EU law from which the retained EU law is derived has been modified by the EU.

If the retained EU law has not been modified on or after IPCD, the court must decide a question of validity, etc. in accordance with relevant retained case law and retained general principles (EUWA 2018, s.6(3). The concepts of retained case law and retained general principles are discussed at **15.6** and **15.7**. It must also have regard, among other things, to the limits of EU competences as they stood immediately before IPCD (see **15.8**).

The Explanatory Notes say (at para.111):

> [Section 6(3)] provides that any question as to the meaning of unmodified retained EU law will be determined in UK courts in accordance with relevant pre-exit CJEU case law and general principles. This means, for example, taking a purposive approach to interpretation where the meaning of the measure is unclear (i.e. considering the purpose of the law from looking at other relevant materials such as the treaty legal base for a measure, its recitals and preambles, and the travaux preparatoires (working papers) leading to the adoption of the measure). It also means applying an interpretation that renders the provision of EU law compatible with the treaties and general principles of EU law. Non-binding instruments, such as recommendations and opinions, would still be available to a court to assist with interpretation of retained EU law after exit.

Interpreting retained EU law in accordance with relevant CJEU case law will therefore involve the UK courts adopting the CJEU's methods of interpretation (see **Chapter 3**).

15.4 MODIFIED RETAINED EU LAW

If the retained EU law under consideration has been modified on or after IPCD, s.6(6) says that a court is not prevented from interpreting it in accordance with relevant retained case law and retained general principles if this is consistent with the 'intention of the modifications'.

While unmodified retained EU law must be interpreted in accordance with retained case law and retained general principles, it does not follow that modified retained EU law must not be interpreted in this way. Section 6(6) permits a UK court to interpret modified retained EU law in a way which is consistent with the intention of the modification.

Ascertaining the intention behind a modification is not a straightforward task. Context will be important but may not provide a clear answer. Given the volume of regulations made under the s.8 deficiencies-correcting power (see **Chapter 17**), it is likely that practitioners will frequently encounter the question of what the 'intention of the modifications' actually is.

However, it is not just modifications made under the s.8 power which are relevant. It would be in the interests of legal certainty for legislation making modifications to make the intention of those modifications clear for the purposes of s.6. In the absence of an indication as to what the intention is, it will be for the court to decide. A court is likely to look at the context. The determination of the intention behind a modification will have a direct bearing on how the retained EU law in question is interpreted, which could in turn lead to the case having a different outcome.

15.5 SCOPE

We turn to the kind of questions that are within the scope of s.6(3) – 'any question as to the validity, meaning or effect of any retained EU law' (note that this wording tracks ECA 1972, s.3(1)). It is worth pausing on 'validity' to clarify the interaction with EUWA 2018, Sched.1, para.1(1). Under EUWA 2018, Sched.1, para.1(1) there is no right in domestic law on or after IPCD to challenge retained EU law (which is domestic law) on the basis that an EU instrument (i.e. EU law) was invalid. This is subject to exceptions (see further **14.6**). Sched.1, para.1(1) rules out a validity challenge on a particular ground as opposed to ruling out validity challenges generally.

Sched.1, para.1(1) is a 'continuity' provision. Under EU law, Member State courts cannot find an EU instrument to be invalid. Only the CJEU can do that. Member State courts can, however, make a reference to the CJEU on the question of validity. Paragraph 1(1) in effect takes this rule and adapts it for the domestic post-IPCD environment. In essence, a domestic court cannot find an EU instrument to be invalid post-IPCD because it could not do so pre-IPCD.

However, para.1(1) leaves open the possibility of challenging the validity of retained EU law other than on the basis that an EU instrument is invalid. So, for example, it would be possible to challenge the validity of EU-derived domestic legislation on the basis that it was *ultra vires* ECA 1972, s.2(2). It is also possible for a minister to make regulations which permit a challenge on the grounds of invalidity in specified circumstances (Sched.1, para.1(2)). Hence, validity challenges are possible in some cases.

Section 6(3) applies whether the facts of the case under consideration have arisen pre- or post-IPCD.

15.6 RETAINED CASE LAW

Next, we consider the concepts of 'retained case law' and 'retained general principles' which are introduced in s.6(3) and defined in s.6(7). The general rule is that a domestic court has to interpret (unmodified) retained EU law in accordance with retained case law and retained general principles.

Retained case law is made up of retained *EU* case law and retained *domestic* case law.

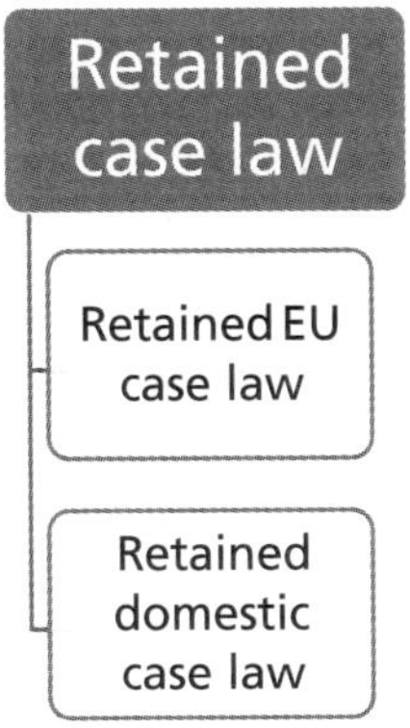

Figure 15.3 Components of retained case law

15.6.1 Retained EU case law

Retained EU case law is defined in s.6(7) as:

'any principles laid down by, and any decisions of, the European Court'

EUWA 2018 does not define what is meant by 'principles' in this context. Given that there is a separate requirement on the courts to interpret retained EU case law in accordance with 'retained general principles', it is reasonable to assume that 'principles' means something other than retained general principles, although the two terms may overlap. It is also possible that the terms 'principles' and 'decisions' overlap. For example, the case of *Marleasing* can conceivably be viewed as laying down principles as well as being a decision. The phrase 'any principles laid down by, and any decisions of' the CJEU is taken from ECA 1972, s.3(1) which indicates an intention to achieve continuity.

'as they have effect in EU law immediately before IP completion day … (as those principles and decisions are modified by or under this Act or by other domestic law from time to time)'

The case law which is relevant for these purposes is CJEU case law as it stood immediately before IPCD but taking into account any subsequent modification by *domestic* law. At first sight, the concept of modifications to case law may seem an odd one. However, the term 'modify' is given a broad meaning under EUWA 2018. It is defined in s.20(1) as follows:

> 'modify' includes amend, repeal or revoke (and related expressions are to be read accordingly)

This is broad enough to include non-textual modifications such as where the Supreme Court departs from retained EU case law (see further **15.9**).

'so far as they … relate to anything to which section 2, 3 or 4 applies'

Retained EU case law applies so far as it relates to EU-derived domestic legislation, retained direct EU legislation and anything which is retained EU law by virtue of s.4.

'and are not excluded by section 5 or Schedule 1'

These exclusions are discussed in **Chapter 14**.

For an illustration of when a question would be decided in accordance with retained EU case law, see the case study at **15.9.2**.

15.6.2 Retained domestic case law

The structure of the definition of 'retained domestic case law' follows the structure for 'retained EU case law' as set out in **15.6.1**, with a reference to 'a court or tribunal in the United Kingdom' in place of a reference to the 'European Court', the term used in EUWA 2018 to refer to the CJEU.

An example of retained domestic case law is *Walker* (see **6.2**).

15.7 RETAINED GENERAL PRINCIPLES OF EU LAW

The structure of the definition of 'retained general principles of EU law' follows the structure for 'retained EU case law' as set out in **15.6.1**, but with a reference to 'the general principles of EU law' in place of a reference to the 'European Court'.

General principles are discussed in detail in **Chapter 6**. It is not made explicit in EUWA 2018 how the general principles continue in domestic law as retained general principles. They may be incorporated into domestic law under EUWA 2018, ss.2, 3 or 4 (see **13.5.4**).

15.8 'LIMITS OF EU COMPETENCES'

As well as interpreting retained EU law in accordance with retained case law and retained general principles of EU law, a court also has to have regard, among other things, to the limits, immediately before IPCD, of EU competences. The Explanatory Notes give national security as an example of a matter which is outside EU competence, as set out in the TEU, Art.4(2).

The concept of the 'limits of EU competences' may be used as an aid to interpretation so that if more than one interpretation of retained EU law is possible, the court should prefer the one which delivers a result that is within EU competence.

The words 'the limits of EU competences' come from the TEU, Art.5 which sets out the principle of conferral (see **8.2**). The purpose of this provision in EUWA 2018 is to ensure that retained EU law is not interpreted in a way that would go beyond the limits of EU competences as they stood immediately before IPCD. However, at that point (as explained at **8.2**), the CJEU's view as to which court ultimately decided the limits of EU competences in the event of a disagreement and the Supreme Court's view diverged. Section 6 does not say expressly how a UK court is to ascertain the limits of EU competences as they stood immediately before IPCD. It remains to be seen how a UK court will apply this provision.

Section 6(3)(b) says that a UK court is to have regard to the limits of EU competence 'among other things'. This leaves room for a court to take into account other (unspecified) matters in interpreting retained EU law.

15.9 CIRCUMSTANCES IN WHICH COURTS ARE NOT BOUND BY RETAINED EU CASE LAW

Section 6(4) introduces a qualification to the general rule that pre-CJEU case law binds UK courts in interpreting retained EU law.

Under s.6(4), the following courts are not bound by retained EU case law:

- the Supreme Court;

- the High Court of Justiciary;[5]
- a relevant court (see **15.9.2**).

There is also special provision in the field of competition law (see the Competition Act 1998, s.60A).

Section 6(4)(c) states that no court is bound by any retained *domestic* case law that it would not otherwise be bound by. This makes clear that the normal doctrine of precedent which determines whether a domestic court is bound by the judgment of another domestic court applies unchanged. For example, the Court of Appeal would not be bound by a judgment of the High Court.

15.9.1 Supreme Court and High Court of Justiciary

In deciding whether to depart from retained EU case law, the Supreme Court and the High Court of Justiciary are to apply the same test that they would apply when deciding whether to depart from their own case law (s.6(5)).

The circumstances in which the Supreme Court may depart from its own case law are set out in a House of Lords Practice Direction (Practice Direction – Judicial Precedent [1966] 3 All ER 77 (HL)) which reads as follows:

> Their Lordships regard the use of precedent as an indispensable foundation upon which to decide what is the law and its application to individual cases. It provides at least some degree of certainty upon which individuals can rely in the conduct of their affairs, as well as a basis for orderly development of legal rules.
>
> Their Lordships nevertheless recognise that too rigid adherence to precedent may lead to injustice in a particular case and also unduly restrict the proper development of the law. They propose, therefore, to modify their present practice and, while treating former decisions of this House as normally binding, to depart from a previous decision when it appears right to do so.
>
> In this connection they will bear in mind the danger of disturbing retrospectively the basis on which contracts, settlements of property and fiscal arrangements have been entered into and also the especial need for certainty as to the criminal law.
>
> This announcement is not intended to affect the use of precedent elsewhere than in this House.

In summary, the test for whether the Supreme Court may depart from its previous case law is 'when it appears right to do so'. This will apply equally to retained EU case law.

15.9.2 Relevant court

The original version of EUWA 2018 which received Royal Assent on 26 June 2018 restricted the ability to depart from retained case law to the Supreme Court and to the High Court of Justiciary. EU(WA)A 2020 added new provisions to EUWA 2018,

[5] The High Court of Justiciary, the highest criminal court in Scotland, is not bound by retained EU law when it is sitting as a court of appeal otherwise than in relation to a compatibility issue or devolution issue or on a reference under the Criminal Procedure (Scotland) Act 1995, s.123(1).

s.6 to allow a minister to make regulations designating a court as a 'relevant court' which, like the Supreme Court and the High Court of Justiciary, would not be bound by retained EU case law. The test that a relevant court applies in deciding whether to depart from retained EU case law is not, however, automatically the same as that for the Supreme Court or the High Court of Justiciary. The test may be set by a minister in regulations.

Under s.6(5A), a minister may make regulations which:

- designate a court as a 'relevant court' which means it is not bound by retained case law so far as is provided for in regulations;
- set out the extent to which, or circumstances in which, a relevant court is not to be bound by retained EU case law;
- set out the test which a relevant court must apply in deciding whether to depart from retained EU case law;
- specify the considerations which are to be relevant to the Supreme Court or High Court of Justiciary in applying the same test as it uses for deciding whether to depart from its own case law;
- specify the considerations which are to be relevant to a relevant court in applying any test set under the regulations for deciding whether to depart from retained EU case law.

Section 6(5B) expands on some of the other provisions that may be made by the s.6(5A) regulations. For example, the regulations may provide for the extent to which, or circumstances in which, a relevant court is not bound by retained domestic case law which relates to retained EU case law.

The regulations can also transfer the setting of the test which a relevant court must apply in deciding whether to depart from retained EU case law to one or more senior members of the judiciary mentioned in s.6(5C).

Before making the s.6(5A) regulations, a Minister must consult:

(a) the President of the Supreme Court,
(b) the Lord Chief Justice of England and Wales,
(c) the Lord President of the Court of Session,
(d) the Lord Chief Justice of Northern Ireland,
(e) the Senior President of Tribunals, and
(f) such other persons as the Minister of the Crown considers appropriate.

The Ministry of Justice published a consultation paper[6] on 2 July 2020 inviting views on its proposals on the use of the s.6(5A) power. The document said (at p.17):

> There is a balance to be struck between the policy aim of encouraging timely departure from retained EU case law, where appropriate, and the negative impacts of driving re-litigation, and therefore case volumes, creating legal uncertainty and reducing confidence in the UK as a forum in which to settle legal disputes.

---

6 'Consultation on the departure from retained EU case law by UK courts and tribunals': **https://assets.publishing.service.gov.uk/government/uploads/system/uploads/attachment_data/file/896830/retained-eu-case-law-consultation.pdf** (accessed 10 November 2020).

The consultation paper put forward two options (at pp.17–18) in terms of which courts should have the power to depart from retained EU case law in addition to the Supreme Court and the High Court of Justiciary:

> Option 1 ...
>
> i. Court of Appeal of England and Wales;
> ii. Court Martial Appeal Court;
> iii. Court of Appeal of Northern Ireland;
> iv. The High Court of Justiciary when sitting as a court of appeal in relation to a compatibility issue or a devolution issue; and
> v. The Inner House of the Court of Session in Scotland.
>
> Option 2 ... In addition to the courts in option 1, this would include:
>
> i. The High Court of England and Wales;
> ii. Outer House of the Court of Session in Scotland;
> iii. The Sheriff Appeal Court in Scotland;
> iv. The High Court of Justiciary sitting at first instance; and
> v. The High Court in Northern Ireland.

The government's response to the consultation was published on 15 October 2020.[7] The consultation attracted 75 responses, of which four were from statutory judicial consultees. The largest number of responses (30) came from the legal services sector. Option 1 was supported by 32 per cent. This figure increased to 56 per cent when including those respondents whose primary preference was for no regulations to be made but who preferred Option 1 if regulations were to be made in any event. Two respondents (3 per cent) supported Option 2.

The government concluded that:

- Option 1 should be adopted with the addition of the Lands Valuation Appeal Court in Scotland and the Registration Appeal Court in Scotland;
- a relevant court should apply the same test adopted by the Supreme Court in deciding whether to depart from its own case law;
- it would not specify any additional factors for the courts to consider.

Regulations under s.6(5A) cannot be made after IPCD (EUWA 2018, s.6(5D)). Draft regulations, the European Union (Withdrawal) Act 2018 (Relevant Court) (Retained EU Case Law) Regulations 2020, were laid before Parliament on 15 October 2020.

7 'Response to the consultation on the departure from retained EU case law by UK courts and tribunals': **https://assets.publishing.service.gov.uk/government/uploads/system/uploads/attachment_data/file/926811/departure-eu-case-law-uk-courts-tribunals-consultation-response.pdf** (accessed 10 November 2020).

Case study: Operation of s.6

This is a fictional example.

A consumer orders a mattress from an online retailer on 31 January 2021. On receipt, she removes the protective packaging to try it out. She decides the mattress is not suitable and contacts the retailer to return it and get a refund. The retailer refuses for hygiene reasons.

The consumer brings a case in the small claims court under the Consumer Contracts (Information, Cancellation and Additional Charges) Regulations 2013 (SI 2013/3134). She argues that the regulations give her a right to cancel for any reason and without incurring any liability. The retailer argues that, under the regulations, there is no right to cancel in the case of a contract for the supply of sealed goods which are not suitable for return due to health protection or hygiene reasons, if they become unsealed after delivery.

The regulations implement Directive 2011/83/EU on consumer rights. They are EU-derived domestic legislation, a category of retained EU law. The case raises a question as to the meaning of retained EU law. That law is unmodified. The court has to decide the question as to the meaning of the retained EU law in accordance with relevant retained case law.

The consumer submits that there is a CJEU case, Case C–681/17 *slewo*, EU:C:2019:255, decided on 27 March 2019, which is on point. The retailer argues that the court should disregard the CJEU case.

In *slewo*, the CJEU held that the removal of a protective film, by a consumer, from a mattress purchased online does not prevent that consumer from exercising their right of withdrawal.

The court considers that case to be relevant. As it is not a 'relevant court' for the purposes of EUWA 2018, s.6(4), it cannot depart from the retained EU case law.[8] Under EUWA 2018, s.6(3)(a), it has to decide the question in accordance with relevant retained case law. It holds that the consumer is entitled to return the mattress.

[8] For the purposes of this example, it is assumed that regulations in the form of the European Union (Withdrawal) Act 2018 (Relevant Court) (Retained EU Case Law) Regulations 2020 laid before Parliament on 15 October 2020 are in force.

CHAPTER 16

Status of retained EU law

16.1 OVERVIEW

This chapter looks at EUWA 2018, s.7. It analyses the system that the Act uses to define the status of retained EU law within the hierarchy of domestic law.

16.2 GENERAL

EUWA 2018, s.7 deals with the status of retained EU law. Knowing where a particular law sits in the domestic legal hierarchy is important because this status affects:

- how that law can be amended;
- how it is scrutinised in Parliament;
- whether it is subject to judicial review;
- whether it can be 'struck down' under HRA 1998;
- the rules of interpretation applied by the courts.

16.2.1 Traditional classification

The traditional classifications of domestic legislation are 'primary legislation' and 'secondary legislation' (also known as delegated or subordinate legislation).

Section 7 does not adopt the traditional classifications for retained EU law. Instead, it takes each category of retained EU law in turn and explains its status. A single system of classification of status is not used. For example, as will be seen, the status of EU-derived domestic legislation is expressed in terms of the kind of legislation it is, while the status of retained direct EU legislation is expressed in terms of how it is modified.

16.2.2 Passage through Parliament

When the European Union (Withdrawal) Bill was introduced in Parliament, it did not assign the status of 'primary legislation' or 'secondary legislation' to retained EU law. Instead, it set out what the status of a particular category of retained EU law was for certain limited purposes. For example, Sched.8 specified that for the purposes of HRA 1998, retained EU direct legislation was to be treated as primary legislation.

Beyond that, the government's intention, as explained in evidence to the House of Lords Select Committee on the Constitution,[1] was to approach the matter on a case-by-case basis and to use the power to make consequential provisions in clause 17 of the Bill (now EUWA 2018, s.23) if there was a particular need to specify the status of a retained EU law for a particular purpose.

This approach came under criticism from the House of Lords Constitution Committee in its report on the European Union (Withdrawal) Bill.[2] The report said:

> 51. As drafted, the Bill gives rise to profound ambiguities about the legal status of retained direct EU law by generally assigning it no particular status while attributing to it (either explicitly or obliquely) particular and different statuses for certain purposes. This is likely to cause confusion and legal uncertainty. In our view, it is essential that all retained direct EU law has the same legal status for all purposes.
>
> 52. We recommend that the legal status that should be accorded to all retained direct EU law for all purposes is that of domestic primary legislation, as directly effective EU law is closely analogous to domestic primary legislation. This will secure legal continuity and certainty post-exit.

Taking on board some of the Committee's recommendations, the government made an amendment to the Bill which eventually became EUWA 2018, s.7. The remainder of this chapter focuses on how EUWA 2018 deals with the issue of the status of retained EU law, taking each category in turn.

16.3 STATUS OF EU-DERIVED DOMESTIC LEGISLATION

Section 7(1A) provides that EU-derived domestic legislation continues to be the same kind of domestic legislation that it was before IPCD. So, an Act of Parliament which is within the definition of EU-derived domestic legislation is still primary legislation. Similarly, regulations which are within the definition of EU-derived domestic legislation remain secondary legislation.

[1] See the uncorrected oral evidence of the Rt Hon Robert Buckland QC MP (then Solicitor General) to the House of Lords Select Committee on the Constitution on Wednesday 13 December 2017, Q47: **http://data.parliament.uk/writtenevidence/committeeevidence.svc/evidencedocument/constitution-committee/european-union-withdrawal-bill/oral/75689.pdf** (accessed 10 November 2020).

[2] Select Committee on the Constitution, *European Union (Withdrawal) Bill* (HL 2017–19, 69).

Table 16.1 Status of EU-derived domestic legislation

EU-derived domestic legislation	Status post-transition period
Pollution Prevention and Control Act 1999	Act of Parliament/primary legislation
Working Time Regulations 1998	Regulations/secondary legislation

16.4 STATUS OF RETAINED DIRECT EU LEGISLATION

Direct EU legislation is subdivided into two categories. The sub-categories are (emphasis added):

- 'retained *direct* principal EU legislation' (s.7(2)); and
- 'retained direct *minor* EU legislation' (s.7(3)).

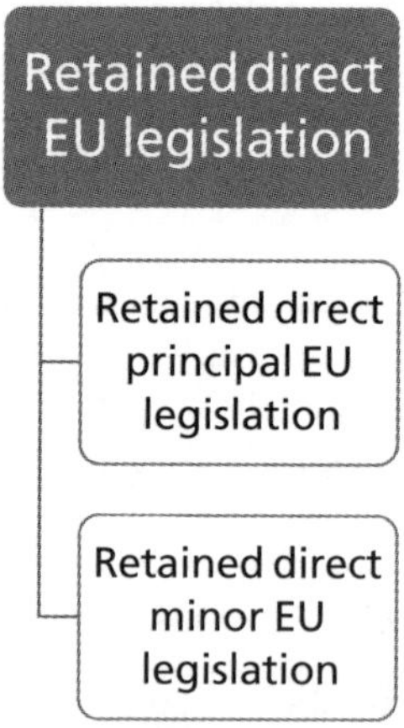

Figure 16.1 Components of retained direct EU legislation

Neither sub-category is given the status of primary or secondary legislation in contrast to the treatment of EU-derived domestic legislation. Instead, s.7 specifies how each of the sub-categories can be modified. As will be seen, retained direct minor EU legislation can be modified more easily than retained direct principal EU legislation. Professor Alison Young poses the pertinent (but unresolved) question:

> … is the means through which a provision is amended a consequence of its status, or is the status of a measure to be determined according to the means through which it can be amended or modified?
>
> (Young, A. (2017) 'Status of EU law post Brexit: Part one', UK Const L Blog (2 May): **https://ukconstitutionallaw.org/**)

The term 'modify' is defined as follows in EUWA 2018, s.20(1):

'modify' includes amend, repeal or revoke (and related expressions are to be read accordingly)

It should be noted that this is broad enough to include non-textual modifications.

Example: A non-textual modification

Article 1 is to be read as if a reference to X were a reference to Y.

16.4.1 Retained direct principal EU legislation

The sub-category 'retained direct principal EU legislation' comprises:

- any EU regulation (other than EU tertiary legislation: see **2.4**) that has been made part of domestic law by EUWA 2018, s.3; and
- any Annex to the EEA Agreement that has been made part of domestic law by EUWA 2018, s.3 and refers to or amends EU regulations,

in both cases, as modified by or under EUWA 2018 or by other domestic law from time to time.

Example

Regulation (EC) No 1007/2009 on trade in seal products is retained direct principal EU legislation.

Modifying retained direct principal EU legislation

Section 7(2) specifies that retained direct principal EU legislation can only be modified by:

- an Act of Parliament;
- other primary legislation (e.g. an Act of the Scottish Parliament);
- subordinate legislation made under specified powers.

Subordinate legislation made under specified powers

The circumstances in which retained direct principal EU legislation can be amended by subordinate legislation are complex. Retained direct principal EU legislation can only be modified by subordinate legislation which has been made using one of the following powers which permits modification, subject to the stated qualifications:

(a) a power under EUWA 2018

For example, the power in EUWA 2018, s.23(1) for a minister to make consequential amendments can be used to amend retained direct principal EU legislation.

(b) a power under an Act other than EUWA 2018

The parent Act must have been passed before EUWA 2018 during the 2017–19 Session of Parliament.[3]

(c) a power under primary legislation

The power must have come into being on or after the passing of EUWA 2018.

(d) a 'Henry VIII power'

A Henry VIII power is a power to make subordinate legislation which is capable of amending or repealing primary legislation. In this context, a Henry VIII power which existed before EUWA 2018 was passed is to be read, as far as possible, as permitting subordinate legislation to be made which modifies retained direct EU legislation.[4]

(e) a power to make subordinate legislation which is not a 'Henry VIII power'[5]

The power in question can be one which existed before EUWA 2018 was passed or it can be a power that came into being on or after the day the Act was passed. In the former case, the power is to be read, as far as possible, as if it allowed a modification of retained direct principal EU legislation but only in so far as the modification is supplementary, incidental or consequential to modifications of retained direct *minor* EU legislation. In the latter case, the power may be exercised, 'so far as applicable and unless the contrary intention appears', to modify retained direct principal EU legislation in so far as the modification is supplementary, incidental or consequential to modifications to retained direct *minor* EU legislation. This is noteworthy in that one might have expected a change to retained direct principal EU legislation to be made first and then reflected in retained direct minor EU legislation rather than the other way round.

(f) a power to make transitional, transitory or savings provisions

The power in question can be one which existed before EUWA 2018 was passed or it can be a power that came into being on or after the day the Act was passed. An existing power to make transitional, transitory or savings provisions is to be read, as

---

[3] A power in such an Act can be exercised before IPCD to modify retained EU law but with the changes coming into force on or after IPCD (Sched.8, para.8(3)). This is also the case for powers exercised by virtue of Sched.8, paras.3, 5, 10 or 11.

[4] This does not apply to a power which can only be used to amend or revoke a Northern Ireland Order in Council.

[5] Also included is a power which cannot be used to amend primary legislation generally but can be used to amend Northern Ireland legislation which is an Order in Council.

far as possible, as if it extended to retained direct EU legislation. Where the power came into being on or after the day the Act was passed, the power may be exercised, 'so far as applicable and unless the contrary intention appears', to modify retained direct EU legislation.

(g) a power to make subordinate legislation conferred on or after EUWA 2018 was passed

A power conferred on or after the day EUWA 2018 was passed and which permits subordinate legislation to be made which amends or revokes retained direct principal EU legislation may also be used, so far as possible and unless the contrary intention appears, to modify any retained direct principal EU legislation other than by amendment or revocation (EUWA 2018, Sched.8, para.11(2)(a)). This would permit non-textual modifications.

16.4.2 Retained direct minor EU legislation

Retained direct minor EU legislation is any retained direct EU legislation which is not retained direct principal EU legislation. This encompasses:

- EU tertiary legislation (which may take the form of a regulation or decision); and
- EU decisions which are not EU tertiary legislation.[6]

Example

Commission Delegated Regulation (EU) 2015/61 to supplement Regulation (EU) 575/2013 with regard to liquidity coverage requirement for Credit Institutions is retained direct minor EU legislation.

Modifying retained direct minor EU legislation

Section 7(3) specifies that retained direct minor EU legislation can only be modified by:

- an Act of Parliament;
- other primary legislation (e.g. an Act of the Scottish Parliament);
- subordinate legislation made under specified powers.

Like retained direct principal EU legislation, retained direct minor EU legislation can only be modified by subordinate legislation which has been made using particular powers. There is a degree of overlap between the powers which can be used to modify both types of retained direct EU legislation. Of the ways that retained direct principal EU legislation can be modified, those set out at **16.4.1** at

[6] See **Chapter 2** for an explanation of regulations, decisions and EU tertiary legislation.

(a), (b), (c), (d), and (f) also apply to retained direct minor EU legislation, *mutatis mutandis*. In addition, retained direct minor EU legislation can be modified using the following power, subject to the stated qualifications:

- **a power to make subordinate legislation**

A power to make subordinate legislation which was conferred *before* EUWA 2018 was passed and which is not a Henry VIII power[7] is to be read, as far as possible, as permitting the modification of retained direct minor EU legislation. Modifications can only be made if they are consistent with any retained direct principal EU legislation or anything within the category of retained EU law established by EUWA 2018, s.4.

A power to make subordinate legislation which was conferred *on or after* the day EUWA 2018 was passed may be used to modify retained direct minor EU legislation as long as the modifications are consistent with any retained direct principal EU legislation or anything within the category of retained EU law established by EUWA 2018, s.4 and unless the contrary intention appears.

16.5 STATUS OF RETAINED EU LAW UNDER EUWA 2018, S.4

The category of retained EU law established by EUWA 2018, s.4 is modified in the same way as retained direct principal EU legislation *mutatis mutandis*. See **16.4.1**.

16.6 SIGNPOSTS

Section 7 is not the only section of EUWA 2018 which is relevant to the status of retained EU law. Section 7(5) 'signposts' several other provisions in the Act about the status of EU law. This book focuses on the signposted provisions which are of most day-to-day relevance to practitioners. Sections 5 and 6 are discussed in **Chapters 14** and **15**.

Also signposted is Sched.8, para.30. For the purposes of HRA 1998, retained direct principal EU legislation is to be treated as primary legislation (Sched.8, para.30(2)). This means, for example, that if retained direct principal EU legislation cannot be construed in accordance with the ECHR, the court cannot set it aside but can issue a declaration of incompatibility. Retained direct minor EU legislation is to be treated as primary legislation so far as it amends any primary legislation but otherwise it is to be treated as subordinate legislation (Sched.8, para.30(3)). See also **14.5** and **18.2.3**.

[7] Or is a power to make subordinate legislation which can be exercised in relation to Northern Ireland legislation which is an Order in Council.

CHAPTER 17

Changes made to retained EU law by 'EU Exit' regulations

17.1 OVERVIEW

This chapter considers EUWA 2018, s.8. Section 8 contains a wide-ranging power for a minister to make regulations which correct deficiencies in retained EU law which arise from withdrawal. As the White Paper explained, this power was needed because provisions of retained EU law would not necessarily make sense or function effectively in a post-IPCD domestic context.

The volume of secondary legislation made using the s.8 power is substantial. Practitioners will need to consider the impact of changes made by s.8 regulations[1] to the retained EU law which is relevant to their area of practice.

The government's initial estimate was that 800–1,000 EU Exit statutory instruments would need to be made. This was later revised down. The House of Lords Constitution Committee said that the scale of the transfer of legislative competence to the government raised 'constitutional concerns of a fundamental nature' regarding the balance of power between Parliament and the Executive.[2]

The deficiencies-correcting regulations can be long and complex. The House of Lords Secondary Legislation Scrutiny Committee raised concerns about a statutory instrument that was more than 600 pages long.[3]

The pace at which the secondary legislation has been produced has in several cases led to amending regulations having to be made, for example to correct drafting errors or to respond to concerns raised by industry.[4]

---

1 Regulations made under s.8 are often referred to as 'EU Exit' or 'onshoring' regulations/statutory instruments.

2 Select Committee on the Constitution, *The 'Great Repeal Bill' and Delegated Powers* (HL 2016–17, 123), para.47.

3 Secondary Legislation Scrutiny Committee (Sub-committee B), *Seventeenth Report* (HL 2017–19, 293).

4 See, for example, the Explanatory Memorandum to the REACH etc. (Amendment etc.) (EU Exit) (No.2) Regulations 2019 (SI 2019/858).

17.2 RATIONALE FOR THE DEFICIENCIES-CORRECTING POWER

As we have seen, EUWA 2018 converts law which was originally made by the EU for the EU and its Member States into UK law. It also preserves law which was originally made by the UK to give effect to law made by the EU for the EU and its Member States. This new body of law, retained EU law, applies in the UK as it stood immediately prior to IPCD. It remains in this form unless and until it is amended, repealed or revoked. This gives rise to a situation where law made in one context applies to another, very different context that was not envisaged when the law was originally made.

Naturally, not all of this law will make sense after IPCD when the UK is no longer a member of the EU[5] and EU law has ceased to apply to it. For example, keeping a legal requirement in retained EU law for the Secretary of State to send a report to the Commission on the measures taken to implement the Directive on the conservation of natural habitats does not make sense when the UK is no longer under an obligation to follow the EU directive.

EUWA 2018 recognises that there will be many such anomalies or, to use the terminology in the Act, 'deficiencies', which need to be ironed out so that retained EU law can operate in the new context. The chosen method of achieving this is by means of a wide-ranging power for ministers to deal with deficiencies under s.8.

17.3 BACKGROUND

While the rationale for the power has been widely accepted, the breadth of the power has come in for criticism. It is a 'Henry VIII power', meaning that it can be used to make subordinate legislation which amends primary legislation. The House of Lords Delegated Powers and Regulatory Reform Committee described the power as 'notable for its width, novelty and uncertainty'[6] while the Hansard Society described the powers in the European Union (Withdrawal) Bill on introduction as 'some of the broadest constitutionally important provisions ever seen in legislation'. Following enactment of the power, attention has switched to how it is being exercised.

Correcting deficiencies is no small task. In March 2017, the government estimated that between 800 and 1,000 statutory instruments would be needed to make the necessary corrections. By March 2019, this had been revised down to 'below 600'.[7] In an average year, the number of statutory instruments is around 3,500. In July 2020, the government estimated that it would lay 250–300 EU Exit statutory instruments between September and December 2020.[8]

---

[5] The UK's membership of the EU came to an end on 31 January 2020. However, EU law continued to apply for the duration of the transition period. See further **10.3** and **20.2**.

[6] Delegated Powers and Regulatory Reform Committee, *European Union (Withdrawal) Bill* (HL 2017–19, 22), para.15.

[7] See letter of 5 March 2019 from the Leader of the House at: **https://old.parliament.uk/documents/commons-committees/european-statutory-instruments/23%2020190305_Leader%20to%20Committee%20Chairs%20-%20Exit%20SIs%20(1).pdf** (accessed 10 November 2020).

[8] See letter of 27 July 2020 from the Leader of the House to the Chair of the European Statutory Instruments Committee at: **https://committees.parliament.uk/publications/2223/documents/20324/default/** (accessed 10 November 2020).

The production of s.8 regulations is the result of a process within government that involves a detailed review of the substantial body of law that will become retained EU law to identify deficiencies, some being more obvious to spot than others. The affected areas are as diverse as financial services, veterinary medicines, plant breeders' rights, aviation and criminal procedure. The review is followed by decisions as to how best to 'rectify' the deficiencies that have been identified.

Even the seemingly straightforward example of altering a legal duty to send information to an EU body raises a number of policy questions. As the House of Lords Delegated Powers and Regulatory Reform Committee identifies:[9]

> Should the information go instead to an existing UK body? Should it go to a newly-created body? Should the requirement be scrapped altogether? Should more or less information be sent to some other body?

The White Paper stated (at para.1.21) that the Bill:

> will not aim to make major changes to policy or establish new legal frameworks in the UK beyond those which are necessary to ensure the law continues to function properly from day one.

When the European Union (Withdrawal) Bill was going through Parliament, ministers made statements to allay concerns as to the breadth of the deficiencies-correcting power, indicating that it would only be used to make technical changes as opposed to significant policy changes. For example, Lord Callanan described the power as:

> ... restricted, both by its purpose – remedying deficiencies arising from withdrawal – and in what it may do. We have always said that significant policy changes will be brought through by primary legislation, receiving proper parliamentary scrutiny.[10]

It remains to be seen how the courts will interpret the scope of the power. As explained in *Craies on Legislation*:

> ... the more general the words by Parliament to delegate a power, the more likely it is that an exercise within the literal meaning of the words will nevertheless be outside the legislature's contemplation.
>
> (Greenberg, D. (ed) (2020) *Craies on Legislation* (12th edn), Sweet & Maxwell, para.1.3.11)[11]

---

9 Delegated Powers and Regulatory Reform Committee, *European Union (Withdrawal) Bill* (HL 2017–19, 22), para.25.

10 Hansard, 7 March 2018, vol.789, col.1212. Steve Baker MP, Parliamentary Under-Secretary of State at the Department for Exiting the European Union said in evidence to the House of Lords Select Committee on the Constitution (13 December 2017, Q53): '... I have to accept that I can say only that we will not make major policy changes, and that those would be brought forward in primary legislation.'

11 Cited with approval by the Supreme Court in *R (on the application of The Public Law Project)* v. *Lord Chancellor* [2016] UKSC 39 at [26].

It is not possible to predict the precise parameters that the courts will impose on a power cast in wide terms. However, applying the principle in *Padfield*,[12] it is likely that a court would approach the power as designed to ensure a properly functioning statute book rather than making broad policy choices about future frameworks.

The use of the power to make the Freedom of Establishment and Free Movement of Services (EU Exit) Regulations 2019 (SI 2019/1401) attracted criticism on the grounds that the regulations brought about a significant change in policy[13] by, among other things, disapplying directly effective rights of establishment and free movement of services derived from articles in the TFEU. However, the matter did not come before the courts.

Given the volume of deficiencies legislation that has had to be made in a short space of time, there have inevitably been errors. A number of statutory amendments made under s.8 have had to be corrected more than once. When considering retained EU law, it is therefore particularly important for practitioners to make sure that they have sight of the most up-to-date modifications. Familiar rules that have been relatively stable may be subject to more frequent change.

A large volume of subordinate legislation made under the s.8 deficiencies-correcting power was made with exit day as the coming into force date. With the advent of the transition period, however, these changes were not required until IPCD. EU(WA)A 2020, Sched.5, para.1(1) defers the coming into force of this body of subordinate legislation until IPCD. There is provision for exceptions to be made.

17.4 SCOPE OF EUWA 2018, S.8(1)

Section 8(1) provides:

> A Minister of the Crown may by regulations make such provision as the Minister considers appropriate to prevent, remedy or mitigate –
>
> (a) any failure of retained EU law to operate effectively, or
> (b) any other deficiency in retained EU law,
>
> arising from the withdrawal of the United Kingdom from the EU.

The terms 'failure' and 'deficiency' are not defined. According to the Explanatory Notes, a 'failure' of retained EU law is:

12 *Padfield* v. *Minister of Agriculture, Fisheries and Food* [1968] AC 997 – a statutory power can validly be used only in the right and proper way which Parliament when conferring it is presumed to have intended.

13 See, for example, HC Deb 21 October 2019, vol.666, col.1 and briefing of the Public Law Project, *Promoting Access to Justice, Upholding the Rule of Law, Ensuring Fair Systems*, published on 18 October 2019 at: **https://publiclawproject.org.uk** (accessed 10 November 2020).

a type of deficiency; a failure means the law doesn't operate effectively whereas deficiency covers a wider range of cases where it does not function appropriately or sensibly.

It is important to note that the deficiency has to arise from withdrawal. This is, however, given a broad meaning. The power can be used in relation to deficiencies arising from any aspect of withdrawal including the end of the implementation period and any other effect of the Withdrawal Agreement. It can also be used to deal with a deficiency that arises from withdrawal taken together with the operation of any provision of EUWA 2018 (see s.8(9)).

There is a power for the devolved authorities corresponding to s.8 which is set out in Sched.2.

17.5 TYPES OF DEFICIENCY

Section 8(2) sets out a non-exhaustive list of the kinds of deficiencies the power can address. For example, it provides that there is a deficiency where the minister considers that retained EU law:

(a) contains provisions that are redundant after the UK has left the EU

Example

The Creative Europe Programme and Europe for Citizens Programme (Revocation) (EU Exit) Regulations 2019 (SI 2019/447) revoke EU Regulation (1295/2013) establishing the Creative Europe Programme and EU Regulation (390/2014) establishing the Europe for Citizens Programme (as converted into domestic law) which put in place mechanisms for the provision of EU funding. Post-IPCD, UK organisations will no longer receive future funding under these EU programmes. The regulations are revoked as they are redundant.

(b) contains provisions on reciprocal arrangements between the UK and the EU or between the UK and EU Member States which are no longer appropriate

---

Example

EU Directive 2014/60/EU, implemented in the UK by the Return of Cultural Objects Regulations 1994 (SI 1994/501 as amended), requires Member States to return objects which have been unlawfully removed from the territory of another Member State.

Post-IPCD, the directive will not apply to the UK as a matter of EU law so Member States will not be required to return objects unlawfully exported from the UK. However, the UK regulations implementing the directive would continue to require the UK to return objects unlawfully removed from an EU Member State.

The Return of Cultural Objects (Revocation) Regulations 2018 (SI 2018/1086), made under EUWA 2018, s.8, revoke the domestic regulations which implement Directive 2014/60/EU.

As set out in the Explanatory Memorandum, this is to avoid a one-sided obligation on the UK to return cultural objects, while unable to enjoy reciprocal rights.

(c) makes provision for other arrangements which involve the EU or are otherwise dependent on the UK's membership of the EU and are no longer appropriate

---

Example

The European Union Budget, and Economic and Monetary Policy (EU Exit) Regulations 2019 (SI 2019/484), made under EUWA 2018, s.8, revoke EU legislation on the EU budget. As the Explanatory Memorandum says, it will no longer be appropriate for EU law regarding the EU budget to apply to the UK.[14]

(d) contains 'EU references'[15] which are no longer appropriate

---

Example

The Genetically Modified Organisms (Contained Use) Regulations 2014 (SI 2014/1663) are retained EU law. The Health and Safety (Amendment) (EU Exit) Regulations 2018 (SI 2018/1370), made under EUWA 2018, s.8, remove a requirement on the relevant UK competent authority to send particular information to the Commission when it is informed of an accidental release of a genetically modified organism. This requirement has been removed on the basis that it would no longer be appropriate to provide such information to the Commission.

In addition, a minister can make regulations to correct a deficiency which they consider is similar to any deficiency listed in s.8(2). There is also a power for a minister to make subordinate legislation which specifies additional deficiencies (see s.8(3)).

The practice is for regulations made using the deficiencies-correcting power to cite s.8(2) as the legal basis as opposed to citing the specific limb of s.8(2). However, the Explanatory Memorandum prepared to accompany the regulations usually goes into more detail as to the precise sub-paragraph of s.8(2) that is being relied on.

17.6 TRANSFER OF FUNCTIONS

The deficiencies-correcting power can be used to give an existing UK public authority the functions that were carried out by an EU entity or a Member State

[14] To the extent that rules with respect to the EU budget apply to the UK under the Withdrawal Agreement, they are dealt with separately.

[15] The term 'EU reference' is defined in EUWA 2018, s.20(1).

public authority. Such functions can also be replaced, abolished or otherwise modified (see s.8(6)).

Example

In the field of financial services, HM Treasury has used the s.8 power to transfer supervisory functions carried out by EU supervisory authorities (such as the European Securities and Markets Authority (ESMA)) to UK regulators. ESMA's function of recognising non-UK Central Counterparties so that they can provide services in the UK has been transferred to the Bank of England. ESMA's function of supervising credit ratings agencies and trade repositories has been transferred to the UK's Financial Conduct Authority.

17.7 LEGISLATIVE SUB-DELEGATION

The power in s.8(1) to make regulations to correct deficiencies is conferred on a minister. There is no express provision that says that the minister can delegate this power. However, the Explanatory Notes point to s.8(5) which says that s.8 regulations can make any provision that could be made by an Act of Parliament. The Notes say that this could include 'sub-delegating the power to a public authority where they are best placed to deal with the deficiencies'.

The government's *Delegated Powers Memorandum*[16] says that the government will only take this approach:

> where existing constitutional arrangements mean that it is more appropriate for the power to be exercised independent of political control.

Whether a specific sub-delegation falls within the power will be a matter of fact and degree on each occasion.

The power has been used to sub-delegate by the Treasury in the Financial Regulators' Powers (Technical Standards etc.) (Amendment etc.) (EU Exit) Regulations 2018 (SI 2018/1115). These regulations, among other things, delegate the deficiencies-correcting power to UK financial regulators to correct deficiencies in Binding Technical Standards, which are a kind of delegated or implementing act.

The Delegated Powers and Regulatory Reform Committee has raised concerns[17] that the sub-delegated rules themselves (which it refers to as tertiary legislation) will bypass parliamentary scrutiny. The lack of parliamentary scrutiny stems from the fact that such rules are not to be made by statutory instrument (Sched.7, para.30) and are therefore not subject to the publication and laying requirements of the Statutory Instruments Act 1946.

[16] Of 13 July 2017, at para.32.

[17] Delegated Powers and Regulatory Reform Committee, *European Union (Withdrawal) Bill* (HL 2017–19, 73), paras.13–16.

In response to the Committee's recommendation that tertiary legislation should be subject to the same parliamentary control as is applicable to secondary legislation, the government said:

> ... The right way to address the exercise of delegated powers transferred, or granted by the SIs under this Bill, is for Parliament to scrutinise the SIs transferring those powers and the conditions they set out closely and carefully.
>
> (Delegated Powers and Regulatory Reform Committee, *European Union (Withdrawal) Bill: Government Response* (HL 2017–19, 119))

The Committee also noted that the time limit in s.8(8) on the availability of the s.8 power (also known as a 'sun-setting provision') does not apply to the exercise of a sub-delegated power.[18] The government's response was to say that:

> There are areas where regular updates are required, for example for the regulation of chemicals the ability to react quickly is of real importance for public safety and health. As such, relevant policy specific delegated powers will be needed after the sunsets of the powers in the Bill to ensure the continued functioning of these regimes.

This illustrates the breadth of the power.

Where powers are delegated, the minister must make a statement explaining why it is appropriate to do so (EUWA 2018, Sched.7, para.30).

17.8 RESTRICTIONS ON THE USE OF THE DEFICIENCIES-CORRECTING POWER

There are a number of restrictions on how the deficiencies-correcting power may be exercised and on what the regulations made under it may do. A change in EU law is not classed as a 'deficiency'. The deficiencies-correcting power cannot therefore be used to 'keep pace' with developments in EU law (see s.8(4)).

Section 8(7) sets out the key restrictions on what the deficiencies-correcting regulations may do. They may not:

> (a) impose or increase taxation or fees,
> (b) make retrospective provision,
> (c) create a relevant criminal offence,
> (d) establish a public authority,
> (e) amend, repeal or revoke the Human Rights Act 1998 or any subordinate legislation made under it, or
> (f) amend or repeal the Scotland Act 1998, the Government of Wales Act 2006 or the Northern Ireland Act 1998 ... [subject to limited exceptions].

The power has to be exercised compatibly with the terms of the Northern Ireland Act 1998, as is the case for all powers under EUWA 2018 (see s.10(1)). Section 10(2) provides that nothing in s.8 authorises regulations which diminish North–

[18] See EUWA 2018, Sched.8, para.40 and Delegated Powers and Regulatory Reform Committee, *European Union (Withdrawal) Bill* (HL 2017–19, 73), para.12.

South cooperation under the Belfast Agreement or introduce border arrangements between Northern Ireland and the Republic of Ireland.

The availability of the deficiencies-correcting power is time-limited. Any deficiencies-correcting regulations must be made within two years of IPCD (s.8(8)).[19]

17.9 PARLIAMENTARY SCRUTINY OF DEFICIENCIES-CORRECTING REGULATIONS

During the passage of the European Union (Withdrawal) Bill, concerns were expressed that the usual parliamentary processes for scrutinising secondary legislation would not provide adequate parliamentary oversight of regulations made under s.8, given the breadth and constitutional significance of the power. To address some of these concerns, a 'sifting' arrangement was introduced, described below.

Regulations made under the s.8 power are scrutinised by Parliament using one of the following procedures:

- the draft affirmative procedure;
- the negative procedure;
- the made affirmative procedure for urgent cases.

Note that none of these procedures affords Parliament the opportunity to amend the regulations.

Before regulations made under s.8(1) are laid (or before a draft is laid), a minister must make certain explanatory statements, for example that in the minister's opinion the instrument does no more than is appropriate (EUWA 2018, Sched.7, para.28).

17.9.1 Draft affirmative procedure

The draft affirmative procedure (see Sched.7, para.1(1) and (2)) has to be used for s.8 regulations which:

- give a UK public authority a function of making an instrument of a legislative character that was exercised by an EU entity;
- relate to fees;
- create or widen a criminal offence;
- create or amend a power to legislate;
- are made under s.8(3)(b) (the power to provide for additional deficiencies).

A minister can, however, choose the draft affirmative procedure even if it is not required.

[19] Note the qualification in **17.7** in relation to the exercise of sub-delegated powers.

Under the draft affirmative procedure, regulations have to be laid in draft before each House of Parliament. They are debated in Parliament and must be approved by a resolution of each House before they can come into force.

17.9.2 Negative procedure

The negative procedure is available for other regulations made under s.8(1), subject to a bespoke 'sifting' process before they are made. The negative procedure involves a lighter form of parliamentary scrutiny. Parliamentary approval is not needed before the regulations come into force; they become law on the day the minister signs them and remain law unless either House 'prays against' (annuls) them within 40 sitting days of the regulations being laid before Parliament.

The sifting procedure operates as shown in Figure 17.1.

Example

In its Seventh Report of Session 2019–21, the European Statutory Instruments Committee recommended that the Communications Act (e-Commerce) (EU Exit) Regulations 2020 (SI 2020/1420) should be subject to the affirmative procedure on the ground that they were of legal and political importance.

17.9.3 Made affirmative procedure

If the minister considers that the situation is urgent, the made affirmative procedure can be used. A draft of the regulations does not have to be laid before Parliament. The regulations can come into force as soon as they are made (i.e. signed by the minister). However, if they are not approved by a resolution of each House within 28 days of being made, they cease to have effect going forward.

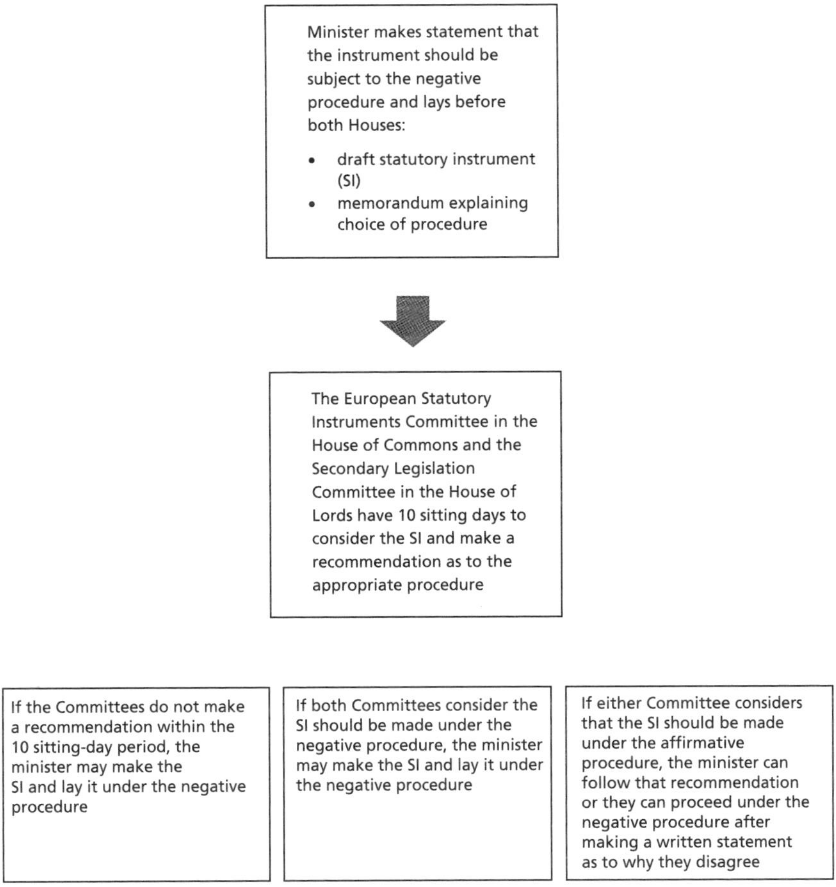

Figure 17.1 Negative procedure with sifting

CHAPTER 18

Miscellaneous provisions

18.1 OVERVIEW

Some of the provisions explained in this chapter are relatively detailed and technical. However, they can have a significant impact on the operation of retained EU law and their importance should not be overlooked.

18.2 CONSEQUENTIAL PROVISIONS

18.2.1 Existing ambulatory references

Some legislation makes reference to other legal instruments. Where the reference is 'ambulatory', this means it is to be read as a reference to the other instrument as that instrument is updated from time to time.

ECA 1972, Sched.2, para.1A enabled ambulatory references to be made when implementing EU law. Primary legislation which implemented EU law can contain ambulatory references. In EU law, cross-references are generally intended to be ambulatory or dynamic. This is set out in the EU institutions' drafting guidance.[1] There is no such presumption in domestic law.

Example

This is a fictional example illustrating the position before IPCD.

Regulations made under ECA 1972, s.2(2) and Sched.2, para.1A prohibit certain chemicals in food. There is an ambulatory reference to an EU decision which lists the chemicals. Where the EU updates the list in the decision, the list in s.2(2) regulations automatically amends to reflect the changes made to the EU decision.

---

[1] See *Joint Practical Guide of the European Parliament, the Council and the Commission for Persons Involved in Drafting of European Union Legislation*, p.52: **https://eur-lex.europa.eu/content/techleg/EN-legislative-drafting-guide.pdf** (accessed 10 November 2020).

Schedule 8 deals with ambulatory references to EU law contained in UK legislation, in direct EU legislation (for example an EU regulation) and in documents relating to that UK legislation or direct EU legislation (such as UK statutory guidance or guidance issued by an EU institution prior to IPCD).[2] These cross-references continue to 'ambulate' (unless the legislator has provided otherwise)[3] but should be read as referring to the UK (not the EU) version of the legislation.[4]

Example

This is a fictional example.

UK domestic regulations made under ECA 1972, s.2(2) prohibit certain chemicals in food. Those regulations are saved by EUWA 2018, s.2 on IPCD. The UK regulations contain an ambulatory reference to an EU decision which lists the chemicals. That EU decision is saved by EUWA 2018, s.3, and a UK body is given the power to amend that decision.

Amendments are made post-IPCD by the UK body to the list of banned chemicals in the decision (now retained direct EU legislation). By virtue of EUWA 2018, Sched.8, para.1(1) the list of prohibited chemicals is updated automatically in the UK domestic regulations, with reference to the UK version of the EU decision.

Where the cross-references are to legislation that is not incorporated (such as directives) the reference 'freezes' to the version of the directive as it stood immediately before IPCD.[5]

Example

This is a fictional example.

A case is brought in the UK a few years after IPCD. The case is about product standards relating to electrical appliances such as kettles and hairdryers. The domestic legislation which regulates this area is EU-derived domestic legislation. The legislation contains an ambulatory reference to the EU directive which it originally implemented. The reference should be interpreted as a reference to the directive as it had effect immediately before IPCD,

---

2 There was some uncertainty as to whether this reference in Sched.8, para.1(1)(iii) as well as the mirroring reference in Sched.8, para.2(1)(iii) might affect ambulatory references in private contracts (HC Deb 17 December 2017, vol.633, col.1169). The City of London Law Society has written a helpful opinion on this subject where it concludes that private contracts are not within the scope of these provisions. Its view is that principles of statutory interpretation support a narrow construction of these provisions which exclude private contracts from scope. Further, the consequences of applying these provisions to private contracts would be significant and inappropriate and would interfere with the principle of freedom of contract. See City of London Law Society, 'Private Contracts and Schedule 8 of the European Union (Withdrawal) Act 2018' at: **www.citysolicitors.org.uk/storage/2018/12/CLLS-endorsed-memorandum-on-private-contracts-and-Schedule.pdf** (accessed 10 November 2020).

3 See the reference to 'unless the contrary intention appears' at Sched.8, para.1(1).

4 This is the effect of Sched.8, para.1(1).

5 This is the effect of Sched.8, para.2(1).

and not to the new version of that directive which regulates product standards in the EU at the time the case is brought.

At the time of writing the draft European Union Withdrawal (Consequential Modifications) (EU Exit) Regulations 2020 insert para.1A into Sched.8. These regulations make provision in relation to ambulatory references in relevant separation agreement law. For example, they ensure that a cross-reference to an EU regulation applied by the Ireland/Northern Ireland Protocol will be to the EU version of the regulation rather than the version retained under EUWA 2018, s.3.

18.2.2 Non-ambulatory references

The position for non-ambulatory references is set out in EUWA 2018, Sched.8, para.2A.[6] The drafting is opaque. In para.2A, cross-references to any of the EU Treaties (as defined in EUWA 2018, s.20(1)), any EU instrument or other document of an EU entity (such as UK statutory guidance or guidance issued by an EU institution) which are in any enactment[7] or in any instrument which is to form part of retained direct EU legislation (such as an EU regulation), are to be read as references to the UK version of the legislation (unless the intention in a particular context is to continue to refer to the EU version).[8] However, this general rule only applies where the reference to the EU legislation is up to date at IPCD.[9] For example, if domestic legislation made in 2015 cross-referred to an EU regulation made in 2013 which was amended in a relevant way[10] by another EU regulation in 2016, the general rule would not apply to that cross-reference. The 2015 legislation would continue to refer post-IPCD to the 2013 version of the EU regulation, rather than the UK version of the regulation. That is because the cross-reference is not up to date at IPCD, because there has been a 'relevant modification' since the cross-reference was made in 2015.

References which are non-ambulatory and are to a directive may also be out of date (for example because the directive has been repealed or amended). There is no general 'fix' for this situation.

Note that some non-ambulatory references are updated by powers in EUWA 2018, s.8.

---

6 At the time of writing the relevant amendments to EUWA 2018 are set out in draft legislation – the European Union Withdrawal (Consequential Modifications) (EU Exit) Regulations 2020. These regulations revoke reg.2 of the European Union (Withdrawal) Act 2018 (Consequential Modifications and Repeals and Revocations) (EU Exit) Regulations 2019 (SI 2019/628).

7 See the definition in EUWA 2018, s.20(1).

8 This is the effect of Sched.8, para.2A(3) and (4).

9 See the reference to there being 'no relevant modification' at Sched.8, para.2A(3)(c).

10 Paragraph 2A(3)(c) refers to a relevant modification as defined at Sched.8, para.2A(7).

18.2.3 Interpretation Act 1978

EUWA 2018, Sched.8, Part 2, paras.18–22 make amendments to the Interpretation Act 1978. For example, a number of definitions which were in ECA 1972 (e.g. 'the EU Treaties') are 'moved across' to the Interpretation Act 1978 to prevent them from being lost on the repeal of ECA 1972.

18.3 GENERAL TRANSITIONAL PROVISIONS

The function of transitional provisions is to set out how the transition from the old law to the new is intended to work.

Schedule 8, Part 3 contains general transitional provisions. The provisions can be summarised as follows: anything done or in force before IPCD (including anything which is in the process of being done) which relates to retained EU law continues to be in force or effective on or after IPCD.

The Explanatory Notes to EUWA 2018 cite an example of licences lawfully issued before IPCD. These will continue to have effect after IPCD.[11] This is subject to specific provision made by regulations under EU(WA)A 2020, s.23(6) (power to make transitional, transitory or saving provision) and s.41(5) (transitional, transitory or saving provision) as well as any other provisions made by or under EUWA 2018 or EU(WA)A 2020 or any other enactment.[12]

For specific transitional provisions see **Appendix C**.

18.4 PUBLICATION BY THE QUEEN'S PRINTER

Schedule 5 requires the Queen's Printer to publish EU regulations, EU decisions, EU tertiary legislation and relevant international agreements (the TEU, TFEU, the Euratom Treaty and the EEA Agreement). This is to ensure that they are accessible after IPCD.

18.5 RULES OF EVIDENCE

In proceedings in the UK, a question as to the meaning or effect of the law of another jurisdiction is treated as a matter of fact. Therefore, where the meaning or effect of the law of another jurisdiction needs to be established, evidence will have to be adduced. The judge will make a finding as to the meaning and effect of the law, based on the evidence before the court.

---

[11] See the Explanatory Notes, para.403. Schedule 1, Part 3 was amended by EU(WA)A 2020. Paragraph 36A made provision for the transition period. See also para.580 to the Explanatory Notes to EU(WA)A 2020.

[12] See EUWA 2018, Sched.8, para.36A(3).

ECA 1972 made provision for the meaning and effect of EU law to be treated as a matter of law.[13] This reflected the status of EU law as part of the law of the Member States.[14]

EUWA 2018 continues the position under ECA 1972. See EUWA 2018, Sched.5, para.3.

18.6 GENERAL PROVISIONS ABOUT POWERS UNDER EUWA 2018

There are some general provisions which apply to the exercise of all powers under EUWA 2018. Of particular note are the following:

- Section 10: all powers are to be exercised compatibly with the Northern Ireland Act 1998.
- Schedule 7, Part 3, para.20: any power to make regulations which is exercisable by a Minister of the Crown is exercisable by statutory instrument. This means that the provisions of the Statutory Instruments Act 1946 apply.
- Schedule 7, Part 3, para.21: this paragraph provides, among other things, that any power under EUWA 2018 may be used to make supplementary, incidental, consequential, transitional, transitory or saving provision. This includes restating any retained EU law in a clearer and more accessible way.

[13] See ECA 1972, s.3, in particular s.3(1), which read: 'For the purposes of all legal proceedings any question as to the meaning or effect of any of the Treaties, or as to the validity, meaning or effect of any EU instrument, shall be treated as a question of law (and, if not referred to the European Court, be for determination as such in accordance with the principles laid down by and any relevant decision of the European Court).'

[14] See, for example, Case 6/64 *Costa* v. *ENEL*, EU:C:1964:66: 'the [EU Treaties have] created [their] own legal system which became an integral part of the legal systems of the Member States and which their courts are bound to apply.'

CHAPTER 19

Devolution and retained EU law

19.1 OVERVIEW

The devolution settlements[1] were crafted during the UK's membership of the EU. The settlements expressly stated that the devolved legislatures could not legislate or act in a manner which was incompatible with EU law.[2] The rules made by the EU in areas that were devolved on a domestic level (e.g. agriculture) had to be complied with by all the constituent parts of the UK.[3] This created, among other things, a consistency of standards within the UK's internal market. The UK's withdrawal from the EU raised questions about how powers in devolved areas which were exercised at EU level during the UK's EU membership would be exercised domestically once the EU legal framework ceased to apply.

19.2 POSITION ON INTRODUCTION OF THE EUROPEAN UNION (WITHDRAWAL) BILL

When the European Union (Withdrawal) Bill was introduced in July 2017, it included provisions in clause 11 and Schedule 3 which removed the restriction on devolved legislatures from acting incompatibly with EU law and replaced it with a provision that devolved legislatures could not modify retained EU law in a devolved area unless a Minister of the Crown first 'released' the area back to the devolved

---

1 The Government of Wales Act 2006 (GOWA 2006), the Northern Ireland Act 1998 (NIA 1998) and the Scotland Act 1998 (Scotland Act 1998).

2 See, for example, GOWA 2006, s.80(8) as originally enacted and the Scotland Act 1998, s.29(2)(d) as originally enacted.

3 That did not, however, mean that the rules adopted to implement EU obligations in devolved areas had to be the same in England, Wales, Northern Ireland and Scotland. In Case C–428/07 *Horvath* v. *Secretary of State for Environment, Food and Rural Affairs*, EU:C:2009:458, a farmer in England challenged a regulation establishing support schemes for farmers under the common agricultural policy. The regulation as implemented in England provided that a failure to maintain public rights of way would lead to a reduction in payments. The rules in Wales, Northern Ireland and Scotland did not contain such a provision. The CJEU held that divergence between the measures adopted by devolved legislatures to implement an EU obligation did not constitute discrimination contrary to EU law. The measures themselves had to be compatible with the obligations stemming from the regulation.

legislatures by Order in Council. The Explanatory Notes said that this would be a transitional arrangement, pending decisions on a long-term common policy approach.

The First Minister of Wales and the First Minister of Scotland issued a joint statement which objected to this approach on the basis that:

> The European Union (Withdrawal) Bill does not return powers from the EU to the devolved administrations, as promised. It returns them solely to the UK government and Parliament, and imposes new restrictions on the Scottish Parliament and [the Welsh Parliament].[4]

The Scottish and Welsh governments entered into discussions with the UK government to agree an alternative.

The House of Commons Public Administration and Constitutional Affairs Committee took evidence on clause 11. In its report,[5] it noted that the clause had been 'the focus of some concern and controversy' and described the debate around it as raising 'fundamental principles about how the relationships between central and devolved government in the UK will be conducted'.

19.3 SEWEL CONVENTION

The European Union (Withdrawal) Bill engaged the Sewel Convention. Under the Sewel Convention, the UK Parliament 'will not normally' legislate on matters within the devolved competence of a devolved legislature without its consent. The consent is given in the form of a legislative consent motion. In September 2017, the First Minister of Wales and the First Minister of Scotland wrote to the Prime Minister to propose amendments to clause 11. The letter said that if the amendments were made, they could consider recommending the Bill to the Scottish Parliament and the Welsh Parliament for their legislative consent.

19.4 CONTINUITY BILLS

The proposed amendments to clause 11 of the European Union (Withdrawal) Bill which were submitted by the Scottish government and the Welsh government to the Prime Minister were defeated in the House of Commons. In February 2018, the Scottish government introduced the UK Withdrawal from the European Union (Legal Continuity) (Scotland) Bill (the 'Scottish Continuity Bill') in the Scottish Parliament and the Welsh government introduced the Law Derived from the European Union (Wales) Bill in the Welsh Parliament (the 'Welsh Continuity Bill').

---

4 Joint Statement from First Ministers of Wales and Scotland in reaction to the EU (Withdrawal) Bill, 13 July 2017, at: **https://gov.wales/joint-statement-first-ministers-wales-and-scotland-reaction-eu-withdrawal-bill** (accessed 10 November 2020).

5 *Devolution and Exiting the EU and Clause 11 of the European Union (Withdrawal) Bill: Issues for Consideration* (HC 2017–19, 484).

These Continuity Bills served a similar purpose to the European Union (Withdrawal) Bill but in relation to matters falling within devolved competence. The Scottish government described the Scottish Continuity Bill as 'contingency planning'. It was intended to fill the gaps which would otherwise be left if consent was not given by the Scottish Parliament to the European Union (Withdrawal) Bill for matters falling within devolved competence. This was on the assumption that matters in devolved areas would be removed from the European Union (Withdrawal) Bill if the Scottish Parliament did not give its consent.

The Scottish Continuity Bill was passed on 21 March 2018. It differed from the European Union (Withdrawal) Bill on some matters of substance. For example, it did not exclude the Charter of Fundamental Rights from becoming part of retained EU law in Scotland. Notably, s.17 required Scottish Ministers to consent to an amendment or repeal of retained EU law by UK Ministers in a devolved area.

In April 2018, the Attorney General and the Advocate General for Scotland made a reference to the Supreme Court under s.33 of the Scotland Act 1998 to establish whether the Scottish Parliament had power to legislate for the continuity of laws relating to devolved matters in Scotland which were the subject of EU law while the UK was a Member State.

In December 2018, the Supreme Court held that the Scottish Continuity Bill as a whole would not be outside the legislative competence of the Scottish Parliament. However, s.17 would be outside the competence of the Scottish Parliament because it would modify the Scotland Act 1998.[6]

The Attorney General also made a reference to the Supreme Court in relation to the Welsh Continuity Bill under s.112(1) of GOWA 2006 but this was withdrawn after agreement was reached with the Welsh government on amendments to clause 11.

In May 2018, the Welsh Parliament approved a motion to consent to the European Union (Withdrawal) Bill but the Scottish Parliament passed a motion not to consent to it. The European Union (Withdrawal) Bill was nevertheless passed in June 2018 with the inclusion of provisions relating to devolved matters. This was the first time the Sewel Convention had not been followed by Parliament.

19.5 RETAINING EU RESTRICTIONS IN DEVOLUTION LEGISLATION

In April 2018, the government had tabled amendments to clause 11 which became EUWA 2018, s.12. At the same time, it published an intergovernmental agreement between the UK and Welsh governments setting out commitments as to how the provisions would work if the amendments were adopted.

EUWA 2018, s.12 removes the requirement on the devolved legislatures not to legislate or act in a way which is incompatible with EU law. It replaces it with a provision that the devolved legislatures cannot modify retained EU law if the modification has been specified in regulations made by a Minister of the Crown (a

6 *Re UK Withdrawal from the European Union (Legal Continuity) (Scotland) Bill* [2018] UKSC 64.

so-called 'freezing power'). In other words, the default position is that the devolved legislatures can act unless 'freezing regulations' are in force.

Before exercising the freezing power, a Minister of the Crown must seek agreement from the relevant devolved government. The draft regulations have to be published and the devolved legislatures have to be given 40 days in which to give consent. Only then can the draft regulations be laid before Parliament. If consent is not given, a minister may go ahead with laying the regulations but must make a statement as to why they are proceeding without consent.

The freezing power expires two years after IPCD. Regulations made under the power expire five years after they come into force. A minister must lay a report before Parliament every three months on the use of the s.12 freezing powers and on matters relating to the common frameworks.[7]

19.6 COMMON FRAMEWORKS

In 2017, the UK, Scottish and Welsh governments agreed that a mechanism would be needed to manage the policy divergence that might occur between different parts of the UK in areas previously covered by EU law. In October 2017, representatives of the UK government and the devolved governments met within the Joint Ministerial Committee on European Negotiations.[8] The Committee issued a communiqué which set out the following agreement on the domestic 'common frameworks' that would replace the outgoing EU framework:

> As the UK leaves the European Union, the Government of the United Kingdom and the devolved administrations agree to work together to establish common approaches in some areas that are currently governed by EU law, but that are otherwise within areas of competence of the devolved administrations or legislatures. A framework will set out a common UK, or GB, approach and how it will be operated and governed. This may consist of common goals, minimum or maximum standards, harmonisation, limits on action, or mutual recognition, depending on the policy area and the objectives being pursued. Frameworks may be implemented by legislation, by executive action, by memorandums of understanding, or by other means depending on the context in which the framework is intended to operate.

The communiqué also set out the principles that would apply to these 'common frameworks'. For example, it was agreed that:

> Common frameworks will be established where they are necessary in order to:
>
> - enable the functioning of the UK internal market, while acknowledging policy divergence;

---

[7] EUWA 2018, Sched.3, para.4.

[8] The Joint Ministerial Committee on European Negotiations (JMC(EN)) is a sub-committee of the Joint Ministerial Committee which was set up to provide central coordination of relations between the UK government and the devolved governments. JMC(EN) is attended by Ministers from the UK and devolved governments. In the absence of a Northern Ireland Executive, a senior civil servant from the Northern Ireland Civil Service would attend.

- ensure compliance with international obligations;
- ensure the UK can negotiate, enter into and implement new trade agreements and international treaties;
- enable the management of common resources;
- administer and provide access to justice in cases with a cross-border element;
- safeguard the security of the UK.

In March 2018, the UK government published the first iteration of the common frameworks analysis, which set out 153 areas where EU law intersected with devolved competence, including 24 areas where legislation may be needed in whole or in part, 82 areas where non-legislative frameworks may be required and 49 areas where no further action was identified. Work to develop future common frameworks is ongoing.

19.7 CORRESPONDING POWERS

The devolved authorities have powers to correct deficiencies arising from withdrawal in areas within devolved competence[9] which correspond to those which a Minister of the Crown has under EUWA 2018, s.8. These powers can be used by a devolved authority acting alone or jointly with a Minister of the Crown. They also have powers to make provision in connection with the implementation period in areas of devolved competence.[10]

19.8 NORTH–SOUTH CO-OPERATION

EUWA 2018, s.10(1) requires a Minister of the Crown or a devolved authority to exercise any powers under EUWA 2018 compatibly with NIA 1998 and with due regard to the joint report from the negotiators of the EU and the UK government on progress during phase 1 of negotiations under the TEU, Art.50.

Section 10(2) relates to the use of the s.8 deficiencies-correcting power and the power in s.23 to make consequential and transitional provisions. These powers cannot be used to diminish North–South co-operation provided for in the Belfast Agreement. Neither can they be used to create or facilitate border arrangements between Northern Ireland and the Republic of Ireland which feature physical infrastructure that did not exist before IPCD and are not in accordance with an agreement between the UK and the EU.

---

9 EUWA 2018, s.11 and Sched.2.

10 EUWA 2018, Sched.2, Part 1A.

CHAPTER 20

European Union (Withdrawal Agreement) Act 2020

20.1 OVERVIEW

The European Union (Withdrawal Agreement) Act 2020 implements the Withdrawal Agreement. Implementation of the Withdrawal Agreement requires amendments to EUWA 2018. This chapter explains the most relevant amendments.

20.2 TRANSITION OR IMPLEMENTATION PERIOD

The UK ceased to be a Member State on 31 January 2020. The TEU and TFEU ceased to apply to it in international law and as a matter of EU law. In domestic law, the European Communities Act 1972 was repealed on exit day by EUWA 2018, s.1. This brought an end to the domestic arrangements for giving effect to EU law in the UK. However, the creation of an implementation period[1] by Part 4 of the Withdrawal Agreement (headed 'Transition')[2] meant that EU law still needed to apply in the UK for a temporary period after exit day. EU(WA)A 2020, Part 1 (ss.1–4) made the changes that were necessary to EUWA 2018 to give effect to the implementation period.

20.2.1 Section 1: Saving of ECA 1972 for implementation period

EU(WA)A 2020, s.1 inserts a new s.1A into EUWA 2018. It saves ECA 1972 but in a modified form so that it gives effect to EU law to the extent required by the Withdrawal Agreement, Part 4. The technical way in which this is achieved is by 'reviving' ECA 1972 so that it has effect as if the Withdrawal Agreement, Part 4 (other than as it relates to the Common Foreign and Security Policy) was included in the definition of 'Treaties' and 'EU Treaties' in ECA 1972, s.1 (see **13.5**). As ECA

[1] The features of the implementation period are explained at **10.3**. The terms 'transition period' and 'implementation period' can be used interchangeably. EU(WA)A 2020 uses the term 'implementation period' whereas the Withdrawal Agreement uses 'transition period' after the concept is first introduced in Art.126 as the 'transition or implementation period'.

[2] The Withdrawal Agreement refers to 'Part Four'. EU(WA)A 2020 refers to 'Part 4'.

1972 was drafted in the context of the UK's membership of the EU, EU(WA)A 2020, s.1 makes a number of modifications so that ECA 1972 works in the context of the transition period when the UK is no longer an EU member. The Explanatory Notes describe this as 'repurposing' ECA 1972. This 'repurposing' continues until IPCD. IPCD is defined as 11.00 p.m. on 31 December 2020.

20.2.2 Section 2: Additional saving for implementation period

EU(WA)A 2020, s.2 inserts a new s.1B into EUWA 2018. It provides that EU-derived domestic legislation continues to have effect in domestic law on and after exit day for the duration of the implementation period. This was necessary to ensure that the effect of EU-derived legislation was preserved despite the repeal of ECA 1972. The concept of EU-derived domestic legislation is explained in **Chapter 11**. In essence, it is domestic legislation which was made to give effect to EU obligations. EU(WA)A 2020, s.2 also introduces a series of what the Explanatory Notes refer to as 'glosses' so that terms in EU-derived domestic legislation which are linked to EU membership are to be read in a way that makes sense in the context of the implementation period. For example, any reference in EU-derived domestic legislation to the 'area of the EU' is to be read as if it included the UK. This 'glossing mechanism' applied for the duration of the implementation period. This was necessary to ensure that EU-related references continued to operate properly despite the UK no longer being a Member State.

20.2.3 Section 3: Supplementary power in connection with implementation period

EU(WA)A 2020, s.3 inserts a new s.8A into EUWA 2018. The section contains a power for ministers to make technical modifications to supplement the glosses and make other corrections if the glosses do not work. There is a corresponding power for devolved authorities in s.4.

20.3 IMPLEMENTATION OF THE WITHDRAWAL AGREEMENT

The main purpose of EU(WA)A 2020 is to implement the Withdrawal Agreement. When the European Union (Withdrawal) Bill was introduced in Parliament in July 2017, negotiations on the Withdrawal Agreement had only just got underway. The Bill contained a broad power for ministers to make secondary legislation to implement a withdrawal agreement but otherwise it did not take account of a withdrawal agreement. The Bill focused on preparing the domestic statute book for the day the UK left the EU. At the time of introduction, there was no agreement between the UK and the EU that there would be an implementation/transition period.

The text of the Withdrawal Agreement was agreed by the UK and EU after EUWA 2018 had received Royal Assent. The Withdrawal Agreement sets out the terms of the UK's withdrawal from the EU. It imposes rights and obligations on the UK and the EU.

The Withdrawal Agreement binds the UK and the EU in international law. It does not automatically have effect in domestic law. This is because the UK is a dualist system. This means that rights and obligations which are created by treaties and which exist, and are binding, on the international plane do not have effect in domestic law unless domestic legislation is made to give effect to them.

In order to make sure that the UK was in a position to meet the obligations it had undertaken on the international plane and to give individuals the benefits of the rights bestowed on them by the Withdrawal Agreement, it was necessary to pass an Act of Parliament to implement the Withdrawal Agreement domestically. The European Union (Withdrawal Agreement) Bill was introduced in Parliament for this purpose.

In order to give effect to what had been agreed in the Withdrawal Agreement, EU(WA)A 2020 had to make a number of changes to the framework set up by EUWA 2018.

20.3.1 Section 5: General implementation of remainder of withdrawal agreement

EU(WA)A 2020, s.5 inserts a new s.7A into EUWA 2018. This new s.7A gives effect to the Withdrawal Agreement, Art.4. That article requires that the provisions of the Withdrawal Agreement and the EU law made applicable by it are to have the same legal effect in the UK as they have in the EU and its Member States and that individuals and legal persons must be able to rely on rights in the Withdrawal Agreement which meet the conditions for having direct effect (i.e. the principles of supremacy and direct effect apply). Article 4 also requires that UK courts disapply domestic law which is inconsistent or incompatible with the Withdrawal Agreement. It further requires that provisions of the Withdrawal Agreement referring to EU law must be interpreted in accordance with CJEU case law made before the end of the transition period. The UK's courts and administrative authorities are also required to have due regard to the relevant case law of the CJEU handed down after the end of the transition period when interpreting and applying the Withdrawal Agreement.

The new s.7A is drafted in a similar way to ECA 1972, s.2(1). It creates a conduit pipe into domestic law for rights and obligations arising under the Withdrawal Agreement so they apply without the need for any further domestic implementing legislation. It also provides that all domestic law (including provisions of EUWA 2018) is to be read and have effect subject to the rights and obligations arising under the Withdrawal Agreement.

20.3.2 Section 6: General implementation of related EEA EFTA and Swiss agreements

EU(WA)A 2020, s.6 inserts a new s.7B into EUWA 2018. This new section gives effect to the EEA EFTA Separation Agreement and the Swiss Citizens' Rights Agreement[3] in the same way as EUWA 2018, s.7A does for the Withdrawal Agreement, by creating a conduit pipe and providing that all enactments are to be read and have effect subject to the two Agreements. The terms of the Withdrawal Agreement, however, take precedence over the EEA EFTA Separation Agreement and the Swiss Citizens' Rights Agreement in the event of incompatibility. There is no provision in the EEA EFTA Separation Agreement or the Swiss Citizens' Rights Agreement requiring them to be implemented in this way. The Explanatory Notes say that it was done to ensure consistency with the way the Withdrawal Agreement was implemented.

20.3.3 Part 3: Citizens' rights

Certain provisions in the Withdrawal Agreement relating to citizens' rights require additional implementation beyond EUWA 2018, s.7A on general implementation of the Withdrawal Agreement. EU(WA)A 2020, Part 3 (ss.7–17) deals with the implementation of these provisions.

20.4 OTHER SUBJECT AREAS

20.4.1 Section 18: Main power in connection with other separation issues

EU(WA)A 2020, s.18 inserts s.8B into EUWA 2018. It gives a Minister of the Crown the power to make regulations to implement the Withdrawal Agreement, Part 3 which deals with other separation issues, for example arrangements for completing police and judicial co-operation in criminal matters which is ongoing at the end of the transition period.

20.4.2 Section 21: Main power in connection with Ireland/Northern Ireland Protocol

EU(WA)A 2020, s.21 inserts s.8C into EUWA 2018. It gives a Minister of the Crown the power to make regulations to implement obligations in the Ireland/ Northern Ireland Protocol beyond what is covered by EUWA 2018, s.7A on general implementation of the Withdrawal Agreement. Section 22 contains corresponding powers for devolved authorities.

---

[3] These terms have the meaning given in EU(WA)A 2020, s.39(1).

20.5 RELATIONSHIP TO EUWA 2018

20.5.1 Section 25: Retention of saved EU law at end of implementation period

EU(WA)A 2020, s.25 amends EUWA 2018, ss.2–5 so that retained EU law comes into being from IPCD instead of exit day and the exclusions in EUWA 2018, s.5 and Sched.1 take effect from IPCD.[4] EU(WA)A 2020, s.25 also inserts a new s.5A into EUWA 2018. Its purpose is to make clear that the temporary status of EU law during the implementation period does not prevent it from having effect at the end of that period as retained EU law.

20.5.2 Section 26: Interpretation of retained EU law and relevant separation agreement law

EU(WA)A 2020, s.26 amends EUWA 2018, s.6 (Interpretation of retained EU law). The changes are discussed in **Chapter 15**. EU(WA)A 2020, s.26 also inserts a new s.7C into EUWA 2018 on the interpretation of 'relevant separation agreement law'. 'Relevant separation agreement law' comprises: EUWA 2018, ss.7A, 7B and 7C; the provisions of the Withdrawal Agreement, EEA EFTA Separation Agreement and Swiss Citizens' Rights Agreement which come through the conduit pipes in ss.7A and 7B; the domestic law made to implement the parts of the Withdrawal Agreement on citizens' rights and other separation issues and the Ireland/Northern Ireland Protocol; the domestic law made to implement the part of the EEA EFTA Separation Agreement on other separation issues; the domestic law made to implement citizens' rights provisions of the EEA EFTA Separation Agreement and the Swiss Citizens' Rights Agreement; EU(WA)A 2020, s.20 (financial provision); and anything else which is domestic law for the purposes of, or otherwise within the scope of, the Withdrawal Agreement (other than Part 4), EEA EFTA Agreement or Swiss Citizens' Rights Agreement.

A question as to the validity, meaning or effect of relevant separation agreement law is to be decided in accordance with the Withdrawal Agreement, EEA EFTA Separation Agreement and Swiss Citizens' Rights Agreement and regard is to be had to ensuring consistency of interpretation where the Agreements contain similar provisions.

In terms of the relationship between retained EU law and relevant separation agreement law, EUWA 2018, s.6(6A) makes clear that the rules for interpreting retained EU law in s.6 are subject to relevant separation agreement law. EUWA 2018, s.5 and Sched.1 are also expressed to be subject to relevant separation agreement law. See also **20.3.1**.

---

[4] Other relevant changes made by s.25 are addressed in **Chapters 11–14**.

20.5.3 Section 27: Dealing with deficiencies in retained EU law

EU(WA)A 2020, s.27 amends EUWA 2018, s.8 (Dealing with deficiencies arising from withdrawal) to extend the power to correct deficiencies so that it can be used to correct deficiencies that result from the end of the implementation period or any other effect of the Withdrawal Agreement.

20.6 OTHER MATTERS

20.6.1 Section 33: Prohibition on extending implementation period

Under the Withdrawal Agreement, Art.132, the UK and EU had the option, before 1 July 2020, to agree to extend the implementation period beyond 31 December 2020 for up to two years. EU(WA)A 2020, s.33 inserted a new s.15A into EUWA 2018 which prevented a UK minister from agreeing to such an extension.

20.6.2 Section 36: Repeal of unnecessary or spent enactments

This section repeals, among other things, the following provisions of EUWA 2018 which are unnecessary or spent:

- s.9 (implementing the Withdrawal Agreement);
- s.16 (maintenance of environmental principles etc.);
- s.18 (customs arrangement as part of the framework for the future partnership);
- s.19 (future interaction with the law and agencies of the EU);
- Sched.2, Part 2 (implementing the Withdrawal Agreement).

20.7 SECTION 38: PARLIAMENTARY SOVEREIGNTY

This section reiterates the principle of parliamentary sovereignty. It recognises that Parliament is sovereign and says that nothing in EU(WA)A 2020 derogates from the sovereignty of Parliament. It states expressly that sovereignty subsists despite the direct applicability of the Withdrawal Agreement, EEA EFTA Separation Agreement and Swiss Citizens' Rights Agreement.

20.8 SCHEDULE 5: CONSEQUENTIAL AND TRANSITIONAL PROVISION ETC.

EUWA 2018 as enacted did not take account of a withdrawal agreement or an implementation period (other than to include a broad power for ministers to implement a withdrawal agreement, a provision which was later repealed). It envisaged that EU law would cease to apply on exit day. A large volume of subordinate legislation which was made to prepare for departure on this basis (in particular subordinate legislation made under EUWA 2018, s.8 deficiencies-correcting power) was accordingly made with exit day as the coming into force date. With the advent of the implementation period, however, these changes were not required until IPCD. Schedule 5, para.1(1) defers the coming into force of this body of subordinate legislation until IPCD. There is provision for exceptions to be made.

APPENDIX A

Direct effect after IPCD

Table A.1 assesses the potential to argue in UK domestic courts that certain aspects of retained EU law have direct effect and can therefore be used to disapply inconsistent provisions of pre-IPCD domestic law.

Table A.1 Direct effect after IPCD[1]

Type of instrument*	Argument about direct effect possible if no existing case law on this point	Argument possible if existing case law on this point	Arguable that the provision has vertical direct effect (i.e. argument against the state)?	Arguable that the provision has horizontal direct effect (i.e. argument in private dispute)?
Treaty[2] article	✓	✓	✓	✓[3]
Charter of Fundamental Rights[4]	X	X	X	X
General principles of EU law[5]	X	X	X	X
EU Regulation	✓	✓	✓	✓

1 For an analysis of direct effect before IPCD see Table 5.1.

2 But see also **13.5** and the difference between the approach in relation to the TEU and TFEU and other international agreements. To determine whether a right in an international agreement has direct effect, the CJEU considers not only whether the provisions are unconditional and sufficiently precise but also whether or not the 'nature and broad logic' of the international agreement precludes direct effect.

3 Note that not all treaty provisions in the TFEU have been successfully invoked horizontally. For example, the TFEU, Arts.34 and 35 are considered not to have horizontal direct effect. See Costa, M. and Peers, S. (2020) *Steiner & Woods EU Law* (14th edn: OUP) at 5.2.3 on p.115.

4 It is important to note that this is subject to transitional provisions (see **Appendix C**). The removal of the Charter from domestic law does not mean that the case law which refers to the Charter no longer applies. Instead, the references in the case law are to be read as if they refer to the source of the right rather than the Charter. See **14.4**.

5 Note that this is subject to transitional provisions (see **Appendix C**).

Type of instrument*	Argument about direct effect possible if no existing case law on this point	Argument possible if existing case law on this point	Arguable that the provision has vertical direct effect (i.e. argument against the state)?	Arguable that the provision has horizontal direct effect (i.e. argument in private dispute)?
EU Directive	X – but scope for argument on the breadth of the 'of a kind' test (see **13.6**)[6]	✓ – but must pass 'of a kind' test (see **13.6**)	✓ – if 'of a kind' test satisfied (see **13.6**)	X
EU Decision[7]	✓	✓	✓	X

* The analysis is the same for regulations, directives or decisions which are tertiary legislation as for secondary legislation.

It is unclear what would happen after IPCD in a case such as *Franz Grad* where the CJEU held that direct effect stemmed from the combined effect of a treaty article, a directive and a decision.[8]

[6] Note, however, that the position is nuanced. EUWA 2018, s.4(2)(b) prevents directly effective rights which arise from an EU directive from being converted into domestic law unless they are 'of a kind' recognised by the CJEU or a UK court before IPCD. However, it is not clear how widely the courts will interpret the words 'of a kind' and it may be that cases in a different context but which are analogous to the case before the court will be deemed to be 'of a kind' recognised before IPCD. See **13.6**.

[7] This is a reference to a decision under the TFEU, Art.288. Decisions under former Art.34(2)(c) of the TEU as it applied before the Lisbon Treaty did not have direct effect.

[8] Case 9/70 *Franz Grad* v. *Finanzamt Traunstein*, EU:C:1970:78.

APPENDIX B

Continued influence of the architecture of ECA 1972 during the transition period and after IPCD

The repeal of the European Communities Act (ECA) 1972 reflects the end of the UK's membership of the European Union.[1]

However, the architecture of ECA 1972 has influenced the design of the post-exit domestic framework. Drafting based on the provisions in ECA 1972 is used:

- during the transition period, in order to comply with the Withdrawal Agreement and to give effect to EU law;
- after the transition period, in order to provide the continuity which is a central aim of retained EU law;
- after the transition period, to give effect to the provisions of the Withdrawal Agreement which come into effect at that point.

Table B.1 illustrates how the drafting in ECA 1972 is woven through each of these 'phases' in the UK legal system. It traces the evolution of the wording in ECA 1972, s.2(1).

[1] The end of the UK's membership of the EU was not brought about by the repeal of ECA 1972 itself. The end of the UK's EU membership took place at the international level, with the completion of the process under the TEU, Art.50, in particular Art.50(3) which states: 'The Treaties shall cease to apply to the State in question from the date of entry into force of the withdrawal agreement.'

Table B.1 The drafting in ECA 1972, s.2(1) through the different 'phases' of EU law in the UK legal system

During EU membership (ECA 1972, s.2(1))	During the transition period (s.1A: Saving for ECA 1972 for implementation period)	After the transition period, as part of retained EU law (s.4: Saving for rights etc. under section 2(1) of ECA 1972)	After the transition period, to give effect to provisions of the Withdrawal Agreement (s.7A: General implementation of remainder of withdrawal agreement)
All such rights, powers, liabilities, obligations and restrictions from time to time created or arising by or under the Treaties, and all such remedies and procedures from time to time provided for by or under the Treaties, as in accordance with the Treaties are without further enactment to be given legal effect or used in the United Kingdom shall be recognised and available in law, and be enforced, allowed and followed accordingly; and the expression 'enforceable EU right' and similar expressions shall be read as referring to one to which this subsection applies.	All such rights, powers, liabilities, obligations and restrictions from time to time created or arising by or under the Treaties, and all such remedies and procedures from time to time provided for by or under the Treaties, as in accordance with the Treaties are without further enactment to be given legal effect or used in the United Kingdom shall be recognised and available in law, and be enforced, allowed and followed accordingly; and the expression 'enforceable EU right' and similar expressions shall be read as referring to one to which this subsection applies.	(1) Any rights, powers, liabilities, obligations, restrictions, remedies and procedures which, immediately before IP completion day – (a) are recognised and available in domestic law by virtue of section 2(1) of the European Communities Act 1972, and (b) are enforced, allowed and followed accordingly, continue on and after IP completion day to be recognised and available in domestic law (and to be enforced, allowed and followed accordingly).	(1) Subsection (2) applies to – (a) all such rights, powers, liabilities, obligations and restrictions from time to time created or arising by or under the withdrawal agreement, and (b) all such remedies and procedures from time to time provided for by or under the withdrawal agreement, as in accordance with the withdrawal agreement are without further enactment to be given legal effect or used in the United Kingdom. (2) The rights, powers, liabilities, obligations, restrictions, remedies and procedures concerned are to be – (a) recognised and available in domestic law, and (b) enforced, allowed and followed accordingly.

APPENDIX C

Specific transitional, transitory and saving provision[1]

Table C.1

Category of exception	Effect on pre-IPCD decisions by courts or tribunals[2]	Effect on proceedings begun, but not finally decided, before a court or tribunal in the UK before IPCD[3]	Effect on conduct which occurred before IPCD and gave rise to criminal liability[4]
Removal of challenges to retained EU law on the basis that the EU instrument was invalid[5]	No effect. Cases which have been decided should not be undone or reopened	SI 2019/673 enables challenges where the challenge is based on the grounds set out in the TFEU, Art.263[6] and relates to proceedings begun but not finally decided in a court or tribunal in the UK before IPCD[7]	No effect. A defendant who was prosecuted after IPCD for behaviour taking place before IPCD would still be able to rely on a defence which applied before IPCD

1 It will be important to check the current position on these matters because this is an area where more regulations may be made. Note also that these provisions are subject to relevant separation agreement law (see EUWA 2018, s.7C). For general transitional provisions, see **18.3**.
2 See EUWA 2018, Sched.8, para.39(2).
3 See EUWA 2018, Sched.8, para.39(3).
4 See EUWA 2018, Sched.8, para.39(4).
5 See EUWA 2018, Sched.1, para.1.
6 The grounds under Art.263 are lack of competence, infringement of an essential procedural requirement, infringement of the EU Treaties or any rule of law relating to their application or misuse of powers.
7 See also the discussion on Sched.1 in relation to the interaction of SI 2019/673 with the Withdrawal Agreement at **14.6.3**.

Category of exception	Effect on pre-IPCD decisions by courts or tribunals[2]	Effect on proceedings begun, but not finally decided, before a court or tribunal in the UK before IPCD[3]	Effect on conduct which occurred before IPCD and gave rise to criminal liability[4]
Removal of the Charter of Fundamental Rights in domestic law[8]	No effect. Cases which have been decided should not be undone or reopened	Cases which rely on the Charter can proceed to conclusion	No transitional/saving provision for this situation. The position as set out in para.39(1) therefore applies. Removal of the Charter of Fundamental Rights in this context therefore applies to matters which occurred before IPCD as well as after IPCD[9]
Removal of the right of action to base a claim on a failure to comply with the general principles of EU law[10]	No effect. Cases which have been decided should not be undone or reopened	Challenges brought on the basis of the general principles can proceed to conclusion. Courts or tribunals can continue to disapply or quash any enactment or other rule of law or quash any conduct or otherwise decide that it is unlawful because it is incompatible with the general principles of EU law	No effect. A defendant who was prosecuted after IPCD for behaviour taking place before IPCD would still be able to rely on a defence which applied before IPCD
Removal of the right to *Francovich* damages[11]	No effect. Cases which have been decided should not be undone or reopened	The right to *Francovich* damages is preserved for these cases	No effect. A defendant who was prosecuted after IPCD for behaviour taking place before IPCD would still be able to rely on a defence which applied before IPCD

8 See EUWA 2018, s.5(4).

9 One example of an area where it might be thought that this would make a difference is in the context of the Charter, Art.50 (right not to be tried or punished twice in criminal proceedings for the same criminal offence). However, see **Appendix D**. It appears that the sources of the Charter right will not provide enforceable rights for individuals after IPCD. However, other sources of law may provide equivalent protections.

10 See EUWA 2018, Sched.1, para.3.

11 See EUWA 2018, Sched.1, para.4.

There are further specific provisions, as follows:

1. **Challenges based on the general principles/ability of courts, etc. to quash conduct, etc. on the basis of a breach of the general principles:**[12]

These cases can continue to be brought[13] provided the proceedings:

- are brought within three years beginning with IPCD
- involve a challenge to anything which occurred before IPCD, and
- involve a challenge that is not for:
  - the disapplication/quashing of an Act of Parliament or a rule of law which is not an enactment, or
  - anything required by, enforcing or giving effect to an Act of Parliament.[14]

2. **Ongoing effect of case law related to the general principles**[15]

A court or tribunal or public body will be able to disapply an enactment/quash conduct, etc. on the basis of a breach of the general principles where a decision is taken after IPCD which is a necessary consequence of any decision of a court or tribunal taken before IPCD, or where that decision is made after IPCD as a result of the transitional provisions in EUWA 2018, Sched.8, para.39. This provision preserves the effect of court decisions made before IPCD.

So where a court disapplied domestic law on the basis that it breached one of the general principles, or where a court did so after IPCD in a case brought within three years beginning with IPCD (see point 1 above[16]), the disapplication of the provision of domestic law would still apply for cases arising after IPCD. An example of where this provision might apply is in cases which are analogous to the facts in *Walker*.[17] So in a case after IPCD another couple could rely on the disapplication of the relevant provisions of the Equality Act 2010 on the basis that they conflict with the general principle of non-discrimination.

3. ***Francovich* damages**[18]

Claims for *Francovich* damages will be capable of being brought after IPCD provided that they are begun within the period of two years beginning with IPCD, where they relate to matters occurring before IPCD.

4. **Direct effect of directives**

The restriction in EUWA 2018, s.4(2)(b) in relation to reliance on the direct effect of directives after IPCD does not apply where the case in question has been commenced before IPCD but is decided on or after IPCD (see Sched.8, para.38). See further **Chapter 13**.

---

[12] See EUWA 2018, Sched.1, para.3.

[13] See EUWA 2018, Sched.8, para.39(5).

[14] In other words, the challenge can be related to secondary legislation or administrative acts. This mirrors the position relating to challenges under HRA 1998. Courts cannot disapply primary legislation under HRA 1998. Instead, primary legislation which breaches HRA 1998 is subject to a declaration of incompatibility (see HRA 1998, s.4). It is not clear how these provisions relate to the differences between retained direct principal EU legislation as compared with retained direct minor EU legislation. See **Chapter 16**.

[15] See EUWA 2018, Sched.8, para.39(6).

[16] In other words, in a challenge brought under EUWA 2018, Sched.8, para.39(5).

[17] *Walker (Appellant)* v. *Innospec Ltd and others (Respondents)* [2017] UKSC 47.

[18] See EUWA 2018, Sched.8, para.39(7).

APPENDIX D

Charter of Fundamental Rights: right-by-right analysis

This table brings together a number of sources including:

- the text of the articles of the Charter;
- the Charter Explanations;
- the government's[1] *Charter of Fundamental Rights of the EU: Right by Right Analysis* of 5 December 2017;
- the Joint Committee on Human Rights'[2] report: *The EU (Withdrawal) Bill: A Right by Right Analysis*;[3] and
- further commentary and analysis.

The table is not intended as a comprehensive analysis. Instead, it aims to give an overview of the relevant rights and to illustrate the complexities which arise as a result of EUWA 2018, s.5(4) and (5) which remove the Charter from domestic law after IPCD. It should be read in conjunction with the commentary in **Chapter 7** on fundamental rights and **Chapter 14** on the exceptions to the saving and incorporation of EU law. Note that the removal of the Charter from domestic law is subject to relevant separation agreement law (see **Chapter 20**).

[1] Note that in this table the government refers to the government in office in 2017.

[2] In this table the Joint Committee on Human Rights is referred to as 'JCHR'.

[3] JCHR, Legislative Scrutiny: *The EU (Withdrawal) Bill: A Right by Right Analysis* (HL HC 2017–19, HL Paper 70, HC 774).

Table D.1

Article	Text of Charter article	Source	Analysis	Basis for claim after IPCD?
Title 1 – Dignity				
Article 1 Human dignity	Human dignity is inviolable. It must be respected and protected	Universal Declaration of Human Rights 1948 General principle of EU law[1]	The Universal Declaration is not a legally binding treaty and does not confer rights on individuals[2] General principles cannot be enforced in UK courts after IPCD[3] Right to human dignity is not a distinct right under the ECHR[4] However, it is arguable that in cases concerning the prohibition of inhuman and degrading treatment, the right under Art.1 does not lead to a different answer from that under the Charter, Art.4 and the ECHR, Art.3[5]	There is no basis for a claim under Art.1 The general principles of EU law cannot be used as the basis for a claim The ECHR, Art.3 as implemented under HRA 1998 may be available as the basis for a claim, but the remedies under HRA 1998 are weaker than for claims under EU law because the courts cannot disapply domestic primary legislation or retained direct principal EU legislation for HRA 1998 claims
Article 2 Right to life	1. Everyone has the right to life 2. No one shall be condemned to the death penalty, or executed	ECHR, Art.2(1) (right to life)[6] ECHR, Protocol 6, Art.1 (abolition of the death penalty)[7]	The ECHR, Art.2 implemented through HRA 1998 Protocol 6, Art.1 is not implemented in domestic law through HRA 1998[8] Protections exist in common law and domestic legislation[9]	The ECHR, Art.2 as implemented under HRA 1998 may be available as the basis for a claim, but the remedies under HRA 1998 are weaker than for claims under EU law because the courts cannot disapply domestic primary legislation or retained direct principal EU legislation for HRA 1998 claims The right is enforceable to the extent that it is protected in common law and domestic legislation

Article	Text of Charter article	Source	Analysis	Basis for claim after IPCD?
Article 3 Right to integrity of the person	1. Everyone has the right to respect for his or her physical and mental integrity 2. In the fields of medicine and biology, the following must be respected in particular: • the free and informed consent of the person concerned, according to the procedures laid down by law • the prohibition of eugenic practices, in particular those aiming at the selection of persons • the prohibition on making the human body and its parts as such a source of financial gain • the prohibition of the reproductive cloning of human beings	General principle of EU law[10] Convention on Human Rights and Biomedicine adopted by the Council of Europe[11] ECHR, Art.8 (right to respect for private and family life)[12] Statute of the International Criminal Court, Art.7(1)(g)[13]	The ECHR, Art.8 is not cited as a source of this right in the Charter Explanations and is not equivalent to Art.3[14] The Convention on Human Rights and Biomedicine has not been signed or ratified by the UK and confers no rights on individuals in domestic law[15] The Statute of the International Criminal Court, Art.7(1)(g) has been implemented in domestic law (International Criminal Court Act 2001) but does not confer rights on individuals[16] The government states that domestic legislation which is relevant to the rights and principles set out in Art.3 will continue to form part of UK law after IPCD.[17] However, the JCHR considers that the domestic legislation cited by the government does not clearly confer rights on individuals (as opposed to prohibiting specific actions)[18] General principles cannot be enforced in UK courts after IPCD[19]	It is not clear whether the sources of this right are enforceable after IPCD The general principles of EU law cannot be used as the basis for a claim The government cites the ECHR, Art.8 as the source of this right. HRA 1998 will be capable of being used as the basis for a claim after IPCD; however, the JCHR does not consider that ECHR, Art.8 and the Charter, Art.3 are equivalent

Article	Text of Charter article	Source	Analysis	Basis for claim after IPCD?
Article 4 Prohibition of torture and inhuman or degrading treatment or punishment	No one shall be subjected to torture or to inhuman or degrading treatment or punishment	ECHR, Art.3[20]	The scope of the ECHR, Art.3, implemented through HRA 1998, is the same as the Charter The government states that the rights under the Charter, Art.4 will continue to be protected through HRA 1998. The government also points to domestic legislation which prohibits torture and inhuman or degrading treatment[21]	The ECHR, Art.3 as implemented under HRA 1998 may be available as the basis for a claim, but the remedies under HRA 1998 are weaker than for claims under EU law because the courts cannot disapply domestic primary legislation or retained direct principal EU legislation for HRA 1998 claims
Article 5 Prohibition of slavery and forced labour	1. No one shall be held in slavery or servitude 2. No one shall be required to perform forced or compulsory labour 3. Trafficking in human beings is prohibited	Art.5(1) and (2) correspond to ECHR, Art.4(1) and (2) (prohibition of slavery and forced labour)[22] Regulation 2016/794 on Europol[23] Chapter VI of the Convention implementing the Schengen Agreement Directive 2011/36/EU on preventing and combating trafficking in human beings[24] International Labour Organization (ILO) Fundamental Conventions[25]	The scope of the ECHR, Art.4, implemented through HRA 1998 , is the same as the Charter The government cites domestic legislation which aims to tackle human trafficking such as the Modern Slavery Act 2015 as protecting this right. However, the JCHR points out that domestic legislation mostly prohibits specific actions rather than conferring rights on individuals[26] ILO conventions are not implemented in domestic law and therefore do not confer rights on individuals[27]	The ECHR, Art.4 as implemented under HRA 1998 may be available as the basis for a claim, but the remedies under HRA 1998 are weaker than for claims under EU law because the courts cannot disapply domestic primary legislation or retained direct principal EU legislation for HRA 1998 claims The right is enforceable to the extent that it is protected in common law and domestic legislation

Article	Text of Charter article	Source	Analysis	Basis for claim after IPCD?
Title II – Freedoms				
Article 6 Right to liberty and security	Everyone has the right to liberty and security of person	ECHR, Art.5 (right to liberty and security)[28]	The scope of the ECHR, Art.5, implemented in HRA 1998, is the same as the Charter[29] The government cites domestic law as protecting this right such as the writ of habeas corpus and the Police and Criminal Evidence Act 1984[30]	The ECHR, Art.5 as implemented under HRA 1998 may be available as the basis for a claim, but the remedies under HRA 1998 are weaker than for claims under EU law because the courts cannot disapply domestic primary legislation or retained direct principal EU legislation for HRA 1998 claims The right is enforceable to the extent that it is protected in common law and domestic legislation
Article 7 Respect for private and family life	Everyone has the right to respect for his or her private and family life, home and communications	ECHR, Art.8 (right to respect for private and family life)[31] General principle of EU law[32]	The scope of the ECHR, Art.8, implemented in domestic law, is the same as the Charter, Art.7 The government also points to domestic legislation as protecting this right such as the Children Act 1989 which ensures that the family lives of children are not interfered with unless it is necessary to do so and the Police and Criminal Evidence Act 1984 which ensures that the right of entry and search in domestic premises is conducted in a proportionate and lawful manner[33]	The ECHR, Art.8 as implemented under HRA 1998 may be available as the basis for a claim, but the remedies under HRA 1998 are weaker than for claims under EU law because the courts cannot disapply domestic primary legislation or retained direct principal EU legislation for HRA 1998 claims The right is enforceable to the extent that it is protected in common law and domestic legislation

Article	Text of Charter article	Source	Analysis	Basis for claim after IPCD?
			General principles cannot be enforced in UK courts after IPCD[34]	The general principles of EU law cannot be used as the basis for a claim
Article 8 Protection of personal data	1. Everyone has the right to the protection of personal data concerning him or her 2. Such data must be processed fairly for specified purposes and on the basis of the consent of the person concerned or some other legitimate basis laid down by law. Everyone has the right of access to data which has been collected concerning him or her, and the right to have it rectified 3. Compliance with these rules shall be subject to control by an independent authority	ECHR, Art.8 (right to respect for private and family life)[35] TFEU, Art.16,[36] TEU, Art.39[37] EU secondary legislation[38] General principle of EU law[39] Council of Europe Convention 108[40]	The ECHR, Art.8 is implemented in domestic law but the Charter, Art.8 'goes further, is more specific and has no counterpart in the ECHR'[41] The TFEU, Art.16(1) contains very similar wording to the Charter, Art.8 and could potentially be used as the basis for a claim if it is saved through EUWA 2018, s.4. However, in order for this argument to succeed the TFEU, Art.16(1) would have to be held to have direct effect. This argument is novel, and the point has not been decided by the CJEU.[42] EUWA 2018, s.4 does not prevent this sort of argument because it saves rights, etc. which flowed into domestic law prior to IPCD without specifying what those rights are Council of Europe Convention 108 has been ratified by the UK and is implemented in the Data Protection Act 2018 The government has placed significant weight on the implementation of data protection rights in EU secondary legislation and domestic legislation in	The ECHR, Art.8 as implemented under HRA 1998 may be available as the basis for a claim, but the remedies under HRA 1998 are weaker than for claims under EU law because the courts cannot disapply domestic primary legislation or retained direct principal EU legislation for HRA 1998 claims A claim under HRA 1998 might not provide the same level of protection, given that the Charter, Art.8 goes further than the ECHR, Art.8. An alternative claim might be based on the argument that the TFEU, Art.16(1) has direct effect. Article 16 could then be used to disapply pre-IPCD domestic law on the basis of incompatibility with the right to protection of personal data as set out in the TFEU, Art.16(1) The 'UK GDPR'46 and the Data Protection Act 2018 contain detailed rights which could be

Article	Text of Charter article	Source	Analysis	Basis for claim after IPCD?
			order to argue that the Charter, Art.8 is incorporated into domestic law. However, there is concern that 'given the vast number of exemptions and derogations from these rights' there is a question as to whether the Data Protection Act 2018 offers 'protection that is equivalent to Article 8 of the Charter'[43] Commentators have pointed out that the Charter, Arts.7 and 8 have been found to provide a 'right to be forgotten' which did not previously exist elsewhere. However, this right is now set out in the GDPR, Art.17 which will be retained under EUWA 2018, s.3, so this right will not be lost after the transition period ends The government also cites the Data Protection Act 2018 as providing protections in this context[44] General principles cannot be enforced in UK courts after IPCD[45]	relied upon in this context, subject to exceptions The general principles of EU law cannot be used as the basis for a claim
Article 9 Right to marry and right to found a family	The right to marry and the right to found a family shall be guaranteed in accordance with the national laws governing the exercise of these rights	ECHR, Art.12 (right to marry)[47]	The scope of the ECHR, Art.12 is the same as the scope of the right in the Charter, although national law may extend the scope of that right (for example to same sex couples)[48]	The ECHR, Art.12 as implemented under HRA 1998 may be available as the basis for a claim, but the remedies under HRA 1998 are weaker than for claims under EU law because the courts cannot

Article	Text of Charter article	Source	Analysis	Basis for claim after IPCD?
			The government also points to domestic legislation as protecting these rights[49]	disapply domestic primary legislation or retained direct principal EU legislation for HRA 1998 claims The right is enforceable to the extent that it is protected in common law and domestic legislation
Article 10 Freedom of thought, conscience and religion	1. Everyone has the right to freedom of thought, conscience and religion. This right includes freedom to change religion or belief and freedom, either alone or in community with others and in public or in private, to manifest religion or belief, in worship, teaching, practice and observance 2. The right to conscientious objection is recognised, in accordance with the national laws governing the exercise of this right	Art.10(1) corresponds to ECHR, Art.9 (freedom of thought, conscience and religion)[50] Art.10(2) corresponds to the constitutional traditions of the Member States[51] as well as ECHR, Art.9[52]	The ECHR, Art.9 is implemented in domestic law through HRA 1998. The ECHR, Art.9 has the same meaning and scope as the Charter, Art.10[53] The government also cites other domestic legislation as protecting this right[54]	The ECHR, Art.9 as implemented under HRA 1998 may be available as the basis for a claim, but the remedies under HRA 1998 are weaker than for claims under EU law because the courts cannot disapply domestic primary legislation or retained direct principal EU legislation for HRA 1998 claims The right is enforceable to the extent that it is protected in common law and domestic legislation

Article	Text of Charter article	Source	Analysis	Basis for claim after IPCD?
Article 11 Freedom of expression and information	1. Everyone has the right to freedom of expression. This right shall include freedom to hold opinions and to receive and impart information and ideas without interference by public authority and regardless of frontiers 2. The freedom and pluralism of the media shall be respected	ECHR, Art.10 (freedom of expression)[55] General principle of EU law[56] Art.11(2) specifies how the right in Art.11(1) applies in the context of freedom of the media[57]	The ECHR, Art.10 is incorporated into domestic law through HRA 1998. The scope and meaning of the ECHR, Art.10 are the same as the Charter, Art.11[58] The government also cites certain domestic legislation as protecting this right[59] General principles cannot be enforced in UK courts after IPCD[60]	The ECHR, Art.10 as implemented under HRA 1998 may be available as the basis for a claim, but the remedies under HRA 1998 are weaker than for claims under EU law because the courts cannot disapply domestic primary legislation or retained direct principal EU legislation for HRA 1998 claims The general principles of EU law cannot be used as the basis for a claim The right is enforceable to the extent that it is protected in common law and domestic legislation
Article 12 Freedom of assembly and of association	1. Everyone has the right to freedom of peaceful assembly and to freedom of association at all levels, in particular in political, trade union and civic matters, which implies the right of everyone to form and to join trade unions for the protection of his or her interests	ECHR, Art.11 (right to freedom of assembly and association)[61] The right to freedom of association and the right to freedom of trade union activity are general principles of EU law[62]	The ECHR, Art.11 is incorporated into domestic law through HRA 1998. However, the scope of the Charter, Art.12 is wider than the ECHR, Art.11 because it applies at EU as well as at national level[63] The Charter, Art.12(2) deals with freedom of assembly for political parties at EU level. After IPCD this provision will not be relevant for the UK[64]	The ECHR, Art.11 as implemented under HRA 1998 may be available as the basis for a claim, but the remedies under HRA 1998 are weaker than for claims under EU law because the courts cannot disapply domestic primary legislation or retained direct principal EU legislation for HRA 1998 claims The elements of the right which protected freedom of assembly and

Article	Text of Charter article	Source	Analysis	Basis for claim after IPCD?
	2. Political parties at Union level contribute to expressing the political will of the citizens of the Union		The government points to a number of domestic statutes which respect these rights[65]	of association at EU level are lost as a consequence of the UK's exit from the EU The general principles of EU law cannot be used as the basis for a claim The right is enforceable to the extent that it is protected in domestic legislation
Article 13 Freedom of the arts and sciences	The arts and scientific research shall be free of constraint. Academic freedom shall be respected	This right is one aspect of the right protected under ECHR, Art.10 (freedom of expression)[66] ECHR, Art.10 has been held to apply to expression in both artistic and scientific contexts[67]	The ECHR, Art.10 is incorporated into domestic law under HRA 1998	The ECHR, Art.10 as implemented under HRA 1998 may be available as the basis for a claim, but the remedies under HRA 1998 are weaker than for claims under EU law because the courts cannot disapply domestic primary legislation or retained direct principal EU legislation for HRA 1998 claims
Article 14 Right to education	1. Everyone has the right to education and to have access to vocational and continuing training 2. This right includes the possibility to receive free compulsory education 3. The freedom to found	The substance of Art.14 corresponds to ECHR, Protocol 1, Art.2 (right to education)[68] The Charter right to have access to vocational and continuing training is based on the Community Charter of the Fundamental Social	The ECHR, Protocol 1, Art.2 is implemented through HRA 1998. Note the UK reservation The scope of the ECHR, Protocol 1, Art.2 is narrower than the Charter, Art.14 as regards rights of access vocational and continuing training as well as the principle of free compulsory education[72]	The ECHR, Protocol 1, Art.2 as implemented under HRA 1998 may be available as the basis for a claim, but the remedies under HRA 1998 are weaker than for claims under EU law because the courts cannot disapply domestic primary legislation or retained direct principal EU legislation for HRA 1998 claims

Article	Text of Charter article	Source	Analysis	Basis for claim after IPCD?
	educational establishments with due respect for democratic principles and the right of parents to ensure the education and teaching of their children in conformity with their religious, philosophical and pedagogical convictions shall be respected, in accordance with the national laws governing the exercise of such freedom and right	Rights of Workers, point 15 and the European Social Charter, Art.10[69] Art.14 is also based on the common constitutional traditions of the Member States[70] Freedom to found educational establishments is part of the right to conduct a business (see the Charter, Art.16)[71]	The UK has ratified the European Social Charter (ESC), Art.10 (right to vocational training) on which the Charter, Art.4 is partly based; however, the ESC is not enforceable – it is a non-justiciable aid to interpretation[73] The Community Charter of the Fundamental Social Rights of Workers ('Community Charter') does not create enforceable rights – it is a 'mere political declaration'[74] The JCHR takes the view that the right to education will have a narrower scope after IPCD[75] The government cites domestic statutes as ensuring access to education[76] The government states that the free movement of workers Regulation 492/2011 gives EU migrant workers and their family members the same rights of access to vocational training under the same conditions as nationals of the member state;[77] however, Art.10 of that Regulation which deals with workers' families including the education of their children ceases to apply in domestic law for the purposes of immigration law on IPCD[78]	Further, the right under HRA 1998 is narrower than the right under the Charter, Art.14 The right is enforceable to the extent that it is protected in domestic law

Article	Text of Charter article	Source	Analysis	Basis for claim after IPCD?
Article 15 Freedom to choose an occupation and right to engage in work	1. Everyone has the right to engage in work and to pursue a freely chosen or accepted occupation 2. Every citizen of the Union has the freedom to seek employment, to work, to exercise the right of establishment and to provide services in any Member State 3. Nationals of third countries who are authorised to work in the territories of the Member States are entitled to working conditions equivalent to those of citizens of the Union	The freedom to choose an occupation is a general principle of EU law[79] The Charter Explanations state that Art.15(1) draws on the revised ESC, Art.1(2) Art.15(2) is based on certain treaty provisions (TFEU, Arts.26, 45, 49 and 56 – freedom of movement for workers, freedom of establishment and freedom to provide services)[80] Art.15(3) is based on TFEU, Art.153(1)(g) and on the ESC, Art.19(4)[81]	Although the UK has ratified the ESC on which Art.15(1) is based, the ESC is not enforceable – it is a non-justiciable aid to interpretation[82] To the extent that the treaty articles on which Art.15 is based are directly applicable they are saved by EUWA 2018, s.4. However, powers under EUWA 2018, s.8 have been used to remove rights within the scope of this article from the UK statute book after IPCD[83] General principles cannot be enforced in UK courts after IPCD[84]	The JCHR states that it is not clear to what extent this right will still be enforceable after IPCD[85] The general principles of EU law cannot be used as the basis for a claim
Article 16 Freedom to conduct a business	The freedom to conduct a business in accordance with Union law and national laws and practices is recognised	The Charter Explanations set out that Art.16 is based on the case law of the CJEU which recognises the freedom to exercise an economic or commercial activity, the freedom of contract and TFEU, Art.119(1) and (3)	The Equality and Human Rights Commission considers that this right will be lost after the transition period has ended[87] General principles cannot be enforced in UK courts after IPCD[88] The extent to which Art.16 conferred an enforceable right before the end of	The JCHR considers that this right is only enforceable to the extent that it is protected in domestic legislation[91] The general principles of EU law cannot be used as the basis for a claim

Article	Text of Charter article	Source	Analysis	Basis for claim after IPCD?
		which recognises free competition The right to carry out an economic activity is a general principle of EU law[86]	the transition period in any event is doubtful[89] The government points to the fact that the domestic framework is 'facilitative' and characterised by 'an absence of restrictions on setting up a business'. It cites examples such as the Companies Acts which allow for the registration of companies subject to complying with certain requirements[90]	
Article 17 Right to property	1. Everyone has the right to own, use, dispose of and bequeath his or her lawfully acquired possessions. No one may be deprived of his or her possessions, except in the public interest and in the cases and under the conditions provided for by law, subject to fair compensation being paid in good time for their loss. The use of property may be regulated by law in so far as is necessary for the general interest	The meaning and scope of Art.17 correspond to ECHR, Protocol 1, Art.1 (protection of property)[92] The protection of intellectual property is an aspect of the right to property[93] The right to property is a general principle of EU law[94]	The ECHR, Protocol 1, Art.1 is implemented in domestic law through HRA 1998 The scope and meaning of Protocol 1, Art.1 are the same as the Charter, Art.17 General principles cannot be enforced in UK courts after IPCD[95] The government also points to various domestic statutes such as the Theft Act 1968 and the Copyright, Designs and Patents Act 1988 as providing protection for this right[96]	The ECHR, Protocol 1, Art.1 as implemented under HRA 1998 may be available as the basis for a claim, but the remedies under HRA 1998 are weaker than for claims under EU law because the courts cannot disapply domestic primary legislation or retained direct principal EU legislation for HRA 1998 claims The general principles of EU law cannot be used as the basis for a claim The right is also enforceable on the basis of protections in domestic law

Article	Text of Charter article	Source	Analysis	Basis for claim after IPCD?
	2. Intellectual property shall be protected			
Article 18 Right to asylum	The right to asylum shall be guaranteed with due respect for the rules of the Geneva Convention of 28 July 1951 and the Protocol of 31 January 1967 relating to the status of refugees and in accordance with the [TEU] and the [TFEU] …	The source of this right is TFEU, Art.78[97] Art.78 requires the Union to respect the Geneva Convention on refugees[98]	The UN Refugee Convention has not been implemented in UK domestic law[99] Art.78 fell within the scope of the UK's Justice and Home Affairs Opt-in Protocol (see Protocol 21 to the EU Treaties). Where the UK did not opt in to measures which fell within the scope of Protocol 21 it was not bound by those measures[100] The government states that it will continue to provide for asylum through domestic law. It also points out that the UK is a party to the 1951 Refugee Convention and the 1967 Protocol[101]	The JCHR's report concludes that 'the sources of Article 18 are not enforceable in the UK' either before or after IPCD[102]
Article 19 Protection in the event of removal, expulsion or extradition	1. Collective expulsions are prohibited 2. No one may be removed, expelled or extradited to a State where there is a serious risk that he or she would be subjected to the death penalty, torture or other inhuman or degrading treatment or punishment	Art.19(1) has the same meaning and scope as the ECHR, Protocol 4, Art.4 (prohibition of collective expulsion)[103] Art.19(1) provides guarantees that every decision is based on a specific examination and that no single measure can be taken to expel all persons having the	The ECHR, Protocol 4, Art.4 has not been implemented under HRA 1998 Although the government's right-by-right analysis states that the ECHR, Art.13 requires fair and effective procedures regarding Art.3 claims, Art.13 has not been implemented under HRA 1998. Domestic courts must take into account ECtHR case law on Art.13. However, the JCHR's report points out that this is not equivalent to an enforceable right under HRA 1998[108]	The JCHR concludes that 'none of the sources of Article 19 will confer an enforceable right upon individuals' after IPCD[110]

Article	Text of Charter article	Source	Analysis	Basis for claim after IPCD?
		nationality of a particular state[104] Art.19 is based in part on Art.13 of the International Covenant on Civil and Political Rights (ICCPR)[105] Art.19(2) incorporates the relevant case law from the ECtHR[106] regarding the ECHR, Art.3 (prohibition of torture)[107]	The ICCPR has not been implemented in domestic law and therefore does not provide enforceable rights before national courts[109]	
Title III – Equality				
Article 20 Equality before the law	Everyone is equal before the law	The source for Art.18 is the general principle of equal treatment[111]	General principles cannot be enforced in UK courts after IPCD[112] The scope of Art.20 is the same as the ECHR, Art.14 (protection from discrimination). The ECHR, Art.14 is implemented through HRA 1998. However, Art.14 is not a free-standing right. It can only be relied upon in conjunction with another right under the ECHR[113] EU-derived domestic legislation which implements EU directives on equality is retained through EUWA 2018, s.2 The government points out that the right also exists at common law and	The right to equality before the law will continue to be enforceable in domestic law where it is implemented through EU-derived domestic legislation or common law. However, after IPCD it will not be possible to assert that provisions of EU directives on equality have direct effect if the rights in question are not of a kind recognised as having direct effect by the CJEU or UK domestic courts in a case before IPCD[115] The ECHR, Art.14 (in conjunction with another right under the ECHR) as implemented under HRA

Article	Text of Charter article	Source	Analysis	Basis for claim after IPCD?
			that the principle of equality before the law is reflected in the rule of law, one of the longest established principles of the UK's constitution[114]	1998 may be available as the basis for a claim, but the remedies under HRA 1998 are weaker than for claims under EU law because the courts cannot disapply domestic primary legislation or retained direct principal EU legislation for HRA 1998 claims The general principles of EU law cannot be used as the basis for a claim The right is enforceable to the extent that it is available through EU-derived domestic legislation or other domestic law
Article 21 Non-discrim-ination	1. Any discrimination based on any ground such as sex, race, colour, ethnic or social origin, genetic features, language, religion or belief, political or any other opinion, membership of a national minority, property, birth, disability, age or sexual orientation shall be prohibited	Art.21(1) draws on TFEU, Art.19,[116] ECHR, Art.14 (protection from discrimination) and the Convention on Human Rights and Biomedicine, Art.11 as regards genetic heritage[117] Art.21(2) corresponds to TFEU, Art.18(1)[118] Art.21 is a more specific expression of the right set out in the Charter,	The ECHR, Art.14 is implemented through HRA 1998. However, Art.14 is not a free-standing right. It can only be relied upon in conjunction with another right under the ECHR The TFEU, Art.18[121] which corresponds to Art.21(2) has been held to be directly effective,[122] and so would provide enforceable rights in domestic law.[123] However, the TFEU, Art.18 will no longer apply in domestic law (at least in so far as it relates to the cessation of freedom of establishment and services)[124] after IPCD	The prohibition against discrimination will continue to be enforceable in domestic law where it is implemented through EU-derived domestic legislation. However, after IPCD it will not be possible to assert that provisions of EU directives on equality have direct effect if the rights in question are not of a kind recognised as having direct effect by the CJEU or UK domestic courts in a case before IPCD[128]

Article	Text of Charter article	Source	Analysis	Basis for claim after IPCD?
	2. Within the scope of application of the Treaties and without prejudice to any of their specific provisions, any discrimination on grounds of nationality shall be prohibited	Art.20[119] The right not to be discriminated against is a general principle of EU law[120]	It may be arguable that the TFEU, Art.19(1), on which Art.21(1) is based, could have direct effect and that this effect is saved through EUWA 2018, s.4. However, this would be a novel argument and the authors are not aware of any case law on this specific point[125] EU-derived domestic legislation[126] which implements rights set out in EU directives is retained through EUWA 2018, s.2, subject to the powers in EUWA 2018, s.8 General principles cannot be enforced in UK courts after IPCD[127]	The ECHR, Art.14 (in conjunction with another right under the ECHR) as implemented under HRA 1998 may be available as the basis for a claim, but the remedies under HRA 1998 are weaker than for claims under EU law because the courts cannot disapply domestic primary legislation or retained direct principal EU legislation for HRA 1998 claims The general principles of EU law cannot be used as the basis for a claim
Article 22 Cultural, religious and linguistic diversity	The Union shall respect cultural, religious and linguistic diversity	The source of Art.22 is TEU, Art.6 and TFEU, Art.167(1) and (4) which deal with culture and respect for cultural and linguistic diversity as well as TEU, Art.3(3)[129]	The government's analysis states that Art.22 sets out a principle which the EU institutions should apply when they legislate, rather than an enforceable legal right[130] The government points to domestic legislation in this area[131] The government also cites the fact that the UK has signed and ratified the European Charter for Regional and Minority Languages[132] To the extent that the relevant articles of the TEU and TFEU contain directly	Respect for cultural, religious and linguistic diversity will be protected to the extent that there is domestic legislation in place which offers these guarantees Rights in the EU Treaties which protect cultural, religious and linguistic diversity may be retained to the extent that they are directly effective

Article	Text of Charter article	Source	Analysis	Basis for claim after IPCD?
			effective rights,[133] these rights will be retained through EUWA 2018, s.4, subject to the powers in s.8	
Article 23 Equality between women and men	Equality between women and men must be ensured in all areas, including employment, work and pay The principle of equality shall not prevent the maintenance or adoption of measures providing for specific advantages in favour of the under-represented sex	TEU, Art.3 and TFEU, Art.8 which set out the objective of promoting equality between men and women[134] TFEU, Art.157[135] Directive 2006/54/EC on the implementation of the principle of equal opportunities and equal treatment of men and women in matters of employment and occupation[136] The government sets out that Art.23 reflects the general principle of equal treatment[137]	The government's position is that the TFEU, Art.157 and Directive 2006/54/EC contain rights: the TEU, Art.3 and TFEU, Art.8 set out principles[138] EU-derived domestic legislation will be retained through EUWA 2018, s.2, subject to the power in s.8[139] The right to equal pay under the TFEU, Art.157 has been held to be directly effective[140] and will therefore be retained through EUWA 2018, s.4 The government also cites the public sector equality duty, the common law duty on public bodies to act reasonably when using their powers and ECHR, Art.14 (protection from discrimination) which requires that the rights and freedoms contained in the ECHR must be applied without discrimination[141] The ECHR, Art.4 is implemented through HRA 1998. However, Art.14 is not a free-standing right. It can only be relied upon in conjunction with another right under the ECHR	The TFEU, Art.157 could be used to disapply pre-IPCD domestic law which conflicts with the right to equal pay The right to equality will be enforceable through EU-derived domestic legislation, other domestic legislation or the common law The ECHR, Art.14 (in conjunction with another right under the ECHR) as implemented under HRA 1998 may be available as the basis for a claim, but the remedies under HRA 1998 are weaker than for claims under EU law because the courts cannot disapply domestic primary legislation or retained direct principal EU legislation for HRA 1998 claims The general principles of EU law cannot be used as the basis for a claim

Article	Text of Charter article	Source	Analysis	Basis for claim after IPCD?
			General principles cannot be enforced in UK courts after IPCD[142]	
Article 24 The rights of the child	1. Children shall have the right to such protection and care as is necessary for their well-being. They may express their views freely. Such views shall be taken into consideration on matters which concern them in accordance with their age and maturity 2. In all actions relating to children, whether taken by public authorities or private institutions, the child's best interests must be a primary consideration 3. Every child shall have the right to maintain on a regular basis a personal relationship and direct contact with both his or her parents, unless that is contrary to his or her interests	UN Convention on the Rights of the Child[143] TFEU, Art.81 deals with civil matters having cross-border implications which may include rights of contact with both parents[144] General principle of EU law[145] The government states that the CJEU has held that the UN Convention is taken into account when the general principles of EU law are applied[146] The government states that the ECHR, Art.8 (right to respect for private and family life) is also relevant and that the ECtHR has drawn on the UN Convention when interpreting Art.8[147]	The UN Convention on the Rights of the Child is not implemented in domestic law and therefore does not confer enforceable rights[148] The JCHR took evidence from witnesses who expressed concern regarding the exclusion of the Charter from the perspective of the protection of children's rights[149] To the extent that the rights of the child overlap with the ECHR, Art.8 they will be implemented through HRA 1998 The rights of the child are retained in domestic law to the extent that they are already protected in national legislation The government cites domestic statutes which it says reflect the UK's commitment to the UN Convention[150] General principles cannot be enforced in UK courts after IPCD	The rights underlying Art.24 will be enforceable to the extent that they are protected in domestic law Where the rights of the child overlap with the ECHR, Art.8, they will be retained through HRA 1998. The ECHR, Art.8 as implemented under HRA 1998 may be available as the basis for a claim, but the remedies under HRA 1998 are weaker than for claims under EU law because the courts cannot disapply domestic primary legislation or retained direct principal EU legislation for HRA 1998 claims The general principles of EU law cannot be used as the basis for a claim

Article	Text of Charter article	Source	Analysis	Basis for claim after IPCD?
Article 25 The rights of the elderly	The Union recognises and respects the rights of the elderly to lead a life of dignity and independence and to participate in social and cultural life	Revised ESC, Art.23 and the Community Charter, Arts.24 and 25[151] The government states that ECHR, Arts.3 (prohibition of torture), 8 (right to respect for private and family life) and 14 (protection from discrimination) are relevant to the rights of the elderly[152]	The government states that given this is a principle and not an enforceable right, therefore the fact that the Charter is not retained in domestic law after IPCD does not remove a free-standing right of challenge for litigants[153] The ECHR, Arts.3, 8 and 14 are implemented in HRA 1998. However, the ECHR, Art.14 is not a free-standing right. It can only be relied upon in conjunction with another right under the ECHR The ESC and Community Charter are non-justiciable aids to interpretation[154] The government points to domestic legislation which protects the rights of the elderly[155]	The JCHR states that the rights of the elderly will only be retained to the extent that they are already provided for in domestic law[156] The ECHR, Arts.8 and 14 (in conjunction with another right under the ECHR) as implemented under HRA 1998 may be available as the basis for a claim, but the remedies under HRA 1998 are weaker than for claims under EU law because the courts cannot disapply domestic primary legislation or retained direct principal EU legislation for HRA 1998 claims
Article 26 Integration of persons with disabilities	The Union recognises and respects the right of persons with disabilities to benefit from measures designed to ensure their independence, social and occupational integration and participation in the life of the community	Revised ESC, Art.15 and the Community Charter, point 26[157]	The government states that Art.26 constitutes guidance to the EU institutions when they legislate, rather than an enforceable right[158] The government states that domestic law protects the rights of persons with disabilities[159] EU legislation in this area cited by the government which protects these rights includes Regulation (EC) No 1107/ 2006 on the rights of disabled persons	This right will be enforceable in so far as it is saved through EUWA 2018, ss.2–4 or through other domestic legislation

Article	Text of Charter article	Source	Analysis	Basis for claim after IPCD?
			and persons with reduced mobility when travelling by air.[160] This regulation will be saved under EUWA 2018, s.3 These rights will be retained to the extent that they are provided for in domestic law[161] The JCHR's report states that a number of organisations had expressed concerns about disability rights as a result of the policy on the Charter and potential regression of rights. The Equality and Human Rights Commission called for the UN Convention on the Rights of Disabled People to be implemented in UK law[162] The ESC and Community Charter are non-justiciable aids to interpretation[163]	
Title IV – Solidarity				
Article 27 Workers' right to inform-ation and consult-ation within the under-taking	Workers or their representatives must, at the appropriate levels, be guaranteed information and consultation in good time in the cases and under the conditions provided for by Union law and national laws and practices	Revised ESC, Art.21[164] Community Charter, points 17 and 18[165] TFEU, Arts.154 and 155[166] Directives: 2002/14/EC (general framework for informing and consulting	The government states that Art.27 on its own does not confer enforceable rights on individuals and simply reflects existing EU legislation, leaving it to Member States to decide whether to go beyond that legislation[168] The government cites domestic legislation which will be saved as EU-derived domestic legislation under	This right will be enforceable in so far as it is saved through retained EU law or other domestic law

Article	Text of Charter article	Source	Analysis	Basis for claim after IPCD?
		employees in the EU), 98/59/EC (collective redundancies), 2001/23/EC (transfers of undertakings), 2009/38/EC (European Works Councils)[167]	EUWA 2018, s.2.[169] The JCHR points out that the relevant legislation will be subject to the powers in s.8 and could be modified[170] The ESC and Community Charter are non-justiciable aids to interpretation[171]	
Article 28 Right of collective bargaining and action	Workers and employers, or their respective organisations, have, in accordance with Union law and national laws and practices, the right to negotiate and conclude collective agreements at the appropriate levels and, in cases of conflicts of interest, to take collective action to defend their interests, including strike action	Revised ESC, Art.6 and the Community Charter, points 12–14[172] ECHR, Art.11 (right to freedom of assembly and association which includes trade unions rights)[173] The modalities and limits for the exercise of collective action (including strike action) come under national laws and practices[174] General principle of EU law[175]	The ECHR, Art.11 is implemented through HRA 1998[176] The right is implemented in other domestic legislation[177] The JCHR points out that the ESC and Community Charter are non-justiciable aids to interpretation[178] General principles cannot be enforced in UK courts after IPCD[179]	The ECHR, Art.11 as implemented under HRA 1998 may be available as the basis for a claim, but the remedies under HRA 1998 are weaker than for claims under EU law because the courts cannot disapply domestic primary legislation or retained direct principal EU legislation for HRA 1998 claims The right will be enforceable to the extent that it is protected in other domestic legislation The general principles of EU law cannot be used as the basis for a claim
Article 29 Right of access to placement services	Everyone has the right of access to a free placement service[180]	ESC, Art.1(3) and the Community Charter, point 13[181]	The government states that Art.29 sets out a principle to guide the EU institutions when they legislate rather than an enforceable right, so no rights will be lost in domestic law on the basis that Art.29 is not incorporated through EUWA 2018[182]	No enforceable right

Article	Text of Charter article	Source	Analysis	Basis for claim after IPCD?
			The government points to the fact that this principle is reflected in legislation which will be saved, for example Art.5 of Regulation 492/2011 on freedom of movement for workers in the EU.[183] However, freedom of movement for workers will be ended through the Immigration and Social Security Co-ordination (EU Withdrawal) Bill (when enacted)[184] The JCHR points out that the ESC and Community Charter are non-justiciable aids to interpretation[185]	
Article 30 Protection in the event of unjustified dismissal	Every worker has the right to protection against unjustified dismissal, in accordance with Union law and national laws and practices	Revised ESC, Art.24[186] Directive 2001/23/EC on the safeguarding of employees' rights in the event of transfers of undertaking[187] Directive 2008/94/EC on the protection of employees in the event of the insolvency of their employer[188]	The government states that Art.30 does not on its own confer enforceable rights on individuals[189] The legislation implementing the relevant directives will be retained under EUWA 2018, s.2[190] The government references the UK's membership of the ILO Fundamental Rights Conventions.[191] However, the JCHR points out that these conventions do not confer enforceable rights on individuals[192] The government points to various domestic legislation in this area[193]	The rights reflected in Art.30 are enforceable after IPCD to the extent that they are implemented in domestic law

Article	Text of Charter article	Source	Analysis	Basis for claim after IPCD?
Article 31 Fair and just working conditions	1. Every worker has the right to working conditions which respect his or her health, safety and dignity 2. Every worker has the right to limitation of maximum working hours, to daily and weekly rest periods and to an annual period of paid leave	Art.31(1) is based on Directive 89/391/EEC on health and safety at work, the ESC, Art.3 and the Community Charter, point 19 and, as regards dignity at work, the revised ESC, Art.26. Working conditions are to be understood in the sense of TFEU, Art.156[194] Art.31(2) is based on Directive 2003/88/EC[195] concerning certain aspects of the organisation of working time, the revised ESC, Art.2 and the Community Charter, point 8[196]	The government's analysis sets out that the CJEU has held that Art.31 does not confer an enforceable right[197] The government points to domestic legislation implementing these rights which will be saved through EUWA 2018, s.2,[198] although amendments could be made to these rights under powers in s.8 or through new domestic legislation The government also cites other domestic legislation in the employment context as well as the existence of employment tribunals[199] The fact that the UK is a party to the ILO Fundamental Conventions including the Discrimination (Employment and Occupation) Convention 1958 is also relied on by the government.[200] However, the ILO Fundamental Conventions do not confer enforceable rights on individuals.[201] The same is true of the ESC and the Community Charter[202]	The rights reflected in Art.31 are enforceable after IPCD to the extent that they are implemented in domestic law
Article 32 Prohibition of child labour and protection	The employment of children is prohibited. The minimum age of admission to employment may not be lower than the minimum	Directive 94/33/EC on the protection of young people at work, the ESC, Art.7 and the Community Charter, points 20–23[203]	Directive 94/33/EC has been implemented in domestic law[204] which will be saved through EUWA 2018, s.2, subject to the powers in s.8 and new domestic legislation	The rights reflected in Art.32 are enforceable after IPCD to the extent that they are implemented in domestic law

Article	Text of Charter article	Source	Analysis	Basis for claim after IPCD?
of young people at work	school-leaving age, without prejudice to such rules as may be more favourable to young people and except for limited derogations Young people admitted to work must have working conditions appropriate to their age and be protected against economic exploitation and any work likely to harm their safety, health or physical, mental, moral or social development or to interfere with their education		The ESC and the Community Charter do not confer enforceable rights[205] The government cites other domestic legislation which protects the rights and best interests of the child[206] The government also cites the fact that the UK is a party to the United Nations Convention on the Rights of the Child; however, the Convention is not directly incorporated in UK-wide domestic law[207]	
Article 33 Family and pro-fessional life	1. The family shall enjoy legal, economic and social protection 2. To reconcile family and professional life, everyone shall have the right to protection from dismissal for a reason connected with maternity and the right to paid maternity leave and to parental leave following the birth or adoption of a child	Art.33(1) is based on the ESC, Art.16[208] Art.33(2) draws on Directive 92/85/EEC on the introduction of measures to encourage improvements in the safety and health of new or expectant mothers[209] Directive 2010/18/EU implementing the revised framework agreement on parental leave[210]	The government states that Art.33 contains both a right and a principle[212] Art.33(1) is a principle which guides the EU institutions when they legislate rather than establishing an enforceable right[213] Art.33(2) sets out enforceable rights which have been implemented in domestic law,[214] although these may be modified through the powers in EUWA 2018, s.8 or repealed by future domestic legislation	The rights reflected in Art.33 are enforceable after IPCD to the extent that they are implemented in domestic law

Article	Text of Charter article	Source	Analysis	Basis for claim after IPCD?
		ESC, Art.8 (protection of maternity) and the revised ESC, Art.27 (right of workers with family responsibilities to equal opportunities and equal treatment)[211] The Charter Explanations make clear that maternity covers the period from conception to weaning	The government states that UK employment law already goes further than many of the standards set out in EU legislation[215] The ESC does not confer enforceable rights[216]	
Article 34 Social security and social assistance	1. The Union recognises and respects the entitlement to social security benefits and social services providing protection in cases such as maternity, illness, industrial accidents, dependency or old age, and in the case of loss of employment, in accordance with the rules laid down by Union law and national laws and practices 2. Everyone residing and moving legally within the European Union is entitled to social	Art.34(1) is based on TFEU, Arts.153 and 156, the ESC, Art.12 and the Community Charter, point 10[217] Art.34(2) is based on the ESC, Arts.12(4) and 13(4) and the Community Charter, point 2, and reflects the rules arising from Regulation (EEC) No 1408/71 and Regulation 492/2011[218] Art.34(3) draws on the ESC, Art.13, the revised ESC, Arts.30 and 31 and the Community Charter, point 10, as reflected in	The government's position is that Art.34 sets out elements of a right and of a principle. Art.34(1) and (3) set out principles to guide the EU institutions when they legislate and do not establish enforceable rights. Therefore the fact that the Charter is not incorporated does not remove a free-standing right in the context of Art.34(1) and (3)[220] The government states that Art.34 as a whole is limited by reference to EU and national law, which means that Art.34 does not create a general entitlement to social security or welfare benefits where there is no EU or domestic law right to them. EU social security law is based on the coordination rather than the	It appears unlikely that the rights reflected in the Charter, Art.34 will be enforceable after IPCD

Article	Text of Charter article	Source	Analysis	Basis for claim after IPCD?
	security benefits and social advantages in accordance with Union law and national laws and practices 3. In order to combat social exclusion and poverty, the Union recognises and respects the right to social and housing assistance so as to ensure a decent existence for all those who lack sufficient resources, in accordance with the rules laid down by Union law and national laws and practices	TFEU, Art.153[219]	harmonisation of national law. Each country remains responsible for its own legislation determining what benefits it pays and to whom[221] The only enforceable right is Art.34(2) which simply restates rights that arise from long-standing provisions on free movement within the EU[222] The government cites various EU regulations dealing with areas such as the free movement of workers,[223] however freedom of movement for workers will be been ended through the Immigration and Social Security Co-ordination (EU Withdrawal) Bill (when enacted)[224] The ESC and the Community Charter do not confer enforceable rights[225]	
Article 35 Health care	Everyone has the right of access to preventative health care and the right to benefit from medical treatment under the conditions established by national laws and practices. A high level of human health protection shall be ensured in the definition	TFEU, Art.168 and ESC, Arts.11 and 13[226]	The government's position is that Art.35 sets out a principle rather than a right[227] but the JCHR has pointed out that this point has not been determined by the CJEU[228] The TFEU, Art.168 would be saved through EUWA 2018, s.4 if it had direct effect, but the drafting of the article makes this unlikely	Art.35 does not give rise to an enforceable right after IPCD

Article	Text of Charter article	Source	Analysis	Basis for claim after IPCD?
	and implementation of all the Union's policies and activities		The ESC is an aid to interpretation but does not give rise to enforceable rights[229]	
Article 36 Access to services of general economic interest	The Union recognises and respects access to services of general economic interest as provided for in national laws and practices, in accordance with the Treaties, in order to promote the social and territorial cohesion of the Union	Art.36 fully reflects TFEU, Art.14[230]	The Charter Explanations confirm that Art.36 does not create new rights The government and the JCHR agree that Art.36 is a principle and does not contain enforceable rights[231] The government also states that this principle will largely fall away once the UK leaves the EU[232]	Art.36 does not give rise to an enforceable right after IPCD
Article 37 Environ-mental protection	A high level of environmental protection and the improvement of the quality of the environment must be integrated into the policies of the Union and ensured in accordance with the principle of sustainable development	TEU, Art.3(3)[233] and TFEU, Arts.11[234] and 191,[235] as well as the provisions of some national constitutions[236]	Both the JCHR and the government consider that this is a principle rather than a right[237] The government also points to the fact that there are numerous pieces of EU legislation in this area which will be incorporated into domestic law as retained EU law[238] The government also makes reference to the precautionary principle and the polluter pays principle which are set out in the Rio Declaration on Environment and Development 1992 to which the UK is a signatory[239] The government also points to the UK's participation in a number of	Art.37 does not confer an enforceable right. Rights in the context of environmental protection will be available to the extent that they are implemented in domestic law after IPCD

Article	Text of Charter article	Source	Analysis	Basis for claim after IPCD?
			multilateral environmental agreements[240]	
Article 38 Consumer protection	Union policies shall ensure a high level of consumer protection	TFEU, Art.169[241]	The Charter Explanations make clear that this is a principle, not a right, and is therefore not enforceable[242] The government points out that consumer rights are protected by a broad spectrum of domestic legislation such as the Consumer Rights Act 2015[243]	Art.38 does not give rise to an enforceable right after IPCD
Title V – Citizens' Rights				
Articles 39–46	These articles are categorised as Citizens' Rights	EU Treaties and secondary legislation	The government and the JCHR take the position that these rights are largely dependent on EU membership and are therefore mostly irrelevant after IPCD[244] The exception is the TFEU, Art.21 which the CJEU has held to have direct effect. However, the Immigration and Social Security Co-ordination (EU Withdrawal) Bill, Sched.1, para.6 removes the right in the TFEU, Art.21 from domestic law[245]	These rights will be mostly irrelevant after IPCD and will therefore not be enforceable

Article	Text of Charter article	Source	Analysis	Basis for claim after IPCD?
Title VI – Justice				
Article 47 Right to an effective remedy and to a fair trial	1. Everyone whose rights and freedoms guaranteed by the law of the Union are violated has the right to an effective remedy before a tribunal in compliance with the conditions laid down in this Article 2. Everyone is entitled to a fair and public hearing within a reasonable time by an independent and impartial tribunal previously established by law. Everyone shall have the possibility of being advised, defended and represented 3. Legal aid shall be made available to those who lack sufficient resources in so far as such aid is necessary to ensure effective access to justice	Art.47(1) is based on ECHR, Art.13 (right to an effective remedy) Art.47(2) corresponds to ECHR, Art.6(1) (right to a fair trial)[246] Art.47(3) reflects the case law of the ECtHR which states that provision should be made for legal aid where the absence of such aid would make it impossible to ensure an effective remedy[247] The right to an effective remedy before a court is a general principle of EU law[248]	The ECHR, Art.6 is implemented in domestic law through HRA 1998 The ECHR, Art.13 is not expressly incorporated into domestic law via HRA 1998[249] Art.47 offers more extensive protections than the ECHR[250] Art.47 is not limited in the same way as Art.6 which does not apply, for example, to decisions regarding immigration status such as deportation hearings[251] The JCHR considers that the scope of the right to an effective remedy and a fair trial may be reduced after IPCD[252] The JCHR cites the case of *Benkharbouche*[253] and states that in the absence of the Charter, Art.47 such cases may result in a different outcome.[254] In *Benkharbouche* the Supreme Court disapplied provisions of the State Immunity Act 1978 on the basis that they breached the Charter, Art.47. If the only remedy available had been under HRA 1998 the Supreme Court would have been limited to making a declaration of incompatibility	The rights reflected in the Charter, Art.47 may be diminished after IPCD[258] The ECHR, Art.6 as implemented under HRA 1998 may be available as the basis for a claim, but the remedies under HRA 1998 are weaker than for claims under EU law because the courts cannot disapply domestic primary legislation or retained direct principal EU legislation for HRA 1998 claims The ECHR, Art.6 is more limited in terms of the protections it offers than the Charter, Art.47 The ECHR, Art.13 is not expressly incorporated into domestic law through HRA 1998 It may be possible to enforce rights reflected in Art.47 on the basis of domestic law and retained EU law, including by bringing a claim for judicial review The general principles of EU law cannot be used as the basis for a claim

Article	Text of Charter article	Source	Analysis	Basis for claim after IPCD?
			The general principles will no longer be enforceable after IPCD[255] The government points to the common law which it asserts protects the rights reflected in Art.47[256] The government also states that 'after [IPCD] domestic law and retained EU law will provide effective routes of challenge and remedies for breaches of rights which derive from EU law and are retained under [EUWA 2018]'. The government cites in particular the availability of judicial review[257]	
Article 48 Presump-tion of innocence and right of defence	1. Everyone who has been charged shall be presumed innocent until proved guilty according to law 2. Respect for the rights of the defence of anyone who has been charged shall be guaranteed	ECHR, Art.6(2) and (3) which deal with the presumption of innocence and minimum rights for individuals charged with a criminal offence[259] The right in Art.48 is a general principle of EU law[260]	The general principles will no longer be enforceable after IPCD[261] The ECHR, Art.6(2) and (3) is implemented through HRA 1998 and has the same meaning and scope as the Charter, Art.48 The government points to various EU measures relating to the rights of suspects which have been implemented in domestic law and will be retained through EUWA 2018, s.2[263] The government also sets out that the presumption of innocence and the right of defence have long been recognised in the UK legal system as reflected in	The ECHR, Art.6 as implemented under HRA 1998 may be available as the basis for a claim, but the remedies under HRA 1998 are weaker than for claims under EU law because the courts cannot disapply domestic primary legislation or retained direct principal EU legislation for HRA 1998 claims This right will be enforceable in so far as it is saved through retained EU law or other domestic law The general principles of EU law cannot be used as the basis for a

Article	Text of Charter article	Source	Analysis	Basis for claim after IPCD?
			common law and domestic legislation[263]	claim
Article 49 Principles of legality and proportionality of criminal offences and penalties	1. No one shall be held guilty of any criminal offence on account of any act or omission which did not constitute a criminal offence under national law or international law at the time when it was committed. Nor shall a heavier penalty be imposed than the one that was applicable at the time the criminal offence was committed. If, subsequent to the commission of a criminal offence, the law provides for a lighter penalty, that penalty shall be applicable 2. This Article shall not prejudice the trial and punishment of any person for any act or omission which, at the time when it was committed, was criminal	ECHR, Art.7 (no punishment without law) and ICCPR, Art.15[264] The principle of 'no punishment without law' and the principle of proportionality in sentencing are general principles of EU law[265]	The general principles will no longer be enforceable after IPCD[266] The government points out that Art.49 only applies to offences that give effect to EU law[267] The ECHR, Art.7 is implemented through HRA 1998[268] The government also states that substantive criminal law in the UK has long recognised the prohibition on retrospective punishment and the importance of proportionality in sentencing as reflected in common law and domestic legislation[269]	The ECHR, Art.7 as implemented under HRA 1998 may be available as the basis for a claim, but the remedies under HRA 1998 are weaker than for claims under EU law because the courts cannot disapply domestic primary legislation or retained direct principal EU legislation for HRA 1998 claims This right will be enforceable in so far as it is available in domestic law The general principles of EU law cannot be used as the basis for a claim

Article	Text of Charter article	Source	Analysis	Basis for claim after IPCD?
	according to the general principles recognised by the community of nations 3. The severity of penalties must not be disproportionate to the criminal offence			
Article 50 Right not to be tried or punished twice in criminal proceedings for the same criminal offence	No one shall be liable to be tried or punished again in criminal proceedings for an offence for which he or she has already been finally acquitted or convicted within the Union in accordance with the law	ECHR, Protocol 7, Art.4 (right not to be tried or punished twice) General principle of EU law[270] EU legislation[271]	The ECHR, Protocol 7, Art.4 is not incorporated in domestic law through HRA 1998 The general principles will no longer be enforceable after IPCD[272] The prohibition on double punishment is recognised in domestic law[273]	The sources of the Charter right will not provide enforceable rights for individuals This right will be enforceable in so far as it is available in domestic law The general principles of EU law cannot be used as the basis for a claim

TABLE NOTES

[1] Case C–377/98 *Netherlands* v. *European Parliament and Council* [2001] ECR I–7079, EU:C:2001:523, paras.70–77.

[2] JCHR Legislative Scrutiny: *The EU (Withdrawal) Bill: A Right by Right Analysis* ('JCHR Legislative Scrutiny') (HL HC 2017–19, HL Paper 70, HC 774).

[3] EUWA 2018, Sched.1, para.3(1) and (2).

[4] JCHR Legislative Scrutiny, p.9, para.20.

[5] See *NS and others*, , para.114.

[6] See the Charter Explanations.

[7] Ibid.

[8] JCHR Legislative Scrutiny, p.9, para.22.

[9] See the government's *Charter of Fundamental Rights of the EU: Right by Right Analysis* ('the government's *Charter Analysis*'), 5 December 2017, p.18.

[10] The government asserts that Art.3 is a general principle of EU law in the government's *Charter Analysis*, p.19, relying on *Netherlands* v. *European Parliament and Council* [– see grounds 70, 78–80.

[11] See the Charter Explanations.

[12] See the government's *Charter Analysis*, p.19. The ECHR, Art.8 protects a person's right to respect for private and family life.

[13] See the Charter Explanations. Eugenics practices involving campaigns for sterilisation, forced pregnancy and compulsory ethnic marriage are all acts deemed to be international crimes.

[14] JCHR Legislative Scrutiny, p.10, para.25. The JCHR's report explains that unlike the ECHR, Art.8, Art.3 'protects physical and mental integrity and provides a number of bioethical guarantees'.

[15] JCHR Legislative Scrutiny, p.10, para.27.

[16] Ibid.

[17] The government's *Charter Analysis*, p.19 cites the Human Fertilisation and Embryology Act 1990 which prohibits reproductive cloning and only enables the testing and selection of embryos for implantation in limited circumstances, and the Human Tissue Act 2004 which prohibits sale of human material for transplantation.

[18] Ibid.

[19] EUWA 2018, Sched.1, para.3(1) and (2).

[20] Ibid.

[21] See the government's *Charter Analysis*, p.21 which states that an example of domestic legislation in this context is the Criminal Justice Act 1988, s.134 which makes torture a criminal offence in the UK.

[22] See the Charter Explanations.

[23] This regulation repealed and replaced Council Decision 2009/371/JHA establishing the European Police (Europol) [2009] OJ L121/37. The government states that Art.5(3) stems from the right to human dignity and is reflected in the legislation establishing Europol. See the government's *Charter Analysis*, p.22.

[24] See the government's *Charter Analysis*, p.22.

[25] Ibid. The conventions cited are the Forced Labour Convention 1930 and the Worst Forms Child Labour Convention 1999.

[26] JCHR Legislative Scrutiny, p.11, para.33.

[27] Ibid.

[28] See the Charter Explanations.

[29] See the Charter Explanations and the government's *Charter Analysis*, p.23.

[30] See the government's *Charter Analysis*, p.23.

[31] See the Charter Explanations.

[32] See the government's *Charter Analysis*, p.24. Cases cited include Case 249/86 *Commission* v. *Germany*, EU:C:1989:204 and Case C–34/13 *Monika Kusionova* v. *SMART Capital*, EU:C:2014:2189.

[33] See the government's *Charter Analysis*, p.24.

[34] EUWA 2018, Sched.1, para.3(1) and (2).

[35] See the Charter Explanations.

[36] The Charter Explanations cite Art.286 of the Treaty establishing the European Community which set out a legal basis for legislation on the processing of personal data by the Community's (later EU's) institutions and the establishment of a supervisory authority to monitor the processing of personal data by the Community's institutions and bodies. The TFEU, Art.16 now sets out the legal basis for the adoption of secondary legislation on the processing of personal data by the EU's institutions and the Member States. Article 16 states:
'1. Everyone has the right to the protection of personal data concerning them.
2. The European Parliament and the Council, acting in accordance with the ordinary legislative procedure, shall lay down the rules relating to the protection of individuals with regard to the processing of personal data by Union institutions, bodies, offices and agencies, and by the Member States when carrying out activities which fall within the scope of Union law, and the rules relating to the free movement of such data. Compliance with these rules shall be subject to the control of independent authorities.'

[37] This is the legal basis for bringing forward secondary legislation on the processing of personal data in the context of the CFSP.

[38] In particular, Regulation (EU) 2016/679 on the protection of natural persons with regard to processing of personal data and on the free movement of such data, and repealing Directive 95/46/EC (General Data Protection Regulation) [2016] OJ L119/1, and Directive (EU) 2016/680 on the protection of natural persons with regard to the processing of personal data by competent authorities for the purposes of the prevention, investigation, detection or prosecution of criminal offences or the execution of criminal penalties, and on the free movement of such data, and repealing Council Framework Decision 2008/977/JHA [2016] OJ L119/89, establishing rules for the protection of individuals with regard to the processing of personal data by competent authorities for purposes of law enforcement (LED). The LED is implemented in the Data Protection Act 2018, Part 3.

[39] See *Stauder* v. *City of Ulm*.

[40] Council of Europe Convention of 28 January 1981 for the Protection of Individuals with regard to Automatic Processing of Personal Data, which has been ratified by the UK and all the Member States.

[41] See *R (Davis & Watson)* v. *Secretary of State for the Home Department* [2015] EWHC 2092 (Admin) at [80].

[42] This point was raised in HM Government (2014) *Review of the Balance of Competences between the United Kingdom and the European Union: Information Rights*, paras.1.74 and 1.75: **https://assets.publishing.service.gov.uk/government/uploads/system/uploads/attachment_data/file/388177/balance-competences-information-rights-dec-2014.pdf** (accessed 10 November 2020). The Liberal Democrat Home Affairs, Justice and Equalities Committee quoted Hijmans, H. and Scirocco, A. (2009) 'Shortcomings in EU data protection in the Third and the Second Pillars: Can the Lisbon Treaty be expected to help?' *Common Market Law Review*, Vol. 46, p.1517. Hijmans and Scirocco stated that there are strong arguments in favour of the TFEU, Art.16(1) having direct effect. They noted the similarity in wording to Art.18 EC on citizenship which the CJEU has already ruled has direct effect. It was noted in the *Review of the Balance of Competences* that this view is not universally accepted, although specific evidence expressing the contrary view was not cited. Durham University argued that the language of the TFEU, which mirrors the language of the Charter, creates a specific right similar to Charter rights.

[43] JCHR Legislative Scrutiny, p.12, para.42.

[44] See the government's *Charter Analysis*, p.25.

[45] EUWA 2018, Sched.1, para.3(1) and (2).

[46] The GDPR will be saved under EUWA 2018, s.3. It will be renamed the 'UK GDPR' using the powers under EUWA 2018, s.8. See the Data Protection, Privacy and Electronic Communications (Amendments etc) (EU Exit) Regulations 2019 (SI 2019/419), reg.2.

[47] See the Charter Explanations.

[48] Ibid.

[49] The government's *Charter Analysis*, p.27 cites examples of legislation protecting rights of marriage and divorce including the Matrimonial Causes Act 1973 and the Civil Partnership Act 2004.

[50] See the Charter Explanations.

[51] Ibid.

[52] See *Bayatyan* v. *Armenia* App No 23459/03 (ECtHR 7 July 2011), paras.106–09.

[53] Ibid.

[54] The government analysis cites examples such as the Public Order Act 1986 which created the offence of incitement to religious hatred. See the government's *Charter Analysis*, p.28.

[55] See the Charter Explanations.

[56] The government's *Charter Analysis*, p.29 cites Case 100/88 *Augustin Oyowe and Amadou Traore* v. *Commission of the European Communities*, EU:C:1989:638. See Case C–415/93 *Bosman*, EU:C:1995:463 and Case 175/73 *Union Syndicale*, EU:C:1974:95.

[57] The Charter Explanations set out that Art.11(2) is based on particular on CJEU case law regarding television, particularly Case C–288/89 *Stichting Collectieve Antennevoorziening Gouda and others*, EU:C:1991:323 (25 July 1991). The Charter Explanations also cite Protocol 29 to the EU treaties which deals with public service broadcasting in the Member States. The Charter Explanations also reference what is now Directive 2010/13/EU on the coordination of certain provisions laid down by law, regulation or administrative action in Member States concerning the provision of audiovisual media services (Audiovisual Media Services Directive) [2010] OJ L95/1.

[58] See the Charter Explanations.

[59] Examples cited by the government include the Contempt of Court Act 1981 which balances freedom of expression with the right to a fair trial. Freedom of speech is also protected under common law. See the government's *Charter Analysis*, p.29.

[60] EUWA 2018, Sched.1, para.3(1) and (2).

[61] See the Charter Explanations.

[62] See the government's *Charter Analysis*, p.30. The government cites *Bosman* and *Union Syndicale*.

[63] See the government's *Charter Analysis*, p.30.

[64] Ibid.

[65] See the government's *Charter Analysis*, p.30. The government points to the Public Order Act 1986 and a number of Trade Union Acts such as the Trade Union and Labour Relations (Consolidation) Act 1992 and the Trade Union Act 2016.

[66] See the Charter Explanations.

[67] See the government's *Charter Analysis*, p.30. The government cites the cases of *Muller* v. *Switzerland*, App No 10737/84 (ECtHR, 24 May 1988) and *Hertel* v. *Switzerland*, App No 25181/94 (1999) 28 EHRR 534.

[68] See the Charter Explanations.

[69] Ibid.

[70] Ibid.

[71] Ibid.

[72] Ibid.

[73] See the government's *Charter Analysis*, p.21. See also O'Cinneide, C. (2018) 'The European Social Charter and the UK: Why it matters', *King's Law Journal*, Vol.29, No.2, 275–96.

[74] See the government's *Charter Analysis*, p.15.

[75] JCHR Legislative Scrutiny, p.15, para.45.

[76] See the government's *Charter Analysis*, pp.32–33. Examples cited include the Education Act 1996, ss.450–458 and the Academies Act 2010, s.1(9) which contain obligations in respect of the provisions of free education at state-funded schools.

[77] See the government's *Charter Analysis*, p.32.

[78] See the Immigration and Social Security Co-ordination (EU Withdrawal) Bill, Sched.1, para.4 (version of the Bill as amended on Report in the House of Lords, 6 October 2020). The explanatory notes to the Bill set out that only the provisions of the Workers Regulation which are specific to immigration cease to have effect. So, for example, para.4 'will prevent an individual claiming they have a right of residence in the UK under Article 10 of the Workers Regulation on the basis their child is in education here; this does not prevent the resident child of an EEA citizen who is legally resident and employed in the UK from being able to rely on Article 10 to access UK education'.

[79] See *Nold KG* v. *Commission*,Case 44/79 *Hauer* v. *Land Rheinland-Pfalz*, EU:C:1979:290 and Case 284/85 *Staatsanwalt* v. *Keller*, EU:C:1986:377. Paragraph 8 of the grounds in the case of *Keller* states 'the freedom to pursue one's trade or profession is part of the general principles of EU law'. See also the Charter Explanations.

[80] See the Charter Explanations.

[81] Ibid.

[82] See the government's *Charter Analysis*, p.15. See also O'Cinneide, C. (2018) 'The European Social Charter and the UK: Why it matters', *King's Law Journal*, Vol.29, No.2, 275–96.

[83] See, for example, the Freedom of Establishment and Free Movement of Services (EU Exit) Regulations 2019 (SI 2019/1401), regs.2 and 3, which remove the application of the TFEU, Art.49 (freedom of establishment) and Art.56 (freedom to provide services) from the UK statute book for the purposes of retained EU law. See the Freedom of Establishment and Free Movement of Services (EU Exit) Regulations 2019: **www.legislation.gov.uk/uksi/2019/1401/made** (accessed 10 November 2020). Note, however, the continuing application of Art.49 in respect of the citizens' rights provisions in the Withdrawal Agreement, Art.13. For a summary of these, see 'Explainer for part 2 (citizens' rights) on the agreement on the withdrawal of the United Kingdom of Great Britain and Northern Ireland from the European Union' (16 October 2020): **www.gov.uk/government/publications/withdrawal-agreement-explainer-for-part-2-citizens-rights** (accessed 10 November 2020).

[84] EUWA 2018, Sched.1, para.3(1) and (2).

[85] See JCHR Legislative Scrutiny, p.14, para.58.

[86] The government's *Charter Analysis*, p.35 cites Case 230/78 *Eridania*, EU:C:1979:216.

[87] See the Equality and Human Rights Commission, House of Lords Committee Stage (2018) 'European Union (Withdrawal) Bill: Supplementary note on the impact of the loss of the EU Charter of Fundamental Rights', 21 February, p.4: **www.equalityhumanrights.com/sites/default/files/note_on_practical_impact_of_loss_of_the_charter.pdf** (accessed 10 November 2020).

[88] EUWA 2018, Sched.1, para.3(1) and (2).

[89] See Rossi, L.S. (2019) 'The *Kücükdeveci* ambiguity: "Derivative" horizontal direct effects for directives?', EU Law Analysis, 25 February. The test of whether provisions of the Charter could have direct effect requires that they are: (i) unconditional in nature, and (ii) mandatory. A provision will be mandatory where it does not need to be implemented in EU or national law. Given the drafting of Art.16 – 'in accordance with Union law and national laws and practices' – it is unlikely that Art.16 would meet the test of being unconditional and so give rise to direct effect. This points to the fact that any gap which arises as a result of the loss of Art.16 of the Charter may not be as significant as some suggest.

[90] See the government's *Charter Analysis*, p.35.

[91] JCHR Legislative Scrutiny, p.14, para.62.

[92] See the Charter Explanations.

[93] Ibid. See, for example, Case C–70/10 *Scarlet Extended*, EU:C:2011:771.

[94] See the government's *Charter Analysis*, p.36 which cites *Hauer* v. *Land Rheinland-Pfalz*, and Case C–479/04 *Laserdisken Aps* v. *Kulturministeriet*, EU:C:2006:549.

[95] EUWA 2018, Sched.1, para.3(1) and (2).

[96] See the government's *Charter Analysis*, p.36.

[97] See the Charter Explanations.

[98] Ibid.

[99] See JCHR Legislative Scrutiny, p.15, para.68.

[100] See the government's explanation of Protocols 19 and 21 to the EU Treaties: https://assets.publishing.service.gov.uk/government/uploads/system/uploads/attachment_data/file/588184/jha-opt-in-background.pdf#:~:text=The%20UK%E2%80%9Fs%20participation%20in%20EU%20legislation%20on%20Justice,collectively%20often%20referred%20to%20as%20the%20Lisbon%20Treaty (accessed 10 November 2020).

[101] See the government's *Charter Analysis*, p.37.

[102] See JCHR Legislative Scrutiny, p.15, para.68.

[103] See the Charter Explanations.

[104] Ibid.

[105] Ibid.

[106] The European Court of Human Rights.

[107] See the Charter Explanations which cite the cases of *Ahmed* v. *Austria*, App No 25964/94 (ECtHR, 17 December 1996), p.2206 and *Soering* v. *the United Kingdom*, App No 14038/88 (ECtHR 7 July 1989).

[108] See JCHR Legislative Scrutiny, p.15, para.70.

[109] Ibid, p.15, para.71.

[110] Ibid, p.15, para.72.

111 See the Charter Explanations which cite Case 283/83 *Firma A. Racke* v. *Hauptzollamt*, EU:C:1984:344, Case C–15/95 *EARL de Kerlast* v. *Unicopa and Cooperative du Trieux*, EU:C:1997:196 and Case C–292/97 *Karlsson and others*, EU:C:2000:202.

112 EUWA 2018, Sched.1, para.3(1) and (2).

113 See JCHR Legislative Scrutiny, p.16, para.75.

114 See the government's *Charter Analysis*, p.39.

115 See EUWA 2018, s.4(2)(b) For further discussion see **13.6**.

116 Article 19 states: '1. Without prejudice to the other provisions of the Treaties and within the limits of the powers conferred by them upon the Union, the Council, acting unanimously in accordance with a special legislative procedure and after obtaining the consent of the European Parliament, may take appropriate action to combat discrimination based on sex, racial or ethnic origin, religion or belief, disability, age or sexual orientation.
2. By way of derogation from paragraph 1, the European Parliament and the Council, acting in accordance with the ordinary legislative procedure, may adopt the basic principles of Union incentive measures, excluding any harmonisation of the laws and regulations of the Member States, to support action taken by the Member States in order to contribute to the achievement of the objectives referred to in paragraph 1.'

117 See the Charter Explanations.

118 Article 18(1) states: 'Within the scope of application of the Treaties, and without prejudice to any special provisions contained therein, any discrimination on grounds of nationality shall be prohibited.' See also the Charter Explanations.

119 See the government's *Charter Analysis*, p.40.

120 Ibid.

121 'Within the scope of application of the Treaties, and without prejudice to any special provisions contained therein, any discrimination on grounds of nationality shall be prohibited. The European Parliament and the Council, acting in accordance with the ordinary legislative procedure, may adopt rules designed to prohibit such discrimination.'

122 See, for example, Case 36/74 *Walrave* v. *Association Union Cycliste Internationale*, EU:C:1974:140.

123 This would have been under EUWA 2018, s.4. However, retained EU law is subject to the powers under s.8 of the Act, which can remove retained EU law from the statute book.

124 See the Freedom of Establishment and Free Movement of Services (EU Exit) Regulations 2019 (SI 2019/1401), reg.4.

125 One difficulty with this argument is that the TFEU, Art.19 does not have the 'mandatory' quality of Art.157, which has been held to have direct effect in *Defrenne*. However, the criteria for direct effect of treaty articles have in the past been applied 'generously' by the CJEU with the result that provisions which do not appear to be clear or precise have been held to have direct effect: see Costa, M. and Peers, S. (2020) *Steiner & Woods EU Law* (14th edn: OUP) at 5.2.3 on p.114.

126 Examples include the Equality Act 2010. See the government's *Charter Analysis*, p.40.

127 EUWA 2018, Sched.1, para.3(1) and (2).

128 See EUWA 2018, s.4(2)(b).

129 See the Charter Explanations.

130 See the government's *Charter Analysis*, p.42.

131 See the government's *Charter Analysis*, p.42. Examples cited include the section of the Belfast (Good Friday) Agreement on Rights, Safeguards and Equality of Opportunity, the Welsh Language (Wales) Measure 2011 which creates a Welsh Language Commissioner and Welsh Language Tribunal and the Gaelic Language (Scotland) Act 2005 which protects Scots Gaelic.

132 See the government's *Charter Analysis*, p.42.

133 The drafting of these articles of the EU Treaties suggests that they are not sufficiently clear, precise and unconditional to have direct effect. However, we are not aware of any case law on this point and the criteria for direct effect of treaty articles have in the past been applied generously by the CJEU, with the result that provisions which do not appear to be clear or precise have been held to have direct effect: see Costa, M. and Peers, S. (2020) *Steiner & Woods EU Law* (14th edn: OUP) at 5.2.3 on p.114.

134 See the Charter Explanations.

135 Ibid.

[136] This directive replaced Council Directive 76/207/EEC on the implementation of the principle of equal treatment for men and women as regards access to employment, vocational training and promotion, and working conditions [1976] OJ L39/40, which is cited in the Charter Explanations.
[137] See the government's *Charter Analysis*, p.43.
[138] Ibid.
[139] The government's *Charter Analysis*, p.43 sets out that the right to equal pay in Art.157(1) and (2) has been implemented in domestic law through the Equality Act 2010.
[140] See *Defrenne*.
[141] See the government's *Charter Analysis*, pp.43–44.
[142] EUWA 2018, Sched.1, para.3(1) and (2).
[143] See the Charter Explanations.
[144] Ibid.
[145] The government cites the case of *HH* v. *Deputy Prosecutor of the Italian Republic, Genoa* [2012] UKSC 25. Rights such as the right for children to express their views and have them taken into account are general principles of EU law. See the government's *Charter Analysis*, p.45.
[146] See the government's *Charter Analysis*, p.45.
[147] Ibid, p.46.
[148] See JCHR Legislative Scrutiny, pp.17–18, para.85.
[149] Ibid, p.18, para.87.
[150] Examples include the Children Acts 1989 and 2004 which set out a range of duties to safeguard children and promote their welfare. See the government's *Charter Analysis*, p.45.
[151] See the Charter Explanations.
[152] See the government's *Charter Analysis*, p.47.
[153] Ibid.
[154] See JCHR Legislative Scrutiny, p.20, para.98.
[155] Examples include the Equality Act 2010 which prohibits age-based discrimination and the Health and Social Care Act 2008 which provides that private and voluntary organisations providing residential care services in England are bound by HRA 1998. See the government's *Charter Analysis*, p.47.
[156] See JCHR Legislative Scrutiny, p.19, para.90.
[157] See the Charter Explanations.
[158] See the government's *Charter Analysis*, p.48. The government points *Glatzel* which confirms that Art.26 is a principle. The CJEU stated that Art.26: 'Cannot by itself confer on individuals a subjective right which they may invoke as such.' See para.78 of the judgment.
[159] See the government's *Charter Analysis*, p.48. Examples include the Equality Act 2010.
[160] See the government's *Charter Analysis*, p.48.
[161] See JCHR Legislative Scrutiny, p.19, para.92.
[162] Ibid, p.19, para.93.
[163] Ibid, p.20, para.98.
[164] See the Charter Explanations.
[165] Ibid.
[166] Ibid.
[167] Directive 95/46/EC has been revoked and replaced.
[168] See the government's *Charter Analysis*, p.49. The government cites Case C–176/12 *Association de Médiation Sociale*, EU:C:2013:491 (see, in particular, para.45).
[169] For example, the Information and Consultation of Employees Regulations 2004 (SI 2004/3426); see the government's *Charter Analysis*, p.49.
[170] See JCHR Legislative Scrutiny, p.19, para.95.
[171] Ibid, p.20, para.98.
[172] See the Charter Explanations.
[173] Ibid.
[174] Ibid.
[175] The government points to Case C–438/05 *The International Transport Workers' Federation and the Finnish Seamen's Union* v. *Viking Line ABP*, EU:C:2007:772 at para.44 and Case C–341/05 *Laval*, EU:C:2007:809 at para.91. See the government's *Charter Analysis*, p.50.
[176] See the government's *Charter Analysis*, p.50.
[177] See the government's *Charter Analysis*, p.50. Examples include the Trade Union and Labour Relations (Consolidation) Act 1992.

178 See JCHR Legislative Scrutiny, p.20, para.98.
179 EUWA 2018, Sched.1, para.3(1) and (2).
180 The government's *Charter Analysis*, p.51 states that the term 'placement services' refers to job placement services such as Jobcentre Plus.
181 See the Charter Explanations.
182 See the government's *Charter Analysis*, p.51.
183 See the government's *Charter Analysis*, p.51. The regulation provides for the freedom of movement of workers in various ways, including rights to residency, equal treatment and access to education.
184 See Sched.1, Part 2, para.4. See the Immigration and Social Security Co-ordination (EU Withdrawal) Bill, Sched.1, para.4 (version of the Bill as amended on Report in the House of Lords, 6 October 2020).
185 See JCHR Legislative Scrutiny, p.20, para.98.
186 See the Charter Explanations.
187 Ibid.
188 The Charter Explanations cite previous legislation which regulated this area.
189 The government relies on the reasoning in *Association de Médiation Sociale* (see, in particular, para.45).
190 See, for example, the Transfer of Undertakings (Protection of Employment) Regulations 2006 (SI 2006/246).
191 See the government's *Charter Analysis*, p.52.
192 See JCHR Legislative Scrutiny, p.20, para.102.
193 For example, the government cites the Employment Rights Act 1996. See the government's *Charter Analysis*, p.52.
194 See the Charter Explanations.
195 This directive replaced Council Directive 93/104/EC concerning certain aspects of the organization of working time [1993] OJ L307/18 which is referenced in the Charter Explanations.
196 See the Charter Explanations.
197 See the government's *Charter Analysis*, p.53 citing *Association de Médiation Sociale* (see, in particular, para.45).
198 Examples include the Working Time Regulations 1998 (SI 1998/1833) and the Management of Health and Safety at Work Regulations 1999 (SI 1999/3242); see the government's *Charter Analysis*, p.53.
199 The government refers to protection from unfair dismissal which is provided through the Employment Rights Act 1996 and the possibility of bringing claims through the employment tribunal; see the government's *Charter Analysis*, p.53.
200 See the government's *Charter Analysis*, p.53.
201 See JCHR Legislative Scrutiny, p.20, para.102.
202 See the government's *Charter Analysis*, p.15.
203 See the Charter Explanations.
204 See the government's *Charter Analysis*, p.54. The legislation cited is the Children and Young Persons Act 1933, as amended.
205 See the government's *Charter Analysis*, p.15.
206 This includes the Children Act 1989, the Adoption and Children Act 2002, the Children and Young Persons Act 1933, as well as the common law. See the government's *Charter Analysis*, p.54.
207 The Equality and Human Rights Commission in its submission to the UN Committee on the Rights of the Child in advance of the public examination of the UK's implementation of the Convention on the Rights of the Child of 16 April 2016 stated at para.4 that: 'The [Commission] regrets that the UK Government has not directly incorporated [the Convention] into UK-wide law … The Commitment of the UK Government to give due consideration to the [Convention] when developing new policy or legislation is currently inadequate and unenforceable.'
Equality and Human Rights Commission (2016) 'Children's Rights in the UK – Updated Submission to the UK Committee on the Rights of the Child in advance of the public examination of the UK's implementation of the Convention on the Rights of the Child', April: **www.equalityhumanrights.com/sites/default/files/childrens_rights_in_the_uk.pdf** (accessed 10 November 2020).
208 See the Charter Explanations.

209 Ibid.

210 This directive replaced the directive referenced in the Charter Explanations – Council Directive 96/34/EC on the framework agreement on parental leave concluded by UNICE, CEEP and the ETUC [1996] OJ L145/4.

211 Ibid.

212 See the government's *Charter Analysis*, p.55.

213 Ibid.

214 Examples cited by the government include the Employment Rights Act 1996 and secondary legislation such as the Maternity and Parental Leave etc. Regulations 1999 (SI 1999/3312). See the government's *Charter Analysis*, p.55.

215 See the government's *Charter Analysis*, p.55.

216 See the government's *Charter Analysis*, p.15.

217 See the Charter Explanations.

218 See the Charter Explanations. Regulation (EEC) No 1612/68 on freedom of movement for workers within the Community [1968] OJ L257/2, which is cited in the Charter Explanations, has been replaced by Regulation (EU) 492/2011 on freedom of movement for workers within the Union [2011] L141/1. The government also cites the EU Social Security Regulation (EC) 883/2004 on the coordination of social security systems [2004] OJ L166/1 as a successor regulation to Regulation (EEC) 1408/71 on the application of social security schemes to employed persons and their families moving within the Community [1971] OJ L149/2. See the government's *Charter Analysis*, p.56.

219 Ibid.

220 See the government's *Charter Analysis*, p.56.

221 See the government's *Charter Analysis*, pp.56–57.

222 Ibid.

223 Examples are the rules resulting from Regulation (EC) 883/2004 on the coordination of social security systems [2004] OJ L166/1 and Regulation (EC) 987/2009 laying down the procedure for implementing Regulation (EC) No 883/2004 on the coordination of social security systems, and Regulation (EU) 492/2011 on freedom of movement for workers within the Union [2011] L141/1.

224 See Sched.1, Part 2, para.4. See the Immigration and Social Security Co-ordination (EU Withdrawal) Bill, Sched.1, para.4 (version of the Bill as amended on Report in the House of Lords, 6 October 2020).

225 See the government's *Charter Analysis*, p.15.

226 See the Charter Explanations.

227 See the government's *Charter Analysis*, p.58.

228 See JCHR Legislative Scrutiny, p.22, para.110. Case C–230/18 *PI* v. *Landespolizeidirektion Tirol*, EU:C:2019:383 does refer to Art.35 as a 'guarantee' (see para.72 of the judgment) but the point is not further elucidated. The Opinion of Advocate General Wathelet of 21 June 2018 in Joined Cases C–391/16, C–77/17 and C–78/17 *M and Others* v. *Commissaire général aux réfugiés et aux apatrides*, EU:C:2019:403 suggests that denial of medical treatment to a refugee could infringe the Charter, Art.35. The judgment in the case refers to Art.35 as an obligation (see para.109). Again, this suggests that Art.35 could confer a right. In pending litigation before the General Court (see Case T–231/20 *Price* v. *Council* EU:T:2020:280) it is alleged that the citizens' rights provisions of the EU-UK Withdrawal Agreement breach Art.35 of the Charter because the Withdrawal Agreement does not provide for the protection of the right to health. However, any judgment on this point if handed down after IPCD would have no application in relation to retained EU law because judgments of the CJEU are not binding on domestic courts after IPCD (see s.6(1)(a)), and the Charter will not apply in domestic law after IPCD. The case could, however, have implications for the interpretation of the Withdrawal Agreement.

229 See the government's *Charter Analysis*, p.15.

230 See the Charter Explanations. Article 14 sets out that given the role of services of general economic interest in the EU's values and in promoting social and territorial cohesion, the EU and the Member States should take care that such services operate on the basis of principles and conditions, particularly economic and financial conditions, which enable them to fulfil their missions.

231 See the government's *Charter Analysis*, p.59 and the JCHR Legislative Scrutiny, p.22, para.111.

232 See the government's *Charter Analysis*, p.59.

[233] The TEU, Art.3(3) states: 'The Union shall establish an internal market. It shall work for the sustainable development of Europe based on balanced economic growth and price stability, a highly competitive social market economy, aiming at full employment and social progress, and a high level of protection and improvement of the quality of the environment. It shall promote scientific and technological advance.'

[234] Article 11 states: 'Environmental protection requirements must be integrated into the definition and implementation of the Union's policies and activities, in particular with a view to promoting sustainable development.'

[235] Article 191(1) sets out that EU policy on the environment should pursue the objective of preserving, protecting and improving the quality of the environment, protecting human health, prudent use of natural resources and promoting measures at international level to deal with regional or worldwide environmental problems, and in particular combating climate change. Article 191(2) sets out that EU policy on the environment aims at a high level of protection. It is based on the precautionary principle as well as the principle that preventive action should be taken, that environmental damage should be rectified at source and that the polluter should pay.

[236] See the Charter Explanations.

[237] See the government's *Charter Analysis*, p.60 and JCHR Legislative Scrutiny, p.22, para.112.

[238] See the government's *Charter Analysis*, p.60.

[239] Ibid.

[240] Ibid.

[241] Article 169(1) states: 'In order to promote the interests of consumers and to ensure a high level of consumer protection, the Union shall contribute to protecting the health, safety and economic interests of consumers, as well as to promoting their right to information, education and to organise themselves in order to safeguard their interest.'

[242] See the government's *Charter Analysis*, p.61 and JCHR Legislative Scrutiny, p.22, para.113.

[243] Ibid.

[244] See JCHR Legislative Scrutiny, p.22, paras.114–115; ibid, pp.62–67; the government's *Charter Analysis*, p.22.

[245] See the Bill as amended on Report in the House of Lords, 6 October 2020.

[246] See the Charter Explanations.

[247] See the Charter Explanations which cite the ECHR judgment of 9 October 1979, Airey, Series A, Volume 32, p.11.

[248] See, for example, Case 222/84 *Marguerite Johnston* v. *Chief Constable of the Royal Ulster Constabulary*, EU:C:1986:206 and Case C–97/91 *Oleificio Borelli* v. *Commission of the European Communities*, EU:C:1992:491 as cited in the Charter Explanations.

[249] The government asserts that HRA 1998 'as a whole ensures that Article 13 is given effect in UK law'. See the government's *Charter Analysis*, p.69.

[250] See the Charter Explanations.

[251] See JCHR Legislative Scrutiny, p.23, para.118, which cites Case C–300/11 *ZZ* v. *Secretary of State for the Home Department*, EU:C:2013:363. In that case the CJEU held that Art.47 applied to deportation hearings and that the individual concerned was entitled to know the reasons for a decision made in closed material proceedings.

[252] See JCHR Legislative Scrutiny, p.23, para.118.

[253] For further discussion of *Benkharbouche* see **4.5.1**.

[254] Although note that the effect of a case that has been decided is not undone: see the specific transitional provisions at **Appendix C**.

[255] EUWA 2018, Sched.1, para.3(1) and (2).

[256] The government cites *R(UNISON)* v. *Lord Chancellor* [2017] UKSC 51 where the Supreme Court held that 'the right of access to justice is not an idea recently imported from the continent of Europe, but has long been embedded in our constitutional law'. The government states that the common law also recognises 'a basic right to procedural fairness' and that the principles of due process and access to justice 'can be traced back to the Magna Carta'. See the government's *Charter Analysis*, p.68.

[257] See the government's *Charter Analysis*, p.69.

[258] JCHR Legislative Scrutiny, p.23, paras.118–120.

[259] See the Charter Explanations.

260 The government cites Case C–344/08 *Rubach*, EU:C:2009:482, Case 85/76 *Hoffman-La Roche* v. *Commission of the European Communities*, EU:C:1979:36 and Case C–419/14 *WebMindLicenses fkt*, EU:C:2015:832. See the government's *Charter Analysis*, p.70.
261 EUWA 2018, Sched.1, para.3(1) and (2).
262 See, for example, Directive 2010/64/EU on interpretation and translation in criminal proceedings [2010] OJ L280/1 and Directive 2012/13/EU on the right to information in criminal proceedings [2012] OJ L142/1. The government states that these directives are implemented through the Criminal Procedure Rules and through the Codes of Practice that accompany the Police and Criminal Evidence Act 1984. The government sets out that this legislation will be retained through EUWA 2018, s.2. See the government's *Charter Analysis*, p.70.
263 See the government's *Charter Analysis*, p.70.
264 See the Charter Explanations.
265 See cases such as Case C–303/05 *Advocaten voor de Wereld VZW* v. *Leden van de Ministeraad*, EU:C:2007:261 and Case 118/75 *Lynne Watson and Alessandro Belmann*, EU:C:1976:106 as cited in the government's *Charter Analysis*, p.72.
266 EUWA 2018, Sched.1, para.3(1) and (2).
267 See the government's *Charter Analysis*, p.72.
268 Ibid.
269 Ibid.
270 See, for example, Case C–238/99 *Limburgse Vinvyl Maatschappij (LVM) and others* v. *Commission of the European Communities*, EU:C:2002:582 and the government's *Charter Analysis*, p.73.
271 Examples include Council Framework Decision 2005/214/JHA on the application of the principle of mutual recognition to financial penalties [2005] OJ L76/16, and the Convention which implements the Schengen Convention as it applies in the UK under Council Decision 2000/365/EC concerning the request of the United Kingdom of Great Britain and Northern Ireland to take part in some of the provisions of the Schengen acquis [2000] OJ L131/43 (see the government's *Charter Analysis*, p.73). Instruments which have been implemented in domestic law are retained under EUWA 2018, s.2. However, note that these instruments have been modified using the power in EUWA 2018, s.8. See for example the Criminal Justice (Amendment etc.) (EU Exit) Regulations 2019 (SI 2019/780). Part 5 of those regulations modifies the retained EU law which was originally enacted to implement Framework Decision 2005/214/JHA on the application of the principle of mutual recognition to financial penalties.
272 EUWA 2018, Sched.1, para.3(1) and (2).
273 The government cites the common law and domestic legislation such as the Criminal Justice Act 2003. See the government's *Charter Analysis*, p.73.

Index